THE MAMMOTH BOOK OF USELESS INFORMATION

AN OFFICIAL USELESS INFORMATION SOCIETY PUBLICATION

NOEL BOTHAM

D1394556

Published by John Blake Publishing Ltd,
3 Bramber Court, 2 Bramber Road,
London W14 9PB, England

www.johnblakepublishing.co.uk

www.facebook.com/Johnblakepub   facebook

twitter.com/johnblakepub   twitter

First published in hardback in 2009
This edition published in paperback in 2012

ISBN: 978-1-85782-811-5

British Library Cataloguing-in-Publication Data:

A catalogue record for this book is available from the British Library.

Design by www.envydesign.co.uk

Printed in Great Britain by CPI Group (UK) Ltd

1 3 5 7 9 10 8 6 4 2

As always to my wife,
Lesley Lewis, with love

CONTENTS

1

INVENTIONS

- Benjamin Franklin invented swim fins.

- The abacus was invented in Egypt in 2000 BC.

- The Greek mathematician Archimedes invented the screw.

- The parachute was invented 120 years before the airplane. It was intended to save people who had to jump from burning buildings.

- The first pull-top can was invented by Ermal Cleon Fraze in 1959, after he had to resort to using his car bumper to open a can of drink.

- Kleenex tissues were originally invented to remove make-up. Maybe that's why they're still called 'facial tissues'.

- Roulette was invented by Blaise Pascal, a French mathematician and scientist.

- In 1916, Jones Wister of Philadelphia, Pennsylvania, invented a rifle for shooting around corners. It had a curved barrel and periscopic sights.

- At the turn of the 19th century, most light bulbs were hand-blown, and the cost of one was equivalent to half a day's pay for the average US worker.

- The first brassiere was invented in 1913 by teenage debutante Mary Phelps Jacob.

- The same man who led the attack on the Alamo, Mexican military general Antonio Lopez de Santa Anna, is also credited with the invention of chewing gum.

- The guillotine was originally called a *louisette*, after Antoine Louis, the French surgeon who invented it. It became known as the guillotine after Joseph Ignace Guillotin, the French physician who advocated it as a more merciful means of execution than the noose or axe.

- Benjamin Franklin invented the rocking chair.

- The modern zipper, the Talon Slide Fastener, was invented in 1913 but didn't catch on until after World War I. The first dresses incorporating the zipper appeared in the 1930s.

- Western Electric invented the loudspeaker, which was initially called a 'loud-speaking telephone'.

- The first VCR, made in 1956, was the size of a piano.

- The Chinese invented eyeglasses. Marco Polo reported seeing many pairs worn by the Chinese as early as 1275, 500 years before lens grinding became an art in the West.

- The first commercial vacuum cleaner was so large it was mounted on a wagon. People threw parties in their homes so guests could watch the new device do its job.

- It has been determined that less than one patented invention in a hundred makes any money for the inventor.

- The rickshaw was invented by the Reverend Jonathan Scobie, an American Baptist minister living in Yokohama, Japan, who built the first model in 1869 in order to transport his wife, who was an invalid. Today it remains a common mode of transportation in the Orient.

- The Ancient Romans invented the arch.

- The shoestring was invented in England in 1790. Prior to this time, all shoes were fastened with buckles.

- The state of Maine was once known as the 'earmuff capital of the world', as earmuffs were invented there by Chester Greenwood in 1873.

- The man who invented shorthand, John Gregg, was deaf.

- Because he felt such an important tool should be public property, English chemist John Walker never patented his invention – matches.

- In 1896, Herman Hollerith founded the Tabulating Machine Company. Twenty-eight years later, in 1924 and after several take-overs, the company became known as International Business Machines (IBM).

- The first mobile car phones were located in the car's boot, taking up nearly half of the space.

- The Nobel Prize resulted from a late change in the will of Alfred Nobel, who did not want to be remembered after his death as a propagator of violence – he invented dynamite.

- Sylvan N. Goldman of Humpty Dumpty Stores and Standard Food Markets developed the shopping trolley so that people could buy more in a single visit to the grocery store. He unveiled his creation in Oklahoma City on 4 June 1937.

- The City and South London Railway opened the world's first deep-level electric railway on 18 December 1890, running from King William Street in the City of London under the River Thames to Stockwell.

- The safety pin was patented in 1849 by Walter Hunt. He sold the patent rights for $400.

- The windmill originated in Iran in AD 644 and was used to grind grain.

- In 1832, the Scottish surgeon Neil Arnott devised waterbeds as a way of improving patients' comfort.

- American Jim Bristoe invented a 30ft-long (9.1m), 2-ton (2.03-tonne) pumpkin cannon that could fire pumpkins up to 5 miles (8 km) at a time.

- Alexander Graham Bell applied for a patent for the telephone three days before he had got it to work. Had Bell waited until he had a working model, Elisha Gray, who filed a patent application the same day, would have been awarded the patent. But the telephone system we use is technically more like that described in Gray's patent.

THE WORLD AND ITS PEOPLE

- Twenty-five per cent of women think money makes a man sexier.

- Pablo Picasso was born dead. His midwife abandoned him on a table, leaving Picasso's uncle to bring him to life with a lungful of cigar smoke.

- Tchaikovsky was financed by a wealthy widow for thirteen years. At her request, they never met.

- The great lover and adventurer Casanova was earning his living as a librarian for a count in Bohemia when he died at the age of 73.

- Today, 6.7 billion people live on the Earth.

- The first person other than royalty to be portrayed on a British stamp was William Shakespeare, in 1964.

- Offered a new pen to write with, 97 per cent of all people will write their own name.

- There are 106 boys born for every 100 girls.

- When Errol Flynn appeared as a contestant on the mid-1950s TV quiz show *The Big Surprise*, he was questioned about sailing and won $30,000.

- The world's population grows by 100 million each year.

- In all, 950 million people in the world are malnourished.

- Actor Montgomery Clift is said to haunt room number 928 of the Roosevelt Hotel in Hollywood, which was home to him for three months while filming *From Here to Eternity* (1953). Hotel guests and employees have reported sensing the actor's presence, or have heard him reciting his lines and playing the trumpet. One guest felt a hand patting her shoulder, while others claim to feel cold spots in the room.

- After Frank Lahainer died in March 1995, in Palm Beach, Florida, his widow Gianna had him embalmed and stored for forty days at a funeral home. It seemed that Frank, worth $300 million, died at an inconvenient time: it was the middle of Palm Beach's social season and Gianna didn't want to miss any of the parties.

- Nuns in the United States have an average life expectancy of seventy-seven years, the longest of any group in the country.

- The men who served as guards along the Great Wall of China in the Middle Ages were often born on the wall, grew up there, married there, died there and were buried within it. Many of these guards never left the wall in their entire lives.

- St George, the patron saint of England, never actually visited England.

- To help create her signature sexy walk, actress Marilyn Monroe sawed off part of the heel of one shoe.

- After his death, the body of Pope Formosus was dug up and tried for various crimes.

- As the official taste-tester for Edy's Grand Ice Cream, John Harrison had his taste buds insured for $1 million.

- Prompted by their immense public appeal, Ancient Roman gladiators performed product endorsements.

- Cleopatra was part Macedonian, part Greek and part Iranian. She was not an Egyptian.

- There are currently six reigning queens in Europe. They are: Queen Elizabeth II of the United Kingdom; Queen Sofia of Spain; Queen Beatrix of the Netherlands; Queen Margrethe II of Denmark; Queen Silvia of Sweden; and Queen Fabiola of Belgium.

- A man hit by a car in New York in 1977 got up uninjured, but lay back down in front of the car when a bystander told him to pretend he was hurt so he could collect insurance money. The car rolled forward and crushed him to death.

- Julius Caesar, Martin Luther King and Jonathan Swift all suffered from Ménière's disease. It is a disorder of the hearing and balance senses, causing progressive deafness and attacks of tinnitus and vertigo.

- King Mithridates VI was so afraid of assassination by poisoning that he gave himself small doses of poison each day in the hope that he would naturally build up a resistance to poisons. When the Romans invaded in 63 BC, to avoid being captured he tried to commit suicide, but he had built up such an immunity that the poison he took had no effect on him. Eventually the king ordered a slave to kill him with his sword.

- Johann Sebastian Bach once walked 230 miles (370km) to hear the organist at Lübeck in Germany.

- Adolf Hitler was fascinated by hands. In his library there was a well-thumbed book containing pictures and drawings of hands belonging to famous people throughout history. He particularly liked to show his guests how closely his own hands resembled those of Frederick the Great, one of his heroes.

- Handel wrote the score of his *Messiah* in just over three weeks.

- US actor Larry Hagman didn't allow smoking on the set of TV series *Dallas*.

- St John was the only one of the twelve apostles to die a natural death.

- The pioneering scientist Marie Curie was not allowed to become a member of the prestigious French Academy because she was a woman.

- In 1994, Los Angeles police arrested a man for dressing as the Grim Reaper – complete with scythe – and standing outside the windows of old people's homes, staring in.

- The composer Richard Wagner was vegetarian, and once published a diatribe against 'the abominable practice of flesh eating'.

- Nazi Adolf Eichmann was originally a travelling salesman for the Vacuum Oil Company of Austria.

- During the 17th century, the Sultan of Turkey ordered that his entire harem of women be drowned and replaced with a new one.

- Henry VII was the only British king to be crowned on the field of battle.

- Ludwig van Beethoven was once arrested for vagrancy.

- In 1759, Emmanuel Swedenborg, speaking to a reception full of local notables in Gothenburg, described in vivid detail the progress of a disastrous fire that was sweeping through Stockholm, 300 miles (483km) away. At six o'clock he told them the fire had just broken out; at eight he told them it had been extinguished only three doors from his home. Two days later, a messenger from Stockholm confirmed every detail.

- When Richard II died, in 1400, a hole was left in the side of his tomb so that people could touch his royal head. However, 376 years later, a schoolboy reportedly took advantage of this and stole his jawbone.

- Julius Caesar wore a laurel wreath to cover the onset of baldness.

- Blackbird, Chief of the Omaha Indians, was buried sitting on his favourite horse.

- Prime Minister William Gladstone, a man of strong Puritan impulses, kept a selection of whips in his cellar with which he regularly chastised himself.

- Irving Berlin composed 3,000 songs in his lifetime but couldn't read music.

- China uses 45 billion chopsticks per year, using 25 million trees to make them.

- President Kaunda of Zambia once threatened to resign if his fellow countrymen didn't stop drinking so much alcohol.

- The Winchester Mansion, in San José, California, was built by Sara Winchester, the widow of gun manufacturer William Winchester. She had been told by a psychic to build a house large enough to house the souls of all those who had been killed by Winchester guns. With stairways and doors that go nowhere, secret rooms and passages, and elevators that only go up one floor, some believe that Sara had the house built in a confusing way so that the spirits wouldn't be able to find her and seek revenge. Obsessed with the number thirteen, every night at the stroke of midnight she would sit down to dinner at a table set for thirteen people, even though she was alone. The house also had thirteen bathrooms, stairways with thirteen steps and so on. Her superstitions meant that she would never give her workmen the day off, afraid that the day she stopped building she would die. One day, however, after many complaints, she finally gave her staff a day off – and that is the day she died.

- It is believed that Handel haunts his former London home. Many who have entered Handel's bedroom, where he died in 1759, have reported seeing a tall, dark shape and sensing a strong smell of perfume. Roman Catholic priests have performed exorcisms in their bid to clear the house of all spirits before it becomes a museum that will be open to the public.

- There are more than 150 million sheep in Australia but only 17 million people, while in New Zealand there are only 4 million people compared with 70 million sheep.

- In Holland, you can be fined for not using a shopping basket at a grocery store.

- On every continent there is a city called Rome.

- The oldest inhabited city is Damascus, Syria.

- The first city in the world to have a population of more than 1 million was London, which today is the thirteenth most populated city.

- The Atlantic Ocean is saltier than the Pacific Ocean.

- Kilts are not native to Scotland. They originated in France.

- One-third of Taiwanese funeral processions include a stripper.

- It is illegal to own a red car in Shanghai, China.

- Antarctica is the only land on our planet that is not owned by any country.

- There is now a cash machine at McMurdo Station in Antarctica, which has a winter population of 200 people. It is the only ATM machine on the continent.

- Major earthquakes have hit Japan on 1 September AD 827, 1 September AD 859, 1 September 1185, 1 September 1649 and 1 September 1923.

- There are ninety-two known cases of nuclear bombs lost at sea.

- In Nepal, cow dung is used for medicinal purposes.

- All the Earth's continents, except Antarctica, are wider at the north than at the south.

- There are no rental cars in Bermuda.

- The richest country in the world is Switzerland, while Mozambique is the poorest.

- Until 1920, Canada was planning on invading the United States.

- In 1956, only 8 per cent of British households had a refrigerator.

- In India, people are legally allowed to marry a dog.

- The Ancient Egyptians trained baboons to wait on tables.

- One day in 1892, residents of Paderborn, Germany, witnessed the appearance of an odd-looking yellow cloud. Out of it fell not only a fierce rain, but also mussels.

- Mount Everest is 1ft (30.5cm) higher today than it was a century ago, and is believed to be still growing.

- Greenland has more ice on it than Iceland does, while Iceland has more grass and trees than Greenland.

- The country of Tanzania has an island called Mafia.

- Panama is the only place in the world where someone can see the sun rise over the Pacific Ocean and set over the Atlantic.

- In Poland, a brewery developed a plumbing problem in which beer was accidentally pumped into the incoming water supply. It meant that residents of the town got free beer on tap for one day.

- The Kingdom of Tonga, in the South Pacific, once issued a stamp shaped like a banana.

- Japanese children can buy a toy in the shape of a small plastic atom bomb.

- Mount Athos, in northern Greece, calls itself an independent country and has a male-only population of about 4,000. No females of any kind, including animals, are allowed. There are twenty monasteries within a space of 20 miles (32km).

- In Cyprus, there is one cinema per every eight people.

- Two hundred and thirty people died when Moradabad, India, was bombed with giant balls of hail more than 2in (5cm) in diameter on 30 April 1888.

- A church steeple in Germany was struck by lightning and destroyed on 18 April 1599. The members of the church rebuilt it, but it was hit by lightning three more times between then and 1783, and rebuilt again and again. Every time it was hit, the date was 18 April.

- Monaco issued a postage stamp honouring Franklin D. Roosevelt, but the picture on the stamp showed six fingers on his left hand.

- The most common place name in Britain is Newton, which occurs 150 times.

- China has more English speakers than the United States.

- The Toltecs, 7th-century native Mexicans, went into battle with wooden swords so as not to kill their enemies.

- In 1821, stones fell on a house in Truro, Cornwall. So remarkable was the event that the local mayor visited the house, though he was unnerved by the rattling of the walls and roof due to the falling stones. Called in to help, the military was unable to determine the source of the stones, and five days later the fall was still going on.

- Belgium is the only country that has never imposed censorship laws on adult films.

- Freelance Dutch prostitutes have to charge sales tax, but can write off items such as condoms and beds.

- The average court fine for drunk driving in Denmark is one month's salary if convicted.

- People in Sweden, Japan and Canada are more likely to know the population of the United States than Americans.

- About 10 per cent of the workforce in Egypt is under 12 years of age.

- The Netherlands is credited with having the most bikes in the world. One bike per person is the national average, with an estimated 16 million bicycles nationwide.

- On a summer's evening in Edinburgh, 1849, there was a loud clap of thunder, after which a large and irregularly shaped mass of ice, estimated to be around 20ft (6m) in circumference, crashed to the ground near a farmhouse.

- The average worker in Japan reportedly takes only half of his or her earned holiday time each year.

- The Amazon's flow is twelve times that of the Mississippi. The South American river disgorges as much water in a day as the Thames carries past London in a year.

- Georgia is the world's top pecan producer.

- People in Siberia often buy milk frozen on a stick.

- The population of Colombia doubles every twenty-two years.

- Sweden is the biggest user of ketchup, spending £2.25 per person a year on it. Australia is the second highest user, spending £1.35 a year, and the United States and Canada are joint third, spending £1.22 a year. The ketchup expenditure of other countries per person is as follows: Germany £0.95, United Kingdom £0.90, Poland and Japan £0.77, France £0.65 and Russia £0.50.

- Eighty per cent of the Australian population live in the cities along the coast.

- The most common name for a pub in Britain is 'The Red Lion'.

- Among the shortest people in the world are the Mbuti Pygmies of the Congo River basin, where the men reach an average of 4ft 6in (1.36m) tall.

- In Tokyo, a bicycle is faster than a car for most trips of less than fifty minutes.

- The world's longest escalator is in Ocean Park, Hong Kong. With a length of 745ft (227m), the escalator boasts a vertical rise of 377ft (115m).

- There is 1 mile (1.6km) of railroad track in Belgium for every 1.5 miles^2 (3.8km^2) of land.

- Fifty per cent of the adult Dutch population has never flown in a plane, and 28 per cent admits a fear of flying.

- The tallest sand dunes in the world are in the Sahara desert. The dunes have enough sand in them to bury the Great Pyramids of Egypt and the Eiffel Tower.

- Asia has the greatest number of working children, totalling 45 million. Africa is second, with 24 million.

- On some Pacific islands, shark teeth are used to make skin tattoos.

- The most-visited cemetery in the world is Cimetière du Père-Lachaise, in Paris. Established in 1805, it contains the tombs of over 1 million people, including: composer Chopin; singer Edith Piaf; writers Oscar Wilde, Molière, Honoré de Balzac, Marcel Proust and Gertrude Stein; artists David, Delacroix, Pissarro, Seurat and Modigliani; actors Sarah Bernhardt, Simone Signoret and Yves Montand; and dancer Isadora Duncan. The most-visited tomb is that of The Doors' former lead singer, Jim Morrison.

- In Japan, some restaurants serve smaller portions to women, even though the charge is the same as for a man's portion.

- The Japanese cremate 93 per cent of their dead, compared with Great Britain, at 67 per cent, and the United States, at just over 12 per cent.

- Approximately one-third of Greenland, the world's largest island, is national park.

- Kulang, China, runs seven centres for recycled toothpicks. People bringing used toothpicks to the recycling centres are paid the equivalent of 35 cents per pound weight.

- Floor-cleaning products in Venezuela have ten times the pine fragrance of British floor-cleaners, as Venezuelan women won't buy a weaker fragrance. They wet-mop their tile floors twice a day, leaving windows and doors open so the scent can waft out to the street and send the message that their houses are clean.

- Windsor Castle is home to the ghosts of King Henry VIII, Queen Elizabeth I, King Charles I and King George III. Henry VIII is supposed to haunt the cloisters near the Deanery with ghostly groans and the sound of dragging footsteps.

- All education through to university level is free in the Eastern European nation of Azerbaijan.

- Canada is the largest importer of American cars.

- No one knows how many people live in Bhutan, a small independent kingdom on the slopes of the Himalayas. As of 1975, no census has ever been taken.

- On average, fifty-one cars a year overshoot and drive into the canals of Amsterdam.

- London cabbies estimate their average driving speed to be 9mph (14km/h) due to increasing traffic congestion.

- The area of Greater Tokyo – meaning the city, its port, Yokohama, and the suburban prefectures of Saitama, Chiba and Kanagawa – contains less than 4 per cent of Japan's land area, but fully one-quarter of its 123 million-plus people.

- Based on population, Chinese Mandarin is the most commonly spoken language in the world. Spanish follows second, with English third and Bengali fourth.

- At about 200 million years old, the Atlantic Ocean is the youngest of the world's oceans.

- In Finland, the awards for best children's fairy tales by children are held on 18 October, known as Satu's Day. The international competition for children ages 7 to 13 has been held since 1993, and its rules are translated into five languages.

- Britain is roughly nine times more densely populated than America, with 588 people per mile^2 (227 people per km^2) as compared with America's 65 people per mile^2 (25 people per km^2).

- In China there are 600 bicycles for every car.

- At London's Drury Lane Theatre, there have been numerous sightings of a ghost described as a soft-green glow, or a handsome young man. During renovation to the theatre in the late 1970s, workers found a skeleton wearing the remnants of a grey riding coat and with a knife sticking out of its ribs. The deceased was found to be a young ghost-hunter who was murdered in 1780.

- Among the tallest people in the world are the Tutsi from Rwanda and Burundi, in central Africa, with the men averaging 6ft (1.8m) in height.

- At 12,000ft (3,658m) above sea level, there is barely enough oxygen in La Paz, Bolivia, to support combustion. The city is nearly fireproof.

- Of the 15,000-odd known species of orchids in the world, 3,000 of them can be found in Brazil.

- Given one square metre per person, all the people in the world could fit on the Indonesian island of Bali, if they stood shoulder to shoulder.

- In a recent five-year period, twenty-four residents of Tokyo died while bowing to other people.

- Australia is home to 500 species of coral.

- A Chinese soap hit it big with consumers in Asia, with the bold claim that users would lose weight by washing with it. The soap was promptly banned.

- One in five people in the world's population live in China.

- In Wales, there are more sheep than people. The human population for Wales is 2,921,000, while there are approximately 5,000,000 sheep.

- The country with the most post offices is India, with over 152,792.

- In Switzerland, when a male reaches 20 years of age he is required to undergo fifteen weeks of military training. Over the next few decades, he has to attend training camps until he has accrued 300 to 1,300 days of active service. Swiss men who live abroad don't have to serve in the Swiss military, but they are required to pay 2 per cent of their income in the form of a military exemption tax. Men who don't qualify for military service also pay the tax, but women aren't required to pay the tax, nor are they expected to serve in the Swiss army.

- Ireland boasts the highest per capita consumption of cereal in the world – 15lb (6.8kg) per person annually.

- The popular American comic strip 'Peanuts' is known as 'Radishes' in Denmark.

- In Cupar, Scotland, in June of 1842, women hanging clothing on clothes-lines in an open area heard a sudden detonation, after which the clothes shot upwards into the air. Eventually, some of the clothing did fall back to the ground, but the rest kept ascending until it disappeared. Even odder, the clothes were carried off to the north, but chimney smoke in that area indicated that the wind was moving to the south.

- The country of Togo has the lowest crime rate in the world, with an average of just eleven reported crimes annually for every 100,000 of the population.

- The state bird of Texas is the mockingbird.

- Contrary to many reports, the Eisenhower Interstate System does not require that one mile in every five must be straight in the United States. The claim that these straight sections are usable as airstrips in times of war or other emergencies does not exist in any federal legislation. Korea and Sweden do use some of their roads as military airstrips, though.

- There are more than 100 offences that carry the death penalty in Iran.

- Airborne sand from the Sahara desert has been picked up 2,000 miles (3,216km) over the ocean.

- With an exchange rate running at an average of 177,000 Ukrainian karbovanets to the US dollar, total assets of just $6 will qualify a person as a Ukrainian millionaire.

- The tallest, longest, fastest and greatest drop roller coaster in the world is the Daidarasaurus in Nagashima Spa Land, Japan. It is 8,133ft (2.479m) long, 318ft (97m) high, has a drop of 307ft (93.5m) and a top speed of 95mph (153km/h).

- Close to 72 per cent of Australia's Aboriginals live in towns and cities.

- Over many centuries of living in the Arctic, Eskimos' bodies have adapted to the cold. Eskimos tend to be short and squat, which brings their arms and legs closer to the heart, so there is less danger of freezing. Extra fat around the torso protects their internal organs from the cold. The metabolism of Eskimos is also set a little higher than that of other peoples. As a result, they burn their food faster to stay warm. Their veins and arteries are also arranged to carry more warming blood to their hands.

- The full name for Britain, the United Kingdom of Great Britain and Northern Ireland, is the third longest country name in the world.

- Greenland ranks as the country with the highest percentage of smoking teenagers, with 56 per cent of 15-year-old boys and 45 per cent of 15-year-old girls smoking a cigarette daily.

- The country of Yemen has the world's highest fertility rate (average number of births per woman), at 7.6, while Switzerland has the world's lowest, at 1.5.

- Studies show that Chinese babies cry less and are more easily consoled than American babies.

- The Gulf Stream carries about 30 billion gallons (136 billion litres) of water every second – six times as much water as all the rivers in the world.

- Roughly 40 per cent of the population of the underdeveloped world is under 15 years old.

- London Heathrow Airport is the busiest international airport in the world, typically handling over 68 million international passengers a year.

- In terms of beer consumption, Britain is ranked seventh in the world, with the average Brit drinking 180 pints a year. The heaviest drinkers are in the Czech Republic, each consuming 281 pints a year on average.

- Japan overtook Sweden as the world's most geriatric nation in 2005.

- Japan is also the largest harvester of seafood in the world, taking 15 per cent of the world's total catch.

- When T.E. Lawrence returned from Arabia, he tried to become anonymous, often using the false names Ross and Shaw.

- In Thailand, the bodies of monks are preserved, once deceased, and placed on public display. However, thanks to an atmosphere of smog, humidity and heat, these corpses still retain teeth, hair and skin decades after their deaths, even though no special techniques are used to preserve the bodies.

- Throughout the South Pacific, no building is taller than the tallest palm tree.

- According to legend, visitors who wish to return to Rome must throw a coin into the city's Trevi fountain.

- Per capita, the Irish eat more chocolate than Americans, Swedes, Danes, French and Italians.

- Portugal was the first European country to start building its overseas empire.

- There are castles on the River Rhine in Germany called the Cat and Mouse castles.

- Munich has a chiming clock on its medieval town hall with two tiers of dancing and jousting figures that emerge twice daily.

- The Parthenon, in Athens, is built in the Doric style of architecture.

- Stockholm is known as the 'Venice of the North'.

- More than 1,000 languages are spoken in Africa.

- Shanghai, China, is sometimes called 'the Paris of the East' and 'the Whore of China'.

- The Spanish Steps are actually in Rome.

- There are no rivers in Saudi Arabia.

- Nearly half the population of Alaska live in one city, Anchorage.

- The Ainu are the aboriginal people of Japan.

- The women of the Tiwi tribe in the South Pacific are married at birth.

- The bulk of the island of Tenerife is the volcanic mountain, Mount Teide.

- The Canary Islands were once known as Blessed or Fortunate Isles.

- Mount Aso, in Japan, is the world's largest volcanic crater.

- Approximately one quarter of the world's population is Chinese.

- Denmark has the oldest flag in the world.

- China has the most borders with other countries.

- Polish people use zloty ('golden') as currency.

- The Romany people were wrongly thought to have come from Egypt, earning them the nickname 'gypsies'.

- Zaire was formerly known as the Belgian Congo.

- Nicaragua is the largest and most sparsely populated state in Central America.

- Colombia's largest export is cocaine.

- 'Himalayas' means 'abode of snow'.

- The Karakoram mountain range is known as the 'roof of the world'.

- Venice consists of 118 islands linked by 400 bridges.

- France is sometimes called the 'Hexagon' because it is roughly six-sided.

- Socrates taught Plato, who in turn taught Aristotle.

- Prime Minister William Gladstone's middle name was Ewart.

- Ronald Reagan was a sports commentator before becoming a Hollywood actor.

- Reagan once advertised Chesterfield cigarettes.

- Four American presidents were assassinated while in office: Lincoln, McKinley, Garfield and Kennedy.

- Linus Pauling is the only man ever to win two individual Nobel prizes; one for peace, the other for chemistry.

- In the 1969 Sydney to Hobart race, British Prime Minister Edward Heath captained the winning team in the yacht *Morning Cloud*.

- President Lincoln's advisor during the Civil War, Frederick Douglass, was born a slave.

- American astronaut John Glenn became a US senator in 1974 but was unsuccessful in his bid to become a Democratic presidential candidate.

- John F. Kennedy was the first Catholic president of the United States.

- Robin Hood became a titled gentleman called the Earl of Huntingdon.

- A fellow prison inmate killed the American serial sex murderer Jeffrey Dahmer in 1994.

- JFK is buried at Arlington National Cemetery, Virginia.

- Nathuran Godse assassinated Gandhi in 1948.

- Malcolm X's daughter, Qubilah Bahiyah Shabazz, was charged with allegedly hiring a hitman to kill the leader of Nation of Islam, Louis Farrakhan.

- When Neil Armstrong and Buzz Aldrin walked on the Moon in 1969, Michael Collins was left behind in the command module.

- John F. Kennedy represented Massachusetts as senator.

- Stella Rimington was the first woman to head MI5.

- Ronald Reagan's Scottish terriers were called Scotch and Soda.

- The Tibetan mountain people use yak's milk as their form of currency.

- Spain literally means 'the land of rabbits'.

- Little pools of unfrozen water can sometimes be found underneath the great icy plains of the Antarctic.

- Ten per cent of the salt mined in the world each year is used to de-ice the roads in the USA.

- The Spanish Inquisition once condemned the entire Netherlands to death for heresy.

- The River Nile has frozen over only twice in living memory – once in the 9th century and again in the 11th century.

- The Angel Falls in Venezuela are nearly twenty times taller than Niagara Falls.

- Dirty snow melts more quickly than clean snow.

- The Scandinavian capital, Stockholm, is built on nine islands connected by bridges.

- The Forth railway bridge in Scotland is a metre (33in) longer in summer than in winter, due to thermal expansion.

- In the Andes, time is often measured by how long it takes to smoke a cigarette.

- Until the 18th century, India produced almost all the world's diamonds.

- The Earth's magnetic field is not permanent.

- On 30 March 1867, Alaska was officially purchased from Russia for about 2 cents an acre. At the time, many politicians believed this purchase of 'wasteland to be a costly folly'.

- During winter, the skating rinks in Moscow cover more than 2,690,980ft^2 (250,000m^2) of land.

- As the Pacific plate moves under its coast, the North Island of New Zealand is getting larger.

- Brazil got its name from the nut, not the other way around.

- If you travel from east to west across the Soviet Union, you will cross seven time zones.

- Sahara means 'desert' in Arabic.

- On 15 January 1867, there was a severe frost in London, and over forty people died in Regent's Park when the ice broke on the main lake and they fell into the freezing waters.

- The water in the Dead Sea is so salty that it is far easier to float than to drown in it.

- The state flag of Alaska was designed by a 13-year-old boy.

- Lightning strikes the Earth about 200 times a second.

- Very hard rain would pour down at the rate of about 20mph (32km/h).

- Discounting Australia, which is generally regarded as a continental land mass, the world's largest island is Greenland.

- No rain has ever been recorded falling in the Atacama Desert in Chile.

- The background radiation in Aberdeen is twice that of the rest of Great Britain.

- About 2 million hydrogen atoms would be required to cover the full stop at the end of this sentence.

- The southernmost tip of Africa is not the Cape of Good Hope, but Cape Agulhas.

- During its lifetime, the Tower of London has had many roles, including that of a zoo.

- Two minor earthquakes occur every minute somewhere in the world.

- In the north of Norway, the sun shines constantly for about fourteen weeks each summer.

- The Polynesian country of Niue is a 65.6-mile^2 (170km^2) limestone rock emerging 197ft (60m) from the Pacific.

- Icelandic phone books are listed by the given name, not the surname.

- The United States, which accounts for 6 per cent of the population of the world, consumes nearly 60 per cent of the world's resources.

- The world's longest freshwater beach is located in Canada.

- Over the years, the Niagara Falls have moved more than 6.8 miles (11km) from their original site.

- The number of births in India each year is greater than the entire population of Australia.

- Yugoslavia is bordered by seven other countries.

- Greenland – so named to attract settlers – was discovered by Eric the Red in the 10th century.

- Within a few years of Columbus's discovery of America, the Spaniards had killed 1.5 million Native Americans.

- Hawaii officially became a part of the USA on 14 June 1900.

- The fastest tectonic movement on Earth is 9.4in (240mm) per year, at the Tonga micro-plate near Samoa.

- If the population of China walked past you in single file, the line would never end because of the rate of reproduction.

- The Earth is actually pear-shaped, the radius to the North Pole being 1.7in (44mm) longer than the South Pole radius.

- In 1908, the Moskva River in Russia rose 29ft 6in (9m), flooding 100 streets and 2,500 houses.

- South Africa produces two-thirds of the world's gold.

- There is about 200 times more gold in the world's oceans than has been mined in our entire history.

- One quarter of Russia is covered by forest.

- There is a rocking stone in Cornwall that, though it weighs many tons, can be rocked with ease.

- The volume of water in the Amazon is greater than the next eight largest rivers in the world combined.

- There is no point in England more than 75 miles (121km) from the ocean.

- England is smaller than New England.

- Nearly a quarter of the population of Poland was killed in World War II.

- There is a town in West Virginia called Looneyville.

- One of the greatest natural disasters of recent centuries occurred when an earthquake hit Tangshan, China, in 1976, killing three-quarters of a million people.

- New York was once called New Amsterdam.

- On Pitcairn Island, it is a criminal offence to shout 'Ship ahoy!' when there is, in fact, no ship in sight.

- The Dead Sea is actually an inland lake.

- There are 6 million trees in the Forest of Martyrs near Jerusalem, symbolising the Jewish death toll in World War II.

- Hawaii's Mount Waialeale is the wettest place in the world – it rains about 90 per cent of the time, about 480in (12,192mm) per annum.

- Between 1075 and 1080, the Norman baron Eudo Dapifer built Colchester Castle around the podium of the Roman temple of Claudius, creating the largest Norman keep in Britain.

- In Tokyo, to buy a three-line classified ad in the newspaper costs £1,800 per day.

- Hawaiian lore teaches that the earth mother Papa mated with the sky father Wakea to give birth to the Hawaiian islands.

- There are many kremlins in the Soviet Union. 'Kremlin' simply means the centre of government, which can be applied to the government buildings in any town.

- The per capita use of soap in Great Britain is 40oz (1,134g) per year. In France, it is only 22.6oz (641g) per year.

- There is a monastery in Ethiopia that can be entered only by climbing up a rope dropped over the edge of a cliff.

- In Turkey, when someone is in mourning they wear purple clothing, not black.

- The desert country of Saudi Arabia must import sand from other countries. This is because the Saudi desert sand is not suitable for building construction.

- In Tibet, some women have special metal instruments with which to pick their noses.

- There is a chemical waste dump in the Soviet Union that is twice as big as the whole state of Vermont.

- Nights in the Tropics are warm because moist air retains heat well. Desert nights get cold rapidly because dry air does not hold heat to the same degree.

- The largest Gothic cathedral is not in Rome or Paris, but on Amsterdam Avenue in New York City: it is the Cathedral of St John the Divine.

- The smallest church in the world is in Kentucky. There is room inside for just three people.

- Only 8.5 per cent of all Alaskans are Eskimos.

- Reno, Nevada, is farther west than Los Angeles, California.

- Twenty-four per cent of Los Angeles, California, consists of roads and parking lots for cars.

- There is a house in Margate, New Jersey, that is made in the shape of an elephant. Another home, in Norman, Oklahoma, is shaped like a chicken.

- There is a house in Massachusetts that is made entirely from newspapers, including the floors, walls and even the furniture.

- Another house, this one in Canada, is made from 18,000 discarded glass bottles.

- The Greek word for brotherly love is *philadelphia*.

- The worst American city to live in, from the viewpoint of air pollution, is St Louis, Missouri.

- Over half of all Americans travel more than a million miles (1.6 million km) in their lifetimes.

- American drivers average about 8,200 miles (13,200km) a year.

3

NUMBERS

- If you multiply 1,089 by 9, you get 9,801. It's reversed itself! This also works with 10,989 or 109,989 or 1,099,989 and so on.

- 1 is the only positive whole number you can add to 1,000,000 and get an answer that's bigger than if you multiply it by 1,000,000.

- $19 = 1 \times 9 + 1 + 9$ and $29 = 2 \times 9 + 2 + 9$. This also works for 39, 49, 59, 69, 79, 89 and 99.

- 153, 370, 371 and 407 are all the 'sum of the cubes of their digits'. In other words, $153 = 1 + 125 + 27$.

- If you divide any square number by 8, you get a remainder of 0, 1 or 4.

- 2 is the only number that gives the same result added to itself as it does times by itself.

- If you multiply 21,978 by 4, it turns backwards.

- There are 12,988,816 different ways to cover a chessboard with 32 dominoes.

- 69 squared = 69^2 = 4,761 and 69 cubed = 69^3 = 328,509. These two answers use all the digits from 0 to 9 between them. As does 18^3 = 5,832 and 184 to the power of 4 = 104,976.

- You can chop a big lump of cheese into a maximum of ninety-three bits with eight straight cuts.

- In the English language, 'forty' is the only number that has all its letters in alphabetical order.

- $1 \div 37 = 0.027027027\ldots$ and $1 \div 27 = 0.037037037\ldots$

- 13^2 = 169 and if you write both numbers backwards you get 31^2 = 961. This also works with 12, because 12^2 = 144 and 21^2 = 441.

- $1/1089 = 0.00091827364554637281\ldots$ (And the numbers in the 9 times table are 9, 18, 27, 36…)

- 8 is the only cube that is 1 less than a square.

- To multiply 10,112,359,550,561,797,752,808,988,764,044, 943,820, 224,719 by 9 you just move the 9 at the very end up to the front. It's the only number that does this.

- The number 4 is the only number in the English language that is spelled with the same number of letters as the number itself.

- $1 \times 9 + 2 = 11$, $12 \times 9 + 3 = 111$, $123 \times 9 + 4 = 1111$ and so on.

- Twenty-nine is the only number that is written with as many strokes as its numerical value! (You need to write 'Y' with three strokes.)

- There are 169,518,829,100,544,000,000,000,000,000 ways to play the first ten moves in a game of chess!

- 3,608,528,850,368,400,786,036,725 has twenty-five digits and divides by 25.

- An 'octillion' is the lowest positive number to contain a letter 'c'.

- One is the only number in the English language to have its letters in reverse alphabetical order.

- The biggest number you can make with three digits and any operators is 9 to the power of 9 to the power of 9. As 9 to the power of $9 = 387,420,489$, the final number is $9^{387,420,489}$ = a number that is over 200 million digits!

- $1 \div 14 = 0.0714285714285714285\ldots$ and 7, 14 and 28 are factors and multiples of 14 and the 5 tells you how many digits 71428 has before they repeat!

- To add all the numbers 1–10, you just divide the 10 by 2 then write the answer out twice = 55. Also all the numbers 1–100 are 100 divided by 2 written twice, i.e. 5,050. This also works for 1–1,000, 1–10,000, 1–100,000, etc!

- 144 is the twelfth number in the Fibonacci series. 144 is also 12^2.

- All the numbers from 12 to 242 added together equal 70^2.

- 1,274,953,680 uses all the digits 0–9 and you can divide it exactly by any number from 1 to 16.

- There is something curious in the properties of the number 9. Any number multiplied by 9 produces a sum of figures that, added together, continually makes 9. For example, all the first multiples of 9 – 18, 27, 36, 45, 54, 63, 72, 81 – add up to 9. Each of them multiplied by any number produces a similar result: 8 x 81 = 648; these added together make 18: 1 and 8 = 9; multiply 648 by itself, the product is 419,904 – the sum of these digits is 27: 2 + 7 = 9. The rule is invariable.

- A mile on land is 5,280ft (1,609m) long. A nautical mile is 6,080ft (1,853m).

- A carat, the measurement of gems, is 200mg, nearly the equivalent of a carb seed on which it was based.

- A pound of gold actually weighs less than a pound of feathers. Explanation: feathers are measured in avoirdupois weight, in which there are 16 oz per pound. Gold is measured in troy weight, with 12oz per pound.

- If you add up the numbers 1–100 consecutively (1 + 2 + 3 + 4 + 5, etc), the total is 5,050.

- The numbers 172 can be found on the back of the US five-dollar bill in the bushes at the base of the Lincoln Memorial.

- 111,111,111 x 111,111,111 = 12,345,678,987,654,321.

4

ARTS AND
ENTERTAINMENT

- Dirk Bogarde's real name was Derek Jules Gaspard Ulric Niven van den Bogaerde.

- In 1944, Barry Fitzgerald got an Oscar nomination in both the Best Actor and Best Supporting Actor categories for the same role in *Going My Way*.

- The first-ever Academy Awards ceremony lasted five minutes, with tickets costing just $10.

- In *Zulu* (1964), some of the Zulu warriors are clearly wearing the wrist watches they were paid with.

- Disney's *Beauty and the Beast* (1991) is the only animated film ever to be nominated for a Best Picture Oscar.

- Judy Garland was 17 years old when she appeared in *The Wizard of Oz* (1939).

- *Star Wars* (1977) was originally called 'The Adventures of Luke Starkiller'. The hero's name was later changed from Starkiller to Skywalker for fear that it sounded too violent.

- The first ever remake was the 1904 re-release of *The Great Train Robbery* (1903).

- A record 8,552 animals were featured in *Around the World in Eighty Days* (1956).

- In 1925, MGM ran a contest to find a new name for Lucille LeSueur. They settled on Joan Crawford.

- The shortest-ever Hollywood marriage is the six-hour union of Rudolph Valentino and Jean Acker.

- Laurence Olivier is the only actor to direct himself in an Oscar-winning performance – in *Hamlet* (1948).

- The only soundtrack to out-gross the movie is that for *Superfly* (1972).

- Paul Newman was the joint owner of an Indy car racing team.

- The date 29 August 1997 is that of Judgement Day in *Terminator 2* (1991).

- The *Braveheart* sword was auctioned in New York in 2001 for $135,000.

- *The Wizard of Oz* was released in England with an X certificate.

- MGM's Irving Thalberg rejected *Gone with the Wind* (1939), saying 'No Civil War picture ever made a nickel!'

- As a prop, E.T. was insured for $1.3 million.

- In *Star Wars*, when the storm troopers break into the control room where R2-D2 and C-3PO are hiding, one of them smacks his head on the door and falls backwards.

- One in twenty American film-goers saw *Star Wars* more than once in 1977, its opening year.

- Actor Henry Winkler, aka the Fonz in US TV series *Happy Days*, was considered for the part of Danny Zuko in *Grease* (1978).

- MGM had a reputation for being the most glamorous film studio, based on its having white telephones.

- Comedian, director, actor and author Billy Crystal has won three Emmy awards for hosting the Oscars.

- In the 1959 film *Ben-Hur*, nine chariots start the chariot race, but six crash and four finish, making a total of ten.

- In *Casablanca* (1942), Humphrey Bogart ad-libbed the line 'Here's looking at you, kid.'

- The names of the companies responsible for the end of the world in the *Terminator* movies, Skynet and Cyberdyne Systems, are actually names of real companies.

- In *Gladiator* (2000), during the battle with the Barbarian Horde, one of the chariots is turned over – revealing a gas cylinder in the back.

- The roar of the T. Rex in *Jurassic Park* (1993) is a blast from a baby elephant mixed with alligator growls and tiger shrieks.

- George Harrison was president of the George Formby Appreciation Society.

- The difference between animated chipmunks Chip 'n' Dale is that Chip has one tooth and Dale has two.

- Billie Holiday was known as 'Lady Day'.

- There are five basic foot positions in ballet.

- Thirteen or more players are needed for a big band.

- The heavy metal band Black Sabbath got their name from a 1963 horror film of the same name starring Boris Karloff.

- Johann Strauss was seven years old when he wrote his first waltz.

- Super-heroine Wonder Woman's real name is Diana Prince.

- Verdi's opera *Aida* was commissioned to celebrate the opening of the Suez Canal in 1869.

- Popeye lives on the Island of Sweetwater.

- The Fine Young Cannibals won Best British Group at the 1990 Brit Awards. The band members returned their trophies, however, saying that the awards show was being used to promote Margaret Thatcher.

- Prince's nickname is 'His Royal Badness'.

- Johnny Cash recorded albums live in Folsom State Prison and San Quentin State Prison, both in California, but contrary to popular belief was never imprisoned himself.

- The TV series *Battlestar Galactica* was the subject of lawsuits from 20th Century Fox, as the company alleged it was a 'steal' from *Star Wars*.

- The cartoon strip 'Peanuts' has appeared in some 2,600 newspapers in seventy-five countries, and has been translated into twenty-one languages.

- Chopin made his debut as a pianist at the age of eight.

- Billy Batson must say the name of the ancient wizard 'Shazam' to transform into Captain Marvel.

- Dolly Parton owns a theme park called Dollywood in the Great Smoky Mountains, Tennessee.

- There are 20,000 television commercials made each year that are aimed exclusively at children in the USA, with 7,000 for sugared breakfast cereals.

- Ancient Chinese artists freely painted scenes of nakedness but would never depict a bare female foot.

- Nearly 80 per cent of Japanese adverts use celebrities, the majority being local stars. Of the foreign celebrities, the most popular are Arnold Schwarzenegger, promoting noodles, and Steven Spielberg, endorsing whiskey.

- The average American sees or hears 560 advertisements a day.

- War photographer Robert Capa's famous photos of D-Day were selected from only 11 exposures that survived the developing process. Although he had shot four rolls of film, most of the photos were ruined by heat.

- In Leonardo da Vinci's famous painting *The Last Supper*, a salt cellar near Judas Iscariot is knocked over. This is said to have started the superstition that spilt salt is unlucky.

- The oldest piano still in existence was built in 1720.

- The average medium-sized piano has about 230 strings, each string having about 165lb (75kg) of tension, with the combined pull of all strings equalling approximately 18 tons (18,288kg).

- X-rays of Leonardo da Vinci's *Mona Lisa* reveal there to be three completely different versions of the same subject, all painted by da Vinci, under the final portrait.

- The sculpture by Auguste Rodin that has come to be called *The Thinker* was not meant to be a profile of a man in thought, but a representation of the poet Dante.

- Because of the precautions taken to prevent photographers from showing the public what occurred on the floor of the New York Stock Exchange, the first published picture of the venue, in 1907, was made through an empty coat sleeve that concealed a camera.

- The harp's ancestor is a hunting bow.

- Violins weigh less than 16oz (approximately 448g) yet resist string tension of over 65lb (29kg).

- It took four months to synchronise the three-minute fight scene between live actors and animated skeletons in *Jason and the Argonauts* (1963).

- The highest-paid animal actors are bears, which can earn $20,000 a day.

- The real names of Fred Astaire and Ginger Rogers were Frederic Austerlitz Jr and Virginia Katherine McMath respectively.

- Film star Audrey Hepburn was fluent in English, French, Dutch, Flemish, Spanish and Italian, and was a member of the Dutch Resistance in World War II from the age of 15.

- 'Success is a great deodorant. It takes away all your past smells.' *Elizabeth Taylor*

- Leonard Nimoy owned a pet store in the 1960s before playing Mr Spock in *Star Trek*.

- 'The duration of a film should not exceed the capacity of the human bladder.' *Alfred Hitchcock*

- In the movie *Rear Window* (1954), Grace Kelly is in a scene arguing with James Stewart, who is sitting in a wheelchair with a cast on his leg. The cast switches from his left leg to his right during the scene.

- In the first *Terminator* (1984), Arnold Schwarzenegger had only seventeen lines of dialogue.

- The man who opened the world's first movie theatre in Paris said, 'The cinema is an invention without any commercial future.'

- In *Camelot* (1967), when King Arthur (Richard Harris) makes a speech praising his subjects and realm, he has a modern Band Aid plaster on his neck.

- Before he became a film actor, Humphrey Bogart, as the house player for an arcade, charged 50 cents a game to people who wanted to play chess.

- David Niven's voice had to be dubbed on in *Curse of the Pink Panther* (1983) by Canadian impersonator Rich Little. Niven was so ill while filming that he could not speak. It was his last role and he died the year the film was released.

- The 1999 movie *South Park: Bigger, Longer and Uncut* has the dubious distinction of containing the most swear words in any film – 399 – and the most offensive gestures – 128.

- *The Bridge on the River Kwai* won seven Oscars, but star Alec Guinness's name was mis-spelled as 'Guiness' in the titles.

- Al Capone is shown living in a sumptuous Chicago mansion in the film *The St Valentine's Day Massacre* (1967). In fact, he lived in a small house in a working-class district of the city.

- Rock matriarch Sharon Osbourne keeps her hands soft with peanut oil – the same concoction she uses to stop the wooden countertops in her kitchen from drying out.

- Hollywood legend Zsa Zsa Gabor hosted the Rubik's cube's launch in America, beginning with a Hollywood party on 5 May 1980.

- US president Gerald Ford once worked as a cover model for *Cosmopolitan* magazine.

- When the decision was made in 1962 that cartoon family *The Flintstones* would have a baby, the child was originally going to be a boy. Later, they decided that a girl would make for better merchandising, such as dolls.

- US rapper Sean 'P. Diddy' Combs is such a fan of Al Pacino's 1983 *Scarface* movie that he has watched it sixty-three times.

- Former TV Superman Dean Cain was a one-time football star in Buffalo, New York. The actor signed for the Buffalo Bills after leaving Princeton University but seriously injured his knee and had to retire before he had played a game for the team.

- Pop diva Jennifer Lopez demanded her on-set trailer on *Shall We Dance?* (2004) be stocked with diet cream soda, despite the fact that the drink is unavailable to buy where the movie was being shot in Winnipeg, Canada. Supplies had to be flown in from Seattle.

- One alternative title considered for sitcom *Friends* was 'Insomnia Café'.

- American funnyman Jerry Seinfeld received £315,000 for a fifteen-minute gig in Las Vegas.

- Will Smith is currently the world's highest-paid actor, taking home a massive $80 million a year.

- While attending America's University of Iowa, actor Ashton Kutcher helped pay his tuition fees by sweeping floors at a local General Mills plant.

- Between takes on movie *Shall We Dance?*, Jennifer Lopez ate strawberry muffins and ice cream on an almost daily basis.

- US singer and actress Hilary Duff is set to launch a new line of canine clothing called Little Dog Duff, named after her own pooch Little Dog.

- Hard rocker Andrew WK has named his new album after his most loyal fans. The Party Hard star has named his album *Wolf* after the WK Wolves who follow him on tour.

- Australian pop beauty Holly Valance's real surname is Vuckadinovic.

- *Alexander* star Colin Farrell often checks into hotels under the name Tom Foolery, while *American Pie* actress Tara Reid regularly adopts the moniker Strawberry Shortcake. *The Truth About Love* star Jennifer Love Hewitt dubs herself Winnie The Pooh.

- *The Osbournes* star Jack Osbourne has had 'Mum' tattooed in a heart on his left shoulder as a special thank-you to mum Sharon, who helped him battle his drug- and alcohol-abuse problems.

- *American Idol* bosses have banned wannabe pop stars from singing Alicia Keys's 'Fallin'' in try-outs, because judges Simon Cowell, Randy Jackson and Paula Abdul are tired of the song.

- *Baywatch*'s Pamela Anderson failed her first driving test when she hit another car. She passed at the fourth attempt.

- Hollywood heartthrob George Clooney bought a couple of *Charlie's Angels* star Lucy Liu's arty collages when she had a brief stint with him on *ER*.

- Pop babe Beyoncé Knowles spends £4,000 a week on personal trainer Mark Jenkins in order to maintain her stunning physique.

- Rap mogul Russell Simmons and his wife have different refrigerators because the DEF JAM founder doesn't want his vegan food mixed with her chicken, fish and dairy products.

- Veteran rocker Bruce Springsteen's triumphant concert at Boston's Fenway Park on 6 September 2003 was the first rock show in the baseball stadium's ninety-one-year history.

- Comedienne Ellen DeGeneres has had a ping-pong table installed on the set of her new chat show *The Ellen DeGeneres Show* to encourage her colleagues to play as hard as they work.

- British women have voted former Spice Girls singer Victoria Beckham as the most boring celebrity to socialise with.

- British singer Robbie Williams refuses to let his lack of a driving licence stop him splashing out on cars. The Los Angeles-based star, who has never passed a driving test, already has a Ferrari and a Jaguar – and now he's looking at a £200,000 Lamborghini Diablo.

- Rappers 50 Cent and Eminem had very simple backstage requests at the MTV Music Video Awards; while other stars were demanding bowls of raw vegetables and expensive alcohol, the rap pair asked for four boxes of Kentucky Fried Chicken and large portions of Mexican treats from Taco Bell.

- Wild-living rocker Ozzy Osbourne has installed a 20ft (12m) water jet at his Los Angeles home in order to deter potential thieves. It will soak anyone who comes near the house without an invitation.

- With an empire consisting of Bad Boy Entertainment, Sean John clothing, Blue Flame marketing and advertising, Justin's restaurants and MTV show *Making The Band 2*, rap mogul Sean 'P. Diddy' Combs, 32, has been ranked twelfth in *Fortune* magazine's Under-40 list, which ranks those below the age of 40 who've become multimillionaires.

- Celebrity parents Will Smith, Madonna, Chris O'Donnell and Kevin Kline are among the many stars who have splashed out on Posh Tots' mini mansions, castles and chalets for their children to play in. The prices for the little homes range from £29,375 to £54,693.

- The Karl Lagerfeld-designed Chanel dress that *Sex in the City*'s Sarah Jessica Parker wore to the 2003 Emmy Awards took 250 hours to make.

- US talk-show host Oprah Winfrey says her two favourite interviews of all time were with Sidney Poitier and Salma Hayek.

- Athens-born rocker Tommy Lee's mother was Miss Greece in 1957.

- Actress Daryl Hannah's brother Don is a skydiving instructor.

- Rocker Simon Le Bon often checks into hotels under the name Shake Yabooty, while rapper Wyclef Jean calls himself Dracula and US singer Brian McKnight opts for Albert Einstein.

- Michael Caine's movie *Secondhand Lions* (2003) was made after the film script topped a magazine list of the ten best scripts never made into a film.

- US actress Drew Barrymore mixed together cream of mushroom soup and stuffing to make her vomit look authentic on the set of comedy *Duplex* (2003).

- Hollywood star Ben Affleck appeared as an extra – playing a basketball player – in the 1992 surprise hit film *Buffy the Vampire Slayer*.

- Czech supermodel Karolina Kurkova's father doubled up as a police chief and a basketball professional when she was a child growing up in Decin.

- Rapper NAS's 30th birthday cake was iced with green marijuana leaves, as a nod to his hemp advocacy.

- Presenters and nominees at the 2003 Emmy Awards received a gift basket worth more than £18,750 featuring speciality phones and a trip to Bora Bora.

- US actress Rena Sofer, who stars in the American version of saucy British sitcom *Coupling*, is an orthodox rabbi.

- Legendary singer Sir Elton John refuses to play white pianos, which he brands 'tasteless'. He also dislikes white limousines, but he can tolerate one item in white – refrigerators.

- US rappers Eminem and Wyclef Jean were born on the same day in the same year, 17 October 1972.

- Rocker Dave Matthews and his wife Ashley have matching wedding bands made out of pressed pennies from the years they were born, 1967 and 1973 respectively.

- Flamboyant comic Eddie Izzard practically managed to sell out his *Sexie* show at New York's City Centre despite having virtually no advertising or promotion.

- Director Quentin Tarantino was so impressed with the bar from the fictitious House of Blue Leaves, created for his movie *Kill Bill, Vol. 1* (2003) he had it installed in his Hollywood home.

- Funnyman Jim Carrey, comedienne Ellen DeGeneres and *Frasier* star Jane Leeves were in the same acting class before hitting fame.

- Actress Uma Thurman carried home rocks from the different locations where she filmed *Kill Bill* for her children Maya, five, and Roan, one.

- *Everybody Loves Raymond* star Ray Romano went to high school with actress Fran Drescher in New York, and refused to be funny in her presence because he couldn't stand her nasal laugh.

- Radiohead star Jonny Greenwood has turned composer – he has penned the score for the human life on Earth TV documentary *Bodysong*.

- Rapper 50 Cent's £2.6 million mansion in Farmington, Connecticut, is the largest in the entire state. The pad used to belong to Mike Tyson and boasts eighteen bedrooms, thirty-eight bathrooms and a man-made waterfall.

- Dublin kebab restaurant Abrakebabra rewarded Westlife singer Bryan McFadden with a gold card to thank him for being their best customer.

- Rapper Eminem's parents once fronted a covers group called Daddy Warbucks.

- Movie funnyman Bill Murray owns a little-league baseball team in St Paul, Minnesota, and helps boost attendances by inviting fans to try out the hot tub he has installed in the stand.

- Football-mad rocker Rod Stewart's fourteen-year-old son with model Rachel Hunter, Liam McAllister Stewart, is named after Scottish international sport hero Gary McAllister.

- *Friends* star Jennifer Aniston wore underwear with a picture of Brad Pitt on it to the 2003 Emmy Awards.

- Welsh actress Catherine Zeta Jones's son Dylan has become so close to his mother's pal George Clooney that he now refers to the actor as 'Uncle George'.

- Reportedly, flamboyant rocker Sir Elton John is having a range of candles made for him with specially designed wicks, as he can't sleep unless he has personally trimmed them before going to bed.

- Staff at supermarket Tesco were so impressed with a special extra-large species of South African avocado that they've christened it the 'J-Lo' after Jennifer Lopez's impressive curves.

- US actor Kevin Costner has twice taken on roles after Harrison Ford turned them down – Ford was the original choice to star in *Dragonfly* (2002) and *JFK* (1991).

- The name of 4-LOM, one of the bounty hunters seen listening to Darth Vader in *The Empire Strikes Back* (1980), stands for: For Love Of Money.

- Hollywood comedian Jim Carrey voted in 2004 at the Beverly Hills City Hall. He had an assistant wait in line for him, however.

- Police in Italy had to come to UK supermodel Naomi Campbell's rescue when a crowd of up to 4,000 men swarmed a beach she was visiting.

- The Russian Imperial Necklace has been loaned out by Joseff jewellers of Hollywood for 1,215 different feature films.

- *Titanic* (1997) star Leonardo DiCaprio says he practised his losing smile for the Oscars – because he knew he wouldn't win the Best Actor trophy.

- There is a new television show on a British cable channel called *Watching Paint Dry*. Viewers watch in real time: gloss, semi-gloss, matt, satin, you name it. Then viewers vote out their least favourite.

- The BBC asked to interview reggae legend Bob Marley in 2005 for a documentary – despite the fact he died in 1981. They sent the Bob Marley Foundation an email saying it would involve him 'spending one or two days with us'.

- Thousands of Britons say they would like Robbie Williams's song 'Angels' played at their funeral.

- In *Star Wars*, a small pair of metal dice can be seen hanging in the *Millennium Falcon*'s cockpit as Chewbacca prepares to depart from Mos Eisley. The dice do not appear in subsequent scenes.

- Zeppo Marx (the unfunny one of the Marx Brothers) had a patent for a wrist watch with a heart monitor.

- A schoolgirl asked band Coldplay for their autographs to sell for charity – and got a triple platinum disc worth £4,000.

- Flamenco dancer José Greco took out an insurance policy through Lloyd's of London against his trousers splitting during a performance.

- Jonathan Davids, lead singer of Korn, played in his high-school bagpipe band.

- Rap artist Sean 'P. Diddy' Combs had his first job aged two when he modelled in an ad for Baskin-Robbins ice-cream shops.

- *E.T.* (1982) director Steven Spielberg is Drew Barrymore's godfather. After seeing her nude in *Playboy* magazine, he sent her a blanket with a note telling her to cover herself up.

- In 1996, 37 per cent of the toys sold in the United States were *Star Wars* products.

- *Speed* (1994) star Sandra Bullock has revealed she uses haemorrhoid cream on her face.

- The Monty Python movie *The Life of Brian* (1979) was banned in Scotland on its release.

- In 1977, the legendary Groucho Marx died three days after Elvis Presley died. Unfortunately, due to the fevered commotion caused by Presley's unanticipated death, the media paid little attention to the passing of this brilliant comic.

- *Men in Black* star Will Smith wants female fans to stop asking him to sign their breasts – because he doesn't want to upset their boyfriends.

- Actor Robert De Niro played the part of the Cowardly Lion in his elementary school's production of *The Wizard of Oz*. De Niro was ten at the time.

- 'Rudolph the Red-Nosed Reindeer' was created in 1939, in Chicago, for the Montgomery Ward department stores for a Christmas promotion. The lyrics were written as a poem, 'Rollo, the Red-nosed Reindeer', by Robert May. Montgomery Ward liked it but didn't like the name Rollo, so they changed it to Rudolph. It wasn't set to music until 1947 and Gene Autry recorded the hit song in 1949.

- The first Michelin Man costume (Bibendum) was worn by none other than Col. Harlan Sanders of Kentucky Fried Chicken fame.

- Former *EastEnders* star Danniella Westbrook buys her millionaire husband clothes on eBay.

- In Estonia, *Teletubbies* is known as *Teletupsuds*.

- *Winnie the Pooh* author A.A. Milne's full name was Alan Alexander Milne.

- *Teletubbies* is filmed in the open on a site in Warwickshire. The dome, hills and rabbits are real. Some of the grass and flowers are real and some are artificial.

- You cannot walk down the Disney parade route without being on at least one camera.

- Actress Jodie Foster was George Lucas's second choice to play the part of Princess Leia in *Star Wars*.

- In 1978, the 'Hollywood' sign was in such a state of disrepair (termites had infested the wooden scaffolding that supports the 15m-high letters) that one of the Os had fallen off.

- After fifty events, the UK claims to be the most successful Eurovision nation – Ireland have won more often, with seven victories to the UK's five, but the UK have finished second an astonishing fifteen times.

- A shocking *EastEnders* storyline featuring Dennis Rickman having an affair with Peggy Mitchell was pulled at the last minute.

- Nicole Richie has six pet rats and gave her *Simple Life* co-star Paris Hilton a rat she called 'Tori Spelling' for Christmas.

- Ex-Van Halen frontman David Lee Roth cancelled the rest of his US tour after injuring himself performing 'a very fast, complicated 15th-century samurai move' during a recent performance.

- In 2004, rocker David Bowie thought he was being stalked by someone dressed as a giant pink rabbit. Bowie noticed the fan at several concerts, but became alarmed when he got on a plane and the bunny was on board.

- The beginning of *The Wizard of Oz* is black and white because colour was not available at that point. When colour was available, the writers decided to start using it for the scenes in Munchkinland.

- Television presenter Johnny Vaughan says his £60,000 sports car was crashed by his pet bulldog, Harvey. Vaughan had stopped his automatic Maserati 3200GT on the way home from a visit to a vet, thinking Harvey needed the toilet, but, when he got out of the vehicle, Harvey jumped across the seat and hit the gear stick into drive.

- Stars received an unusual gift in their goodie bag at this year's Oscars – a vacuum cleaner.

- The computer Hal in *2001: Space Odyssey* (1968) got his name from the producers of the film. HAL are the letters before IBM (H comes before I, A before B and L before M).

- Napoleon Bonaparte is the historical figure most often portrayed in movies. He has been featured in 194 movies. By comparison, Jesus Christ features in 152 and Abraham Lincoln in 137.

- While on a training schedule and drinking protein drinks to enhance her muscles, Hollywood superstar Halle Berry confessed she couldn't stop breaking wind as a result of the drinks.

- Chewbacca's name is inspired by the name of Chebika City, in Tunisia, near the place where the Tatooine scenes in *Star Wars* where shot.

- Glamour model Jordan once said she fancied a six-in-a-bed romp with five other celebrities – but not the Beckhams.

- In 1965, auditions were held for TV show *The Monkees*. Some of the people who responded (but were not hired) were Stephen Stills, Harry Nilsson and songwriter Paul Williams.

- *American Beauty* (1999) star Kevin Spacey's older brother is a professional Rod Stewart impersonator.

- A BBC children's presenter was reprimanded for wearing a T-shirt that contained a risqué slogan. Dominic Wood was rapped for wearing a 'Morning Wood' T-shirt on his *Dick and Dom in da Bungalow* show.

- Irish singer Ronan Keating had to abandon a filming session when he was flashed at by streakers in Phuket, Thailand.

- A mouse caused £7,000 worth of damage to BBC television presenter Sue Barker's Ferrari.

- David Letterman was voted Class Smart Alec at his home-town high school, Broad Ripple High.

- La Boca in southern Buenos Aires, Argentina, is the birthplace of the tango.

- *Basic Instinct* (1992) star Sharon Stone is a member of MENSA.

- The *Millennium Falcon* in *Star Wars* was originally inspired by the shape of a hamburger with an olive on the side.

- Singer Lenny Kravitz kept a marijuana joint he'd shared with Rolling Stone Mick Jagger for a year as a tribute.

- In *The Empire Strikes Back*, legendary actor Alec Guinness performed all his appearances in six hours.

- The Swedish pop group ABBA recently turned down an offer of £1 billion to reunite.

- In 1962, the Mashed Potato, the Loco-Motion, the Frug, the Monkey and the Funky Chicken were all popular dances.

- *Friends* star Lisa Kudrow has a degree in biology from Vassar College.

- Hollywood legend Paul Newman was colour-blind.

- *Miss Congeniality* (2000) star Sandra Bullock is allergic to horses.

- US actress Lara Flynn Boyle is dyslexic.

- *9 ½ Weeks* Star Kim Basinger has suffered panic attacks during which she cannot leave the house.

- *Austin Powers* star Mike Myers has an aversion to being touched.

- *Charlie and the Chocolate Factory* (2005) star Johnny Depp is afraid of clowns.

- *Four Weddings and a Funeral* (1994) actress Andie MacDowell worked at McDonald's and Pizza Hut as a teenager.

- US funnyman Steve Martin once worked at Disneyland selling maps and guidebooks.

- *Matrix* star Keanu Reeves's father has served time in prison for cocaine possession.

- *Cheers* actor Woody Harrelson's father has served time in prison for murder.

- *Red Dragon* (2002) actor Edward Norton's father invented the shopping mall.

- *ER* actress Julianna Margulies's father wrote the 'Plop-Plop, Fizz-Fizz' Alka-Seltzer commercial.

- The great-uncle of *Baywatch* star David Hasselhoff was Karl Hasselhoff, the inventor of inflatable sheep.

- Singer Eric Clapton owns one-fifth of the planet Mars.

- In the film *Forrest Gump* (1994), all the still photos show Forrest with his eyes closed.

- Toto the dog was paid £65 per week while filming *The Wizard of Oz*.

- Kelsey Grammar sings and plays the piano for the theme song of *Frasier*.

- The director of 2005's *Charlie and the Chocolate Factory*, Tim Burton, spent millions on training squirrels to crack nuts to recreate the 'Nut Room' scene.

- Cinderella's slippers were originally made out of fur. The story was changed in the 1600s by a translator.

- Pupils at a US school have been offered counselling after a teacher showed them clips of Mel Gibson's film *The Passion of the Christ* (2004).

- A fan of *Pop Idol* runner-up Gareth Gates missed meeting him when he turned up at her home because her dad had the television on too loud.

- An elderly actor who broke his leg on stage during a performance of Nobel Prize winner Dario Fo's *The Accidental Death of an Anarchist* in Bosnia had to endure laughs and taunts from the audience who thought his cries of pain were part of the show.

- Pinocchio was made of pine.

- In the opening scene of *Raiders of the Lost Ark* (1981), Indy escapes with the golden idol in a seaplane with the registration number OB-3PO. This of course refers to Obi-wan and C-3PO from *Star Wars*.

- The 'Mexican Hat Dance' is the official dance of Mexico.

- Professional ballerinas use about twelve pairs of toe shoes per week.

- US singer Macy Gray has stunned fans by performing naked on stage – apart from a pair of designer shoes.

- For *Star Wars*' 20th anniversary, the first episode film renovation cost as much as the original movie.

- Former Generation-X singer Billy Idol has revealed he shaves his grey pubic hair.

- Over eight years of *Seinfeld*, 'Cosmo' Kramer went through Jerry Seinfeld's apartment door 284 times.

- Actress Elizabeth Hurley has twelve piercings in her ears and a pierced nose.

- Buskers in Budapest are to have to take a yearly exam to protect tourists from musically incompetent beggars.

- A rock fan who paid £1,000 for a guitar signed by Queen's Brian May rubbed off the signature with his sleeve when he played it.

- In all three *Godfather* films, when you see oranges there is a death (or a very close call) coming up soon.

- Prince Charles sent a bottle of whisky to recovering alcoholic Ozzy Osbourne after his quad bike crash.

- When director George Lucas was mixing the *American Graffiti* (1973) soundtrack, he numbered the reels of film starting with an 'R' and numbered the dialogue starting with a 'D'. Sound designer Walter Murch would ask George for Reel 2, Dialogue 2 by saying 'R2D2'. George liked the way that sounded so much he integrated it into another project he was working on.

- Singer Janet Jackson's boob flash at the Super Bowl has become the most searched event in the history of the Internet.

- It was illegal to sell *E.T.* dolls in France because there is a law there against selling dolls without human faces.

- DJ Jo Whiley has gone under the knife to have a third nipple removed. She had thought it was a mole until doctors informed her otherwise.

- The Paramount logo contains twenty-two stars.

- Donald Duck lives at 1313 Webfoot Walk, Duckburg, Calisota.

- The small actor hiding inside R2-D2 is named Kenny Baker. He is less than 4ft (1.2m) tall.

- Canadian singer Bryan Adams's song 'Everything I Do (I Do It For You)' is the track most couples pick for the first dance at their weddings.

- By the time an American child finishes primary school he will have witnessed 8,000 murders and 100,000 acts of violence on television.

- Veteran crooner Tony Christie has landed a £50,000 contract to become the face of Stilton cheese.

- Sections of the under-construction Death Star in *Star Wars* resemble the San Francisco skyline, the silhouette of a favourite city of George Lucas.

- In 1912, the Archbishop of Paris declared dancing the tango a sin.

- Karmuela Searlel, one of the many Tarzans, was mauled to death on the set by a raging elephant.

- The most popular TV show in Venezuela is the *Miss Venezuela Pageant*.

- A man who lost £20,000 worth of prizes on ITV1's *Ant and Dec's Saturday Night Takeaway* crashed his car after leaving the studio.

- *Return of the Jedi* (1983) was originally titled 'Revenge of the Jedi' – but later underwent a title change, because, according to director George Lucas, a Jedi would never take revenge.

- Television presenter Nick Owen was turned away from a football club bar that is named after him. The BBC *Midlands Today* presenter was trying to get into the Nick Owen bar at Luton Town Football Club, but was refused entry because the bar was full.

- Scenes showing Irish actor Colin Farrell's penis have been cut from a film he's made – because it's too distracting for audiences.

- Jackie Stallone, mother of *Rocky* star Sylvester, says she believes her dogs possess psychic powers because they predicted George W. Bush would win the US election.

5

THE THINGS PEOPLE SAY

● 'After doing *One Fine Day* and playing a paediatrician on ER, I'll never have kids. I'm going to have a vasectomy.'

George Clooney

● 'Alex Ferguson is the best manager I've ever had at this level. Well, he's the only manager I've actually had at this level. But he's the best manager I've ever had.'

David Beckham, when at Manchester United

● 'Once you've been really "bad" in a movie, there's a certain kind of fearlessness you develop.'

Jack Nicholson

● 'I carried my Oscar to bed with me. My first and only three-way happened that night.'

Halle Berry

● 'No one is more enslaved than a slave who doesn't think they're enslaved.'

Kate Beckinsale

● 'I'd like to put on buckskins and a ponytail and go underwater with a reed, hiding from the Indians... To me, that's sexy!'

Kevin Costner

● 'My biggest nightmare is I'm driving home and get sick and go to hospital. I say, "Please help me." And the people say, "Hey, you look like ..." And I'm dying while they're wondering whether I'm Barbra Streisand.'

Barbra Streisand

● 'What's the point of doing something good if nobody's watching?'

Nicole Kidman

● 'I'm in trouble because I'm normal and slightly arrogant. A lot of people don't like themselves and I happen to be totally in love with myself.'

Mike Tyson

● 'I do have big tits. Always had 'em – pushed 'em up, whacked 'em around. Why not make fun of 'em? I've made a fortune with 'em.'

Dolly Parton

● 'I owe a lot to my parents, especially my mother and father.'

Greg Norman

● 'I have to be careful to get out before I become the grotesque caricature of a hatchet-faced woman with big knockers.'

Jamie Lee Curtis

● 'The biggest misconception people have about me is that I'm stupid.'

Billy Idol

● 'When I was in prison, I was wrapped up in all those deep books. That Tolstoy crap – people shouldn't read that stuff.'

Mike Tyson

● 'Just let the wardrobe do the acting.'

Jack Nicholson

● 'Big girls need big diamonds.'

Elizabeth Taylor

● 'Nothing irritates me more than chronic laziness in others. Mind you, it's only mental sloth I object to. Physical sloth can be heavenly.'

Elizabeth Hurley

● 'I'm only two years older than Brad Pitt, but I look a lot older, which used to greatly frustrate me. It doesn't any more. I don't have to fit into that category and get trounced by Tom Cruise and Brad.'

George Clooney

- 'If I can get you to laugh with me, you like me better, which makes you more open to my ideas. And, if I can persuade you to laugh at the particular point I make, by laughing at it you acknowledge its truth.'

  John Cleese

- 'I used to do drugs, but don't tell anyone or it will ruin my image.'

  Courtney Love

- 'I think that everyone should get married at least once, so you can see what a silly, outdated institution it is.'

  Madonna

- 'I never diet. I smoke. I drink now and then. I never work out. I work very hard, and I am worth every cent.'

  Naomi Campbell

- 'I have a love interest in every one of my films – a gun.'

  Arnold Schwarzenegger

- 'Just standing around looking beautiful is so boring.'

  Michelle Pfeiffer

- 'I know there are nights when I have power, when I could put on something and walk in somewhere, and if there is a man who doesn't look at me, it's because he's gay.'

  Kathleen Turner

- 'If you're going to kick authority in the teeth, you might as well use two feet.'

  Keith Richards

- 'I paid a worker at New York's zoo to reopen it just for me and Robin [Tyson's ex-wife]. When we got to the gorilla cage, there was one big silverback gorilla there just bullying all the other gorillas. They were so powerful but their eyes were like an innocent infant. I offered the attendant $10,000 to open the cage and let me smash that silverback's snotbox! He declined.'

  Mike Tyson

- 'Children always understand. They have open minds. They have built-in shit detectors.'

  Madonna

'How people keep correcting us when we are young! There is always some bad habit or other they tell us we ought to get over. Yet most bad habits are tools to help us through life.'

  Jack Nicklaus

- 'I definitely want Brooklyn to be christened, but I don't know into what religion yet.'

  David Beckham

- 'I always listen to *NSYNC's "Tearin' Up My Heart". It reminds me to wear a bra.'

  Britney Spears

- 'He who laughs most learns best.'

  John Cleese

- 'Everyone probably thinks that I'm a raving nymphomaniac, that I have an insatiable sexual appetite, when the truth is I'd rather read a book.'

  Madonna

- 'I'm not a woman, I'm a force of nature.'

  Courtney Love

- 'A word to the wise ain't necessary, it's the stupid ones who need the advice.'

  Bill Cosby

- 'I feel safe in white because, deep down inside, I'm an angel.'

  Sean 'P. Diddy' Combs

- 'I'm staggered by the question of what it's like to be a multimillionaire. I always have to remind myself that I am.'

  Bruce Willis

- 'I had a huge crush on Olga Korbut, the gymnast. The only other person was Cliff Richard, which is embarrassing – it means that when I was seven I had bad taste and was presumably gay.'

  Hugh Grant

- 'I've gone for each type: the rough guy; the nerdy, sweet, lovable guy; and the slick guy. I don't really have a type. Men in general are a good thing.'

  Jennifer Aniston

● 'Firstly, Tamzin who? Secondly, I think it's disrespectful. And thirdly, as if, love.'

Victoria Beckham, on hearing that Tamzin Outhwaite wouldn't mind a night with husband David

● 'I fell off my pink cloud with a thud.'

Elizabeth Taylor

● 'I won't be happy till I'm as famous as God.'

Madonna, a long time ago

● 'You have to be careful with the clitoris because, if the piercer doesn't know what he's doing, it can be numbed for good.'

Janet Jackson

● 'Yeah I flirt, I'm not blind and I'm not dead!'

Dolly Parton

● 'There is no off position on the genius switch.'

David Letterman

● 'I only get ill when I give up drugs.'

Keith Richards

● 'I'm rich, freakin' rich. It's crazy.'

Britney Spears

● 'I was the first woman to burn my bra – it took the fire department four days to put it out.'

Dolly Parton

- 'Picasso had his pink period and his blue period. I am in my blonde period right now.'

  Hugh Hefner

- 'Brad [Pitt], poor geezer, was blown up, thrown around, burned, slapped, frozen. But never a moan or a whine. Now that's what I call a real star.'

  Guy Ritchie

- 'I'm taking my rats. Those are my friends for the tour. Thelma and Louise. They're so cute.'

  Pink

- 'After about twenty years of marriage, I'm finally starting to scratch the surface of that one [what women want]. And I think the answer lies somewhere between conversation and chocolate.'

  Mel Gibson

- 'Me and Janet really are two different people.'

  Michael Jackson

- 'Violence is one of the most fun things to watch.'

  Quentin Tarantino

- I used to smoke two packs a day and I just hate being a non-smoker... but I will never consider myself a non-smoker because I always find smokers the most interesting people at the table.'

  Michelle Pfeiffer

- 'With two movies opening this summer, I have no relaxing time at all. Whatever I have is spent in a drunken stupor.'

  Hugh Grant

- 'I hope people realise that there is a brain underneath the hair and a heart underneath the boobs.'

  Dolly Parton

- 'It was no great tragedy being Judy Garland's daughter. I had tremendously interesting childhood years – except they had little to do with being a child.'

  Liza Minnelli

- 'I don't know much about football. I know what a goal is, which is surely the main thing about football.'

  Victoria Beckham

- 'Charlton Heston admitted he had a drinking problem, and I said to myself, "Thank God this guy doesn't own any guns!" '

  David Letterman

- 'I've only slept with men I've been married to. How many women can make that claim?'

  Elizabeth Taylor

- 'I knew I was a winner back in the late Sixties. I knew I was destined for great things. People will say that kind of thinking is totally immodest. I agree. Modesty is not a word that applies to me in any way – I hope it never will.'

  Arnold Schwarzenegger

- 'Cameron Diaz was so cute at the MTV Movie Awards when she pulled her skirt up and wiped her armpits.'

  Pink

- 'Everybody loves you when they are about to come.'

  Madonna

- 'I look just like the girls next door... if you happen to live next door to an amusement park.'

  Dolly Parton

- 'I tell you what really turns my toes up: love scenes with sixty-eight-year-old men and actresses young enough to be their granddaughter.'

  Mel Gibson

- 'I try and take lots of vitamins and I don't drink. I do smoke, though. I'd be insufferable if I didn't smoke, you'd have to push me off a balcony I'd be so boring.'

  Kate Beckinsale

- 'It's tiny [his butt], what can I do?'

  Ricky Martin

- 'I want to die before my wife, and the reason is this. If it is true that when you die, your soul goes up to judgement, I don't want my wife up there ahead of me to tell them things.'

  Bill Cosby

- 'All musicians are fun to get drunk with, except the ones who are cleaning up their act. We steer clear of those.'

  Rod Stewart, on intolerance for low tolerance

- 'I didn't pay that much attention to the election. Nobody really grabbed me. The earthquakes in California worry me, so I'm hoping Arnold [Schwarzenegger] might take care of them.'

  Dolly Parton, who was once asked to run for the post of Governor for her native Tennessee

- 'That's the kind of face you hang on your door in Africa.'

  Comedienne Joan Rivers, on perma-tanned fashion queen Donatella Versace

- 'He's claiming abuse. I pay my wife good money for a little abuse; a good spanking sometimes. I don't know what he's complaining about.'

  Cuba Gooding, Jr, on David Gest's lawsuit against Liza Minnelli for physical abuse

- 'In Hollywood now when people die they don't say, "Did he leave a will?" but "Did he leave a diary?" '

  Liza Minnelli

- 'Did you ever see the customers in health-food stores? They are pale, skinny people who look half-dead. In a steak house, you see robust, ruddy people. They're dying, of course, but they look terrific.'

  Bill Cosby

• 'Health food may be good for the conscience but Oreos taste a hell of a lot better.'

Robert Redford

• 'There are, I think, three countries left in the world where I can go and I'm not as well known as I am here. I'm a pretty big star, folks – I don't have to tell you. Superstar, I guess you could say.'

Bruce Willis

• 'It was definitely different from kissing a girl. He had a bunch of stray hairs on his lip. The worst part was that we had to do thirty takes.'

Jason Biggs, on locking lips with Seann William Scott in American Wedding

• '*USA Today* has come out with a new survey – apparently, three out of every four people make up 75 per cent of the population.'

David Letterman

• 'I dress sexily – but not in an obvious way. Sexy in a virginal way.'

Victoria Beckham

• 'I used to desire many, many things, but now I have just one desire, and that's to get rid of all my other desires.'

John Cleese

• 'I am a survivor. I am like a cockroach, you just can't get rid of me.'

Madonna

- 'I would seriously question whether anybody is really foolish enough to really say what they mean. Sometimes I think that civilisation as we know it would kind of break down if we all were completely honest.'

  Elizabeth Hurley

- 'The moral of filmmaking in Britain is that you will be screwed by the weather.'

  Hugh Grant

- 'It costs a lot of money to look this cheap.'

  Dolly Parton

- 'I am not going to be no señorita.'

  Victoria Beckham, on moving to Spain

- 'When the sun comes up, I have morals again.'

  Elizabeth Taylor

- 'We covered "Hey Jude". My father panicked, misunderstanding the lyrics and thinking our lead singer was belting out "Hey Jew" to a roomful of Holocaust survivors.'

  Ben Stiller

- 'Wherever we've travelled in this great land of ours, we've found that people everywhere are about 90 per cent water.'

  David Letterman

- 'Why does a woman work ten years to change a man's habits and then complain that he's not the man she married?'

  Barbra Streisand

- 'I'm still me even after all that's happened.'

  Victoria Beckham

- 'New York now leads the world's great cities in the number of people around whom you shouldn't make a sudden move.'

  David Letterman

- 'The one thing I remember about Christmas was that my father used to take me out in a boat about ten miles offshore on Christmas Day, and I used to have to swim back. Extraordinary. It was a ritual. Mind you, that wasn't the hard part. The difficult bit was getting out of the sack.'

  John Cleese

- 'My body is like breakfast, lunch and dinner. I don't think about it, I just have it.'

  Arnold Schwarzenegger

- 'There is a new billboard outside Times Square. It keeps an up-to-the-minute count of gun-related crimes in New York. Some goofball is going to shoot someone just to see the numbers move.'

  David Letterman

- 'Human beings are the only creatures on Earth that allow their children to come back home.'

  Bill Cosby

- 'You find out who your real friends are when you're involved in a scandal.'

  Elizabeth Taylor

- 'I've always had confidence. Before I was famous, that confidence got me into trouble. After I got famous, it just got me into more trouble.'

  Bruce Willis

- 'I always thought I should be treated like a star.'

  Madonna

- 'I'd kill myself if I was as fat as Marilyn Monroe.'

  Elizabeth Hurley

- 'If someone had told me years ago that sharing a sense of humour was so vital to partnerships, I could have avoided a lot of sex!'

  Kate Beckinsale

- 'If you haven't got it, fake it! Too short? Wear big high heels. But do practise walking!'

  Victoria Beckham

- 'Women are like elephants. I like to watch them, but I wouldn't want to own one.'

  W.C. Fields

- 'I like to have a martini, two at the very most. After three I'm under the table. After four I'm under my host.'

  Dorothy Parker

- 'I myself have never been able to find out precisely what feminism is; I only know that people call me a feminist whenever I express sentiments that differentiate me from a doormat or a prostitute.'

  Irish writer Rebecca West

- 'If you want to see a comic strip, you should see me in the shower.'

  Groucho Marx

- 'A verbal contract isn't worth the paper it's written on.'

  Sam Goldwyn

- 'To find out a girl's faults, praise her to her girlfriends.'

  Benjamin Franklin

- 'Coping with the language shouldn't be a problem. I can't speak English.'

  Footballer Paul Gascoigne, on moving to Italian club Lazio

- 'A pun is the lowest form of humour – when you don't think of it first.'

  US pianist and actor Oscar Levant

- 'I want a sandwich named after me.'

  US comic Jon Stewart

- 'I love New York City; I've got a gun.'

  Basketball player Charles Barkley

- 'No one knows my ability the way I do. I am pushing against it all the time.'

  John Steinbeck

- 'It's just a job. Grass grows, birds fly, waves pound the sand. I beat people up.'

  Muhammad Ali

- 'Maybe there is no actual place called hell. Maybe hell is just having to listen to our grandparents breathe through their noses when they're eating sandwiches.'

  Jim Carrey

- 'A billion here, a billion there, sooner or later it adds up to real money.'

  Congressman Everett Dirksen

- 'If I hadn't been a woman, I'd have been a drag queen.'

  Dolly Parton

- 'I get to go to lots of overseas places, like Canada.'

  Britney Spears

- 'Middle age is when your age starts to show around your middle.'

  Bob Hope

- 'I've been on a calendar, but I've never been on time.'

  Marilyn Monroe

- 'The only place where success comes before work is in a dictionary.'

  Vidal Sassoon

- 'Time you enjoy wasting was not wasted.'

  John Lennon

- 'If you would be singing like this two thousand years ago, people would have stoned you.'

  Simon Cowell, speaking on Pop Idol

- 'Our nation must come together to unite.'

  George W. Bush

- 'I'm not saying my wife's a bad cook, but she uses a smoke alarm as a timer.'

  Comic Bob Monkhouse

- 'For me, their biggest threat is when they get into the attacking part of the field.'

  Football pundit Ron Atkinson

- 'Sex is better than talk. Talk is what you suffer through so you can get to sex.'

  Woody Allen

- 'TV has brought murder back into the home where it belongs.'

  Alfred Hitchcock

- 'When you are down and out, something always turns up – usually the noses of your friends.'

  Orson Welles

- 'Wise men talk because they have something to say. Fools talk because they have to say something.'

  Plato

- 'Football players win football games.'

  Chuck Knox, American football coach

- 'Traditionally, most of Australia's imports come from overseas.'

  Former Australian cabinet minister Keppel Enderby

- 'I wanted to perform, I wanted to write songs and I wanted to get lots of chicks.'

  Musician James Taylor, when asked why he got into music

- 'Beer is proof that God loves us and wants us to be happy.'

  Benjamin Franklin

- 'I'm not against half-naked girls – not as often as I'd like to be…'

  Benny Hill

- 'Ever wonder if illiterate people get the full effect of alphabet soup?'

  US comic John Mendoza

- 'Love is the only force capable of transforming an enemy into a friend.'

  Martin Luther King, Jr

- 'After *The Wizard of Oz* I was typecast as a lion, and there aren't all that many parts for lions.'

  Actor Bert Lahr

- 'I've had a wonderful evening, but this wasn't it.'

  Groucho Marx

- 'I can answer you in two words – im possible.'

  Sam Goldwyn

- 'Everything I buy is vintage and smells funny. Maybe that's why I don't have a boyfriend.'

  Lucy Liu

- 'I don't listen to music. I hate all music.'

  Johnny Rotten, Sex Pistols vocalist

- 'Because young men are so goddamn disappointing!'

  Harrison Ford, commenting on why women like older leading men

- 'Everybody stands – that's our policy. If Jesus Christ comes on the show, guess what? It's like, "Stand right here, Jesus, we got Papa Roach coming up at number six."'

  MTV host Carson Daly

- 'I think that the film *Clueless* was very deep. I think it was deep in the way that it was very light. I think lightness has to come from a very deep place if it's true lightness.'

  Alicia Silverstone

- 'Cocaine is God's way of saying you're making too much money.'

  Robin Williams

- 'I've always wanted to be a spy, and frankly I'm a little surprised that British Intelligence has never approached me.'

  Elizabeth Hurley

- 'Women are meant to be loved, not to be understood.'

  Oscar Wilde

- 'The only reason we're 7–0 is because we've won all seven of our games.'

  David Garcia, baseball team manager

- 'It's about the two Ms – movement and positioning.'

  Ron Atkinson

- 'Run for office? No. I've slept with too many women, I've done too many drugs and I've been to too many parties.'

  George Clooney

- 'With all due respect to the world's great drummers – it ain't brain surgery.'

  Mickey Dolenz, The Monkees' singer and drummer

- 'I'm living on a one-way, dead-end street. I don't know how I got there.'

  Stephen Wright

- ''Twas a woman who drove me to drink. I never had the courtesy to thank her.'

  W.C. Fields

- 'I'd love to be a pop idol. Of course, my groupies are now between forty and fifty.'

  Kevin Bacon

- 'There's nothing sexier than a lapsed Catholic.'

  Woody Allen

- 'I've given up reading books. I find it takes my mind off myself.'

  Oscar Levant

- 'Gentlemen – include me out.'

  Sam Goldwyn

- 'A bit of lusting after someone does wonders for the skin.'

  Elizabeth Hurley

- 'What does this Frenchman know about football? He wears glasses and looks like a schoolteacher. Does he even speak English properly?'

  Arsenal captain Tony Adams, speaking about new boss Arsène Wenger

- 'Those are my principles. If you don't like them, I have others.'

  Groucho Marx

- 'Retire? I'm going to stay in show business until I'm the only one left.'

  George Burns at age 90

- 'Feminism is just a way for ugly women to get into the mainstream of America.'

  Right-wing talk-show host Rush Limbaugh

- 'Security is the essential road-block to achieving the road-map to peace.'

  George W. Bush

- 'I do my best work when I'm in pain and turmoil.'

  Sting

- 'The largest crowd ever in the state of Las Vegas.'

  Mark Jones, TV Broadcaster

- 'An eye for an eye makes the whole world blind.'

  Gandhi

- 'Some are born great, some achieve greatness and some hire PR officers.'

  Pulitzer Prize-winning author Daniel J. Boorstin

- 'God heals and the doctor takes the fee.'

  Benjamin Franklin

- 'There are worst things than death. If you've ever spent an evening with an insurance salesman, you know exactly what I mean.'

  Woody Allen

- 'The keeper was unsighted – he still didn't see it.'

  Ron Atkinson

- 'All those who believe in telekinesis, raise my hand.'

  Stephen Wright

- 'I've been accused of vulgarity. I say that's bullshit.'

  Mel Brooks

- 'Once I shot an elephant in my pyjamas. How he got into my pyjamas, I'll never know.'

  Groucho Marx

- 'My audience loves to see Britney get her head cut off.'

  Alice Cooper

- 'You've also got to measure in order to begin to effect change that's just more – when there's more than talk, there's just actual – a paradigm shift.'

  George W. Bush

- 'Let's bring it up to date with some snappy 19th-century dialogue.'

  Sam Goldwyn

- 'Roses are red, violets are blue, I'm schizophrenic, and so am I.'

  Oscar Levant

- 'All of the Mets' road wins against Los Angeles this year have been at Dodger Stadium.'

  Sportscaster Ralph Kiner

- 'After two days in hospital I took a turn for the nurse.'

  W.C. Fields

- 'I grew up with six brothers. That's how I learned to dance – waiting for the bathroom.'

  Bob Hope

- 'Thanks, you don't look so hot yourself.'

  Baseball player Yogi Berra, after being told he looked cool

- 'The last time I was inside a woman was when I was inside the Statue of Liberty.'

  Woody Allen

- 'In Australia, not reading poetry is the national pastime.'

  US poet Phyllis McGinley

- 'I think the American people – I hope the American – I don't think, let me – I hope the American people trust me.'

  George W. Bush

- 'Never hold discussions with the monkey when the organ grinder is in the room.'

  Winston Churchill

- 'The light at the end of the tunnel has been turned off due to budget cuts.'

  US comic Stephen Wright

- 'We're going to turn this team around 360 degrees.'

  Basketball player Jason Kidd

- 'What we want is a story that starts with an earthquake and works its way up to a climax.'

  Sam Goldwyn

- 'Guests, like fish, begin to smell after three days.'

  Benjamin Franklin

- 'An author who speaks about their own books is almost as bad as a mother who speaks about her own children.'

  Benjamin Disraeli

- 'I don't bring God into my life to… to, you know, kind of be a political person.'

  George W. Bush

- 'A man's got to believe in something. I believe I'll have another drink.'

  W.C. Fields

- 'Of all the things I've lost, I miss my mind the most.'

  Mark Twain

- 'Zero–zero is a big score.'

  Ron Atkinson

- 'There's a fine line between genius and insanity. I have erased this line.'

  Oscar Levant

- 'This film cost $31 million. With that kind of money, I could have invaded some country.'

  Clint Eastwood

- 'Immature poets imitate; mature poets steal.'

  T.S. Eliot

- 'It's amazing I won. I was running against peace, prosperity and incumbency.'

  George W. Bush, speaking to the Swedish Prime Minister and unaware that a live television camera was still rolling

- 'I was married by a judge. I should have asked for a jury.'

  Groucho Marx

- 'Wise men don't need advice. Fools won't take it.'

  Benjamin Franklin

- 'It took me fifteen years to discover that I had no talent for writing, but I couldn't give it up because by that time I was too famous.'

  US actor, author and humorist Robert Benchley

- 'I trust the people.'

  George W. Bush before the election

- 'People can't be trusted.'

  George W. Bush after the election

- 'Critics are to authors what dogs are to lamp-posts.'

  US author Jeffrey Robinson

- 'How did I get to Hollywood? By train.'

  Filmmaker John Ford

- 'Buy land. They've stopped making it.'

  Mark Twain

6

COFFEE

- 'Coffee should be black as hell, strong as death and sweet as love.' — Turkish proverb

- The Arabs are generally believed to have been the first people to have brewed coffee.

- Fifty-two per cent of Americans drink coffee.

- An acre of coffee trees can produce up to 10,000lb (4,536kg) of coffee cherries. That amounts to approximately 2,000lb (907kg) of beans after hulling or milling.

- A scientific report from the University of California found that the steam rising from a cup of coffee contains the same amount of antioxidants as three oranges. The antioxidants are heterocyclic compounds, which prevent cancer and heart disease.

- The habit of adding sugar to coffee is believed to have started in 1715, in the court of Louis XIV.

- Coffee trees produce highly aromatic, short-lived flowers with a scent somewhere between jasmine and orange. These blossoms produce cranberry-sized coffee cherries. It takes four to five years to yield a commercial harvest.

- Australians consume 60 per cent more coffee than tea, a six-fold increase since 1940.

- Advertisements for coffee in London in 1657 claimed that the beverage was a cure for scurvy, gout and other ills.

- After the decaffeinating process, processing companies no longer throw the caffeine away; they sell it to pharmaceutical companies.

- After the coffee beans are roasted, and when they begin to cool, they release about 700 chemical substances that make up the vaporising aromas.

- An Arabica coffee tree can produce up to 12lb (5.4kg) of coffee a year, depending on soil and climate.

- Hawaii features an annual Kona Festival, a coffee-picking contest. Each year, the winner becomes a state celebrity.

- Beethoven was a coffee lover, and so particular about his coffee that he always counted out sixty beans for each cup when he prepared his brew.

- Before roasting, some green coffee beans are stored for years. Experts believe that certain beans improve with age, when stored properly.

- By 1850, the manual coffee grinder had found its way to most upper-middle-class kitchens of the Western world.

- Before the first French café in the late 18th century, coffee was sold by street vendors in Europe in the Arab fashion. The Arabs were the forerunners of the pavement espresso carts of today.

- Brazil accounts for almost one-third of the world's coffee production, producing over 3.3 billion lb (1.5 billion kg) of coffee each year.

- Caffeine is on the International Olympic Committee list of prohibited substances. Athletes who test positive for more than 12 micrograms of caffeine per millilitre of urine may be banned from the Olympic Games. This level may be reached after drinking about five cups of coffee.

- Citrus has been added to coffee for several hundred years.

- Coffee as a medicine reached its highest and lowest point in the 17th century in England. Wild medical contraptions to administer a mixture of coffee and an assortment of heated butter, honey and oil became treatments for the sick. Soon, tea replaced coffee as the national beverage.

- Coffee is graded according to three criteria: bean quality (altitude and species), quality of preparation and size of bean.

- Coffee trees are self-pollinating.

- Coffee beans are similar to grapes that produce wine in that they are affected by the temperature, soil conditions, altitude, rainfall, drainage and degree of ripeness when picked.

- Coffee is generally roasted between 400°F and 425°F (204–218°C).

- The longer it is roasted, the darker the roast. Roasting time is usually from ten to twenty minutes.

- Coffee is grown commercially in over forty-five countries throughout the world.

- Coffee is the most popular beverage worldwide, with over 400 billion cups consumed each year.

- The drink's popularity may be attributed to the fact that just about all flavours mix well with it.

- A coffee recipe from *Kitchen Directory and American Housewife* (1844): 'Use a tablespoonful ground to a pint of boiling water [less than a quarter of what we would use today]. Boil in tin pot twenty to twenty-five minutes. If boiled longer it will not taste fresh and lively. Let stand four or five minutes to settle, pour off grounds into a coffee pot or urn.'

- Coffee represents 75 per cent of all the caffeine consumed in the United States.

- Coffee sacks are usually made of hemp and weigh approximately 132lb (60kg) when they are full of green coffee beans. It takes over 600,000 beans to fill a coffee sack.

- Coffee trees are evergreen and grow to heights above 15ft (4.6m) but are normally pruned to around 8ft (2.4m) in order to facilitate harvesting.

- Coffee was first known in Europe as 'Arabian Wine'.

- Along with beer and peanut butter, coffee is on a list of the 'ten most recognisable odours'.

- As a world commodity, coffee is second only to oil.

- During World War II, the US Government used 260 million lb (118 million kg) of instant coffee.

- During the American Civil War, the Union soldiers were issued 8lb (3.6kg) of ground roasted coffee as part of their personal ration of 100lb (45.4kg) of food. And they had another choice: 10lb (4.54kg) of green coffee beans.

- Frederick the Great had his coffee made with champagne and a bit of mustard.

- Commercially flavoured coffee beans are flavoured after they are roasted and partially cooled to around 100 degrees. Then the flavour is applied, when the coffee beans' pores are open and therefore more receptive to flavour absorption.

- Dark roasted coffees actually have less caffeine than medium roasts. The longer a coffee is roasted, the more caffeine burns off during the process.

- Finely grinding coffee beans and boiling them in water creates what is known as 'Turkish coffee'. It is still made this way today in Turkey and Greece.

- 'Hard Bean' means the coffee was grown at an altitude above 5,000ft (1,524m).

- Hawaii is the only state of the United States in which coffee is commercially grown, and the coffee is harvested between November and April.

- Iced coffee in a can has been popular in Japan since 1945.

- In Japan, coffee shops are called Kissaten.

- If you like your espresso coffee sweet, you should use granulated sugar, which dissolves more quickly, rather than sugar cubes; white sugar rather than brown sugar; and real sugar rather than sweeteners, which alter the taste of the coffee.

- In 1670, Dorothy Jones of Boston was granted a licence to sell coffee, and so became the first American coffee trader.

- In 1727, using seedlings smuggled from Paris, coffee plants were first cultivated in Brazil. Brazil is now by far the world's largest producer of coffee.

- In 1900, coffee was often delivered door-to-door in the United States by horse-pulled wagons.

- In 1990, over $4 billion worth of coffee was imported into the United States.

- In early America, coffee was usually taken between meals and after dinner.

- Espresso is considered so essential to daily life in Italy that the price is regulated by the government.

- In the 16th century, Turkish women could divorce their husbands if the man failed to keep his family's pot filled with coffee.

- In Sumatra, workers on coffee plantations gather the world's most expensive coffee by following a gourmet marsupial that consumes only the choicest coffee beans. By picking through what it excretes, they obtain the world's most expensive coffee – 'Kopi Luwak', which sells for over $100 per pound.

- In the 14th century, the Arabs started to cultivate coffee plants. The first commercially grown and harvested coffee originated in the Arabian Peninsula near the port of Mocha.

- In the last three centuries, 90 per cent of all people living in the Western world have switched from tea to coffee.

- In 1763, there were over 200 coffee shops in Venice.

- In 1790, there were two coffee-related firsts in the United States: the first wholesale coffee roasting company and the first newspaper advertisement featuring coffee.

- Irish cream and hazelnut are the most popular whole-bean coffee flavourings.

- The first coffee mill appeared in London during the 17th century.

- Italy now has over 200,000 coffee bars, and the number is still growing.

- Over 5 million people in Brazil are employed by the coffee trade. Most of those are involved with the cultivation and harvesting of more than 3 billion coffee plants.

- Italians do not drink espresso during meals. It is considered to be a separate thing and is given its own time.

- Jamaica Blue Mountain is often regarded as the best coffee in the world.

- Japan ranks number three in the world for coffee consumption.

- Large doses of caffeine can be lethal: 0.4oz (10g), or 100 cups of coffee over four hours, can kill the average human.

- 'Latte' is the Italian word for milk. So, if you order a latte in Italy, you'll be served a glass of milk.

- Lloyd's of London began as Edward Lloyd's coffeehouse.

- Milk as an additive to coffee became popular in the 1680s, when a French physician recommended that *café au lait* be used for medicinal purposes.

- The official Coffee Day in Japan is 1 October.

- Only about 20 per cent of harvested coffee beans are considered to be premium beans of the highest quality.

- Over 10,000 coffee cafés, plus several thousand vending machines with both hot and cold coffee, serve the needs of Tokyo alone.

- More than fifty-three countries worldwide grow coffee, but all of them lie along the equator between the Tropics of Cancer and Capricorn.

- Over-roasted coffee beans are highly flammable during the roasting process.

- Raw coffee beans, soaked in water and spices, are chewed like sweets in many parts of Africa.

- Regular coffee drinkers have about one-third fewer asthma symptoms than non-coffee drinkers, according to a Harvard researcher who studied the drinking habits of 20,000 people.

- Special studies conducted on the human body reveal it will usually absorb up to about 0.01oz (300mg) of caffeine at a given time – about three normal cups. Additional amounts are just cast off, providing no further stimulation. The human body dissipates 20 per cent of the caffeine in the system each hour.

- Roasted coffee beans start to lose small amounts of flavour within two weeks. Ground coffee begins to lose its flavour in an hour. Brewed coffee and espresso loses flavour within minutes.

- Espresso vendors report an increase in decaffeinated sales in the month of January due to New Year's resolutions to decrease caffeine intake.

- Scandinavia has the world's highest per capita annual coffee consumption: 26.4lb (12kg).

- Italy has an annual consumption per capita of only 10lb (4.54kg).

- The 2,000 Arabica coffee cherries it takes to make a roasted pound of coffee are normally picked by hand as they ripen. Since each cherry contains two beans, it takes about 4,000 Arabica beans to make a pound of roasted coffee.

- The Arabica is the original coffee plant and still grows wild in Ethiopia. The Arabica coffee tree is an evergreen and in the wild will grow to a height of 14–20ft (4.3–6.1m).

- The average annual coffee consumption of an American adult is 26.7 gallons (121.4 litres), or over 400 cups.

- The aroma and flavour derived from coffee is a result of the little beads of the oily substance called coffee essence, coffeol, or coffee oil. This is not an actual oil, since it dissolves in water.

- The first Parisian café opened in 1689 to serve coffee.

- The average age of an Italian barista is 48 years old. A barista is a respected job title in Italy.

- The average cup of coffee contains more than 1,000 different chemical components, none of which is tasted in isolation but only as part of the overall flavour.

- The drip pot was invented by a Frenchman in around 1800.

- The coffee filter was invented in 1908 by Melitta Benz, a German homemaker, when she lined a tin cup with blotter paper to filter the coffee grinds.

- The coffee tree produces its first full crop when it is about five years old. Thereafter, it produces consistently for fifteen or twenty years.

- The most widely accepted legend associated with the discovery of coffee is of a goatherd named Kaldi of Ethiopia. In around AD 800–850, Kaldi was amazed to see his goats behaving in a frisky manner after eating the leaves and berries of a coffee shrub. And, of course, he had to try them himself!

- The Europeans first added chocolate to their coffee in the 17th century.

- The first commercial espresso machine was manufactured in Italy in 1906.

- French philosopher Voltaire reportedly drank fifty cups of coffee a day.

- The largest coffee importer centre in the USA is located in the city of New Orleans.

- The heavy tea tax imposed on the colonies in 1773, which led to the Boston Tea Party, resulted in America switching from tea to coffee. Drinking coffee was seen as an expression of freedom.

- The United States is the world's largest consumer of coffee, importing 16 to 20 million bags (2.5 million lb; 1.1 million kg) annually, representing one-third of all coffee exported. More than half of the United States' population consumes coffee. The typical coffee drinker has 3.4 cups of coffee per day. That translates into more than 450,000,000 cups of coffee daily for the USA.

- The word 'cappuccino' has several derivations, the original of which arose in the 16th century. The Capuchin order of friars, established after 1525, played an important role in bringing Catholicism back to Reformation Europe. Its Italian name came from the long pointed cowl, or *cappuccino* – 'hood' – that was worn as part of the order's habit. The French version of cappuccino was *capuchin*, from which came the English Capuchin. In Italian, the word 'cappuccino' went on to describe espresso coffee mixed or topped with steamed milk or cream, so called because the colour of the coffee resembled the colour of the habit of a Capuchin friar. The first use of 'cappuccino' in English is recorded in 1948 in a work about San Francisco. There is also another story that suggests the term comes from the fact that the coffee is dark, like the monk's robe, and the drink's pale surface is likened to the colour of the monk's head.

- The vast majority of coffees available to consumers are blends of different beans.

- Until the 18th century, coffee was almost always boiled.

- The word 'tip' dates back to the old London coffeehouses. Conspicuously placed brass boxes etched with the inscription 'To Insure Promptness' encouraged customers to pay for efficient service. The resulting acronym, TIP, has become a byword.

- 'Those British are sophisticated people, in almost everything except their choice of coffee. They still drink instant ten-to-one over fresh brewed.'
  Anon

- Turkey began to roast and grind the coffee bean in the 13th century. By the 16th century, the country had become the chief distributor of coffee, with markets established in Egypt, Syria, Persia and Venice, Italy.

- Until the late 19th century, people roasted their coffee at home using popcorn poppers and stove-top frying pans.

- William Penn purchased a pound of coffee in New York in 1683 for $4.68.

- There are about 30mg of caffeine in the average chocolate bar, while a cup of coffee contains around 100–150mg.

7

SUPERLATIVES

- The average Miss America winner is 5ft 6.6in (1.72m) tall.

- The tallest Miss America contestant – Jeanne Robertson – was 6ft 2in (1.88m).

- The perfect height for a female fashion model is said to be 5ft 9.5in (1.81m).

- The perfect height for a male model is allegedly 6ft (1.83m).

- The tallest US president was Abraham Lincoln, at 6ft 4in (1.95m).

- The shortest US president was James Madison, at 5ft 4in (1.64m).

- The USS *Enterprise* was built in Newport VA and launched in 1960; it remains the largest warship ever built and the first nuclear-powered aircraft carrier. It is the eighth ship and the second aircraft carrier to be called *Enterprise*. At 1,123ft (342m) long and 250ft (76m) high, the ship is both the longest and tallest warship ever built. With a top speed of over 30 knots (34.5mph; 55.6km/h), it is also the fastest carrier in the US fleet. Weighing in at 90,000 tons (91,444 tonnes), the 'Big E', as it is dubbed by sailors, is home to over 5,000 officers and crew members.

- The only mammal species in which the female is normally taller than the male is a type of antelope called the okapi.

- The largest web-footed bird is the albatross, which also has the largest wingspan.

- On 31 July 1994, Simon Sang Sung of Singapore turned a single piece of dough into 8,192 noodles in 59.29 seconds.

- At 12 years old, an African named Ernest Loftus made his first entry in his diary and continued every day for 91 years.

- In 1925, Toronto, Ontario, was home to what was then the biggest swimming pool in the world. It held 2,000 swimmers, and was 300 x 75ft (91.4 x 22.9m). It is still in operation.

- In the original Ian Fleming books, the character Dr No was 6ft 6in (1.98m) tall. The character Auric Goldfinger was only 5ft (1.52m).

- The highest parachute jump ever made was on 16 August 1960 as a part of the Air Force research programme, Project Excelsior. Air Force Captain Joseph W. Kittinger, Jr, stepped off a platform raised to 102,800ft (31,333m) over Tularosa, New Mexico by a high-altitude balloon. To survive the altitude, Kittinger wore a pressure suit similar to those for astronauts. After 4 minutes, 36 seconds of free fall, he reached a speed of 714mph (1,149km/h) and became the only human to break the sound barrier without being enclosed in a machine of any kind. He dropped 84,700ft (25,817m) before opening his parachute, and landed safely 13 minutes, 45 seconds after jumping.

- In 1876 the average Western man was 5ft 5in (1.65m) tall, 4in shorter than today's average. Half of that increase, a full 2in (5cm) on average, has been since 1960s according to the US Department of Health and Human Services.

- Tsar Peter the Great stood 6ft 6.75in (2m) tall, an incredible height for the 18th century.

- The tallest bird alive today is the ostrich.

- With 252 lanes, the Tokyo World Lanes Bowling Centre is the largest bowling establishment in the world.

- The tallest mammal is the giraffe.

- The tallest snake is the king cobra, which can rear itself up to 6ft (1.83m) and spread its 'hood' 9in (22.9cm) wide.

- Berjaya Times Square in Kuala Lumpur, Malaysia, is currently the largest shopping mall in the world. It has space for more than 1,000 retail shops, 1,200 luxury service suites, 65 food outlets to suit many tastes and entertainment attractions such as Asia's largest indoor theme park, Cosmo World, and Malaysia's first-ever IMAX 2D and 3D theatre, which is located on the tenth floor.

- The Giant Sequoia (*Sequoiadendron giganteum*) is the largest living organism on Earth, and is native, primarily, to the Sierra Nevada Mountains of eastern California. The largest Sequoia is the General Sherman tree, with a height of 250ft (76m) and a diameter near the base of 24ft 8in (7.5m). The trunk of the tree weighs almost 1,400 tons (1,422 tonnes).

- The tallest man on record was Robert Wadlow of Illinois, USA. He was 8ft 11.1in (2.72m) tall, and at the time of his death at the age of 22 he weighed 490lb (222kg).

- The tallest woman ever recorded, Trijntje Cornelisdochter, was born in 1616 in Holland. She was 8ft 4in (2.54m) tall when she died, aged 17, in 1633.

- The tallest married couple were Anna Hanen Swan (1846–88), and Martin Van Buren Bates (1845–1919). She was 7ft 5.5in (2.27m) and Martin stood 7ft 2.5in (2.19m) when they married at the Church of St Martin-in-the-Fields, London, on 17 June 1871.

- At 891ft (272m) tall, the 1.6-mile-long (2.6-km) Millau Bridge is the tallest road bridge in the world. It crosses the Tarn Valley, in France's Massif Central mountains, and opened in 2004. The suspension bridge hangs on seven towers, the tallest being 1,122ft (345m) tall. It was constructed over three years at a cost of 394 million euros.

- Released in 2002, the sci-fi comedy *The Adventures of Pluto Nash* is the biggest Hollywood bomb in terms of loss. The movie had a gross budget of $100 million, but only earned $4.41 million at the US box office.

- The Caterpillar 797B dump truck is currently the largest in the world and has a load capacity of 380 tons (386 tonnes). It is powered by a turbocharged diesel engine making 3,550 horsepower. The dump truck is 21ft 6in (6.6m) tall, 28ft (8.5m) wide and 47.7ft (14.5m) long and has an empty operating weight of 278 tons (282 tonnes). Each tyre is 13ft (4m) tall, weighs 4 tons (4.1 tonnes) and costs $25,000.00.

- The largest cruise ship in the world, launched in 2009, is Royal Caribbean's 220,000-ton *Genesis*. With a length of 1,180ft (360m), it will carry 6,400 passengers. From the bridge, the captain will be able to move the ship in any direction – forward, backward, sideways – with the flick of a joystick. No tugboats required.

- The CargoLifter hangar, located in Brand, Germany, on a former Soviet military airport, is the largest self-supporting hangar in the world. At 1,181ft (360m) long, 689ft (210m) wide and 351ft (107m) high, the hangar was designed to accommodate the planned CargoLifter CL 160, an 853ft-long (260m) airship.

- The tallest man-made structure in the world is the CN Tower located in Toronto, Canada, at 1,815ft (553m).

- The biggest hog ever recorded was a creature named Big Boy, who weighed in at 1,904lb (864kg).

- The *Hindenburg* (LZ 129), built by the Zeppelin Company of Germany in 1936, was the largest aircraft ever built and flown. It was 804ft (245m) long, with a maximum diameter of 135ft (41m) and boasted a 200ft-long (61m) promenade deck. The *Hindenburg* flew at a top speed of 82mph (132km/h), cutting the transatlantic travel time by more than two-thirds, and could lift 112 tons (114 tonnes) beyond its own weight. It was used in transatlantic service for a year before crashing in May 1937.

- The average US adult male is 5ft 9.1in (1.75m) tall, but 3.9 per cent of US men are 6ft 2in (1.88m) or taller.

- The average US adult female is 5ft 3.7in (1.61m) tall, but 0.7 per cent of US women are 5ft 10in (1.77m) or taller.

- The minimum height for a US astronaut is 4ft 10.5in (1.49m), and the minimum height for a US Space Shuttle pilot is 5ft 4in (1.62m).

- The maximum height for all US Space Shuttle crew members is 6ft 4in (1.93m).

- The longest Monopoly game ever played was 1,680 hours long – that's 70 straight days!

- With faces standing 60ft (18.3m) tall and 500ft (152.4m) up, the Mount Rushmore National Monument is the largest art object in the world. The four faces of American presidents George Washington, Thomas Jefferson, Theodore Roosevelt and Abraham Lincoln are carved into the face of Mount Rushmore in the Black Hills of South Dakota. Sculptor Gutzon Borglum began carving the mountain on 10 August 1927 and, along with 400 workers, worked on the monument until his death in 1941. It was never completed.

- More than a dozen writers worked on *The Adventures of Pluto Nash*, which features Eddie Murphy as a nightclub owner on the Moon, struggling to keep control of his club when a wealthy casino owner tries to take over. It was shelved for almost two years before being released.

- The largest cabbage ever grown weighed 144lb (65.3kg).

- The largest book ever published was *Bhutan: A Visual Odyssey Across the Kingdom*, by Michael Hawley, in 2003. Each book is 5 x 7ft (1.5 x 2.1m), comprises 112 pages and weighs 133lb (60.3kg). The book, which costs $2,000 to produce, is sold along with its easel-like stand for $10,000.

- The longest-running theatre play is the murder mystery *The Mousetrap*, originally called 'Three Blind Mice'. It was written by Agatha Christie in 1947 as a thirty-minute radio play to celebrate Queen Mary's 80th birthday. Performance number 20,807 on 25 November 2002 marked its fiftieth anniversary as the world's longest-running play. The performance was attended by the Queen, then celebrating her fiftieth year on the throne. The play has been seen by over 10 million people and performed in forty-four different countries, and is still running in London – in its fifty-seventh year.

- The world's tallest mountains, the Himalayas, are also the fastest-growing. Their growth – about half an inch (1.3cm) a year – is caused by the pressure exerted by two of the Earth's continental plates.

- Belgian driver Jenatzy was the first to reach a speed of over 100 km/h (62mph) in his electrically powered car *La Jamais Contente* in 1899.

- *Linn's Stamp News* is the world's largest weekly newspaper for stamp collectors.

- The Bible is the number-one book to be shoplifted in America.

- At the 2004 French Open, Fabrice Santoro and Arnaud Clement played the longest match since the open era of professional tennis began in 1968. The match began on Monday, 24 May, but play was suspended in the fifth set when darkness fell. The game resumed the next day and Santoro finally beat Clement 16–14 to win the fifth set. The seventy-one-game marathon lasted a total of 6 hours, 33 minutes on court.

- The heaviest man recorded was Brower Minnoch of Bainbridge, USA, who was admitted to University Hospital, Seattle, saturated with fluid and suffering from heart and respiratory failure, weighing more than 1,400lb (635kg). After sixteen months in hospital, he was discharged at 476lb (216kg), but was readmitted two years later after regaining almost 200lb (91kg). When he died in 1983, he weighed more than 798lb (362kg).

- The longest monopoly game in a bathtub lasted ninety-nine hours.

- The smallest fish in the world is the *Paedocypris progenetica,* a member of the Carp family, which is found in Indonesia and Sumatra. It grows to 0.31in (0.8cm).

- The longest snake ever found is a reticulated python that was discovered in Sulawesi Island, Indonesia in 1912. It was 33ft (10m) long. The largest snake ever held in captivity was a python named Colossus, who lived at the Pittsburgh Zoo in Pennsylvania. At the time of her death she was 28ft 6in (8.7m) long, had a girth of 37.5in (95.3cm) and weighed an estimated 320lb (145kg).

- The cheetah is the fastest mammal on Earth and can accelerate from 0 to 45mph (72km/h) in two seconds. Top speeds of 71mph (114km/h) can be maintained for up to 300yd (274m). The fastest cheetahs have been clocked at over 90mph (144km/h).

- The world's largest weather vane sits on the shores of White Lake in Montague, Michigan. It's 48ft (14.6m) tall with a 26ft (7.9m) wind arrow and adorned with a 14ft (4.3m) replica of a 19th-century Great Lakes schooner.

- The world's largest coffee pot is located in Davidson, Saskatchewan. It measures 24ft (7.3m) tall, is made of sheet metal and can hold 150,000 8oz (227g) cups of coffee.

- The highest wind velocity ever recorded in the USA was 231mph (372km/h), in New Hampshire, in 1934.

- The world's largest yo-yo is in the National Yo-Yo Museum in Chico, California. Named 'Big Yo', the 256lb (116kg) yo-yo is an exact scale replica of a Tom Kuhn 'No Jive 3 in 1 Yo-Yo'. Fifty inches (127cm) tall and 31.5in (80cm) wide, the yo-yo was made in 1979.

- The largest school in the world is in the Philippines, with an enrolment of about 25,000.

- Victor Hugo's *Les Misérables* contains one of the longest sentences in the French language – 823 words without a full stop.

- The longest unicycle journey was from Chicago to Los Angeles. It was made by Steve McPeak in 1968 and took him six weeks.

- The biggest bell is the Tsar Kolokol, which was cast in the Kremlin in 1733. It weighs 216 tons (219 tonnes), but was cracked in an accident and never rung.

- Shakespeare's most talkative character is Hamlet. None of his other characters has as many lines in a single play, although Falstaff, who appears in several plays, has more lines in total.

- France had the first supermarket in the world. It was started by relatives of the people who began the Texas Big Bear supermarket chain.

- China's Great Wall, the world's longest wall, stretches for over 1,500 miles (2,414km).

- During a game of tennis, Howard Kinsey and Mrs R. Roark struck the ball back and forth 2,001 consecutive times.

8

THE ROMANS

- Slaves are thought to have constituted up to 40 per cent of the Roman population.

- The slaves' standard sales contract stated that they were 'non-returnable, except for epilepsy'.

- Romans used to believe that walnuts could cure head ailments, since their shape was similar to that of a brain.

- In the 3rd century, Romans believed that the lemon was an antidote for all poisons.

- In Ancient Rome, the law stated that prostitutes were to either dye their hair blonde or wear a blonde wig to separate themselves from the respectable brunette female citizens of Rome.

- Wealthy Romans, both men and women, would have all their body hair plucked, including pubic hair.

- Unwanted Roman babies were usually left on rubbish heaps to die.

- One Roman 'cure' for stomach ache was to wash your feet and then drink the water.

- Another 'remedy' was to swallow a small amount of lead, which would cure your stomach ache, but could also kill you.

- Slaves generally came from conquered peoples, but even a free man unable to pay back his debts could be sold into slavery.

- It was an offence to obstruct the flow of water, punishable by a fine of 10,000 sesterces.

- Some Roman dishes were extremely exotic and included teats from a sow's udder, or lamb's womb stuffed with sausage meat. A recipe survives for a platter of small songbirds in asparagus sauce.

- Roman emperors ate flamingo tongues, which were considered a delicacy. They also feasted on parrotfish livers, baked dormice, pheasant brains, badgers' earlobes and wolves' nipples.

- Public toilets – rectangular-shaped rooms, some seating up to 100 people – contained rows of long, stone benches, each with a row of keyhole-shaped openings cut into it. Water running down drains underneath the benches would flush waste away into the sewers. Sponge-sticks were used instead of toilet paper.

- In the time of Ancient Rome, gladiators would fight to the death as a form of popular entertainment in the Colosseum. Spectators would sometimes shout 'Quasso cruris', the Latin equivalent of 'Break a leg'. This meant that the will of the crowd was that it wished the loser good luck by requesting that he be kept alive and only be crippled by having his leg broken. 'Break a leg' is still meant to bring good luck, particularly among actors when said before a performance.

- Rome's Circus Maximus was the biggest stadium, with seating for 250,000, and was mainly used for chariot racing.

- As far as public facilities were concerned, urinal pots and public toilets served the public need. Urine from men's public urinals was sold as a commodity. Fullers (the Roman version of a not-so-dry cleaner) would empty the urinal pots and use the ammonia-rich urine for laundering and bleaching togas and tunics!

- At one time, Ancient Romans used human urine as an ingredient in their toothpaste and as a hair product.

- Asparagus was so prized a delicacy in Ancient Rome that it was rushed by chariot to the Alps, where it was deep frozen for six months to last until the Feast of Epicurius – God of Edible Delicacies.

- The Roman language, Latin, became the basis for many other languages, such as Spanish, Italian, Portuguese and French, and still influences us today.

- According to a legend, the city of Rome was founded by twins Romulus and Remus, who were raised by a female wolf.

- Many of the legal systems of Europe and Latin America are based on sets of laws devised by the Romans.

- They invented numerals that are still used today.

- They played a wide variety of board games, including dice (tesserae), Roman chess (latrunculi), merels, duodecim scripta, tic-tac-toe (terni lapilli), Roman backgammon (tabula) and others.

- The Romans were the first to create sculptures that actually resembled the people they were supposed to portray.

- They enjoyed a variety of ball games, including handball (expulsim ludere), soccer and field hockey.

- The ancient city of Rome at one time boasted 2 million residents.

- Capital punishment was often carried out in the amphitheatre as part of the morning entertainment, requiring condemned criminals to either face wild animals without the benefit of weapons and armour or, unprotected by any kind of armour, to fight each other with swords to the death.

- In the 2nd century AD, the Romans produced glass vessels at a rate that would not be seen again in the civilised world for more than 1,000 years.

- While 'Roman' is actually the root word for 'romance', there wasn't a lot of it in Ancient Rome when it came to marriage. There was no one to conduct the ceremony, and no legal record made of it. A marriage was recognised when a man and woman agreed to live together, or when there was evidence of a dowry having been paid.

- Divorce was a lot simpler, though – you just packed up and left!

- In Ancient Rome, there were two ways of telling the time: the sundial or the water clock. The day had twelve hours and the night had twelve hours. Noon was always the sixth hour of the day, and midnight the sixth hour of the night, no matter what the season, or the fact that the length of hours changed according to the time of year.

- Some Roman toilets had seats with basins underneath that emptied into the sewer system. In rare buildings, there was evidence of a cistern above the seats, so that the toilet could be flushed.

- The ancient city of Rome was on the site of the present city of Rome, the capital of Italy.

- The Forum was the main focal point and meeting place of a Roman city and the site of religious and civic buildings.

- Spartacus was an escaped Roman slave who led an army of 90,000 escaped slaves against the might of the Romans. He was eventually defeated and killed in 72 BC.

- Roman boys were educated and expected to be able to read, write and count, and, most importantly, to be effective speakers. Other important subjects taught to boys were Roman law, Roman history, Roman customs and respect for the Roman gods. Physical education and training were also important, as the Ancient Romans expected their young citizens to be prepared to serve and, if necessary, fight in the Roman Army.

- For recreation, Roman boys played at war, using wooden swords. They played board games, walked on stilts, flew kites and made models. They also played with hobby horses and hoops.

- Most boys of wealthy Roman families would have been educated in schools away from the home, while those from poorer Roman families would have been educated at home by their fathers.

- Roman boys who attended school went seven days a week – there were no days off at the weekend. But they would get a day off when there was a religious festival or celebration and there were a lot of these.

- When a Roman boy reached adulthood some time between the ages of 14 and 17, he was entitled to wear the pure white toga of a man and Roman citizen.

- Roman girls were not allowed to fall in love and choose their own husbands – a marriage would have been arranged for them by their families.

- Hadrian's Wall was begun in AD 122 on the orders of the Emperor Hadrian when he visited Britain. It was built of stone and turf, and was 80 miles (129km) long, 19ft (5.8m) high and 10ft (3m) wide.

- In ancient Rome, it was considered a sign of leadership to be born with a crooked nose.

- People would buy food on the way to and from the games, and sometimes animals that had been slaughtered in the games were quickly cooked and served up, including giraffe and lion meat!

- The Ancient Romans were as fond of 'fast food' and 'snack food' as we are today. There were literally thousands of corner food shops and taverns serving food and wine in Ancient Rome.

- In the days of the early Roman Empire, emperors had their busts sculpted. Sometimes the sculptors were not too careful, or a bit shaky after a late night. Subsequently, some of the busts appeared to depict pock-marked emperors. To conceal their mistakes, the sculptors filled in the cracks and holes with wax. After the statues had been standing in the sun for a time, however, the wax melted, leaving the pock marks visible. The outraged emperors decreed that from henceforth, all sculptors should sign their name on the bottom and vow that their work contained no wax. So in the days of the later Roman Empire, underneath the sculpted busts would be the chiselled declaration: 'Sin Cere' (or 'Without wax') and the artist's name. This caught on. Hence, 'Yours, sincerely.'

- The Romans used to clean themselves with olive oil, since they did not have any soap. They would pour the oil on their bodies and then use a 'strigil', a type of blade, to scrape off any dirt along with the oil.

9

STATISTICS

- At -40°C (-40°F), a person loses about 14.4 calories per hour by breathing.

- One million Americans, about 3,000 each day, take up smoking each year. Most of them are children.

- In 1933, Mickey Mouse, an animated cartoon character, received 800,000 fan letters.

- If you attempted to count all the stars in a galaxy at a rate of one every second, it would take around 3,000 years to count them all.

- Less than 3 per cent of Nestlé's sales are for chocolate.

- The average chocolate bar has eight insects' legs in it.

- There are two credit cards for every person in the United States.

- The average person will spend two weeks over their lifetime waiting for a traffic light to change.

- More than 2,500 left-handed people are killed every year from using right-handed products.

- February 1865 and February 1999 are the only months in recorded history not to have a full moon.

- The most common name in the world is Mohammed.

- More people are killed by donkeys annually than are killed in plane crashes.

- The only two days of the year in which there are no professional sports games in the USA (MLB, NBA, NHL or NFL) are the day before and the day after the Major League All-Star Game.

- Only one person in 2 billion will live to be 116 or older.

- You share your birthday with at least 9 million other people in the world.

- It is estimated that, at any one time, 0.7 per cent of the world's population are drunk.

- The tip of a 0.3in-long (0.8cm) hour hand on a wrist watch travels at 0.00000275 mph (0.00000443km/h).

- One thing that humans do more than anything in their entire life is sleep. Most Westerners sleep more than six to eight hours a day, which is on average around twenty-four years of one's life!

- It takes about half a gallon (2.3 litres) of water to cook a pot of macaroni, and about a gallon (4.5 litres) to clean the pot.

- A man's beard contains between 7,000 and 15,000 hairs.

- A hair is 70 per cent easier to cut when soaked in warm water for two minutes.

- Women's hair is about half the diameter of men's hair.

- During an average lifetime, a man will spend 3,350 hours removing 27ft 6in (8.4m) of stubble.

- Four million children die each year from inhaling smoke from indoor cooking fires that burn wood and dung.

- Less than 1 per cent of China's 500 cities have clean air; respiratory disease is China's leading cause of death.

- The number of cars on the planet is increasing three times faster than the population growth.

- It took 1,175 animators working in Disney Studios in Burbank, California, Orlando, Florida and Paris to complete the animated Tarzan. Because of the time differences, production was able to occur around the clock for more than three years.

- The most expensive commercial ever made is one of the most famous. The 1984 Apple Macintosh commercial that introduced Macintosh to the world ran only once during the 1984 Super Bowl. It was directed by Ridley Scott, and cost $600,000–$1 million to make.

- The average human eats eight spiders in a lifetime at night.

- About 17 per cent of humans are left-handed. The same is true of chimpanzees and gorillas.

- Banging your head against a wall uses 150 calories an hour.

- The entire length of all eyelashes shed by a human in a lifetime is over 98ft (30m).

- No president of the United States was an only child.

- The average woman consumes 6lb (2.7kg) of lipstick in her lifetime.

- It only takes 7lb (3.2kg) of pressure to rip off your ear.

- In all, $26 billion in ransom has been paid out in the USA in the past twenty years.

- You use more calories eating celery than there are in the celery itself.

- On average, there are 178 sesame seeds on each McDonald's Big Mac bun.

- There are 1 million ants for every person in the world.

- Odds of being killed by a dog – 1 in 700,000.

- Odds of dying while in the bathtub – 1 in 1 million.

- Odds of being killed by poisoning – 1 in 86,000.

- Odds of being killed by freezing – 1 in 3 million.

- Odds of being killed by lightning – 1 in 2 million.

- Odds of being killed in a car crash – 1 in 5,000.

- Odds of being killed in a tornado – 1 in 2 million.

- Odds of being killed by falling out of bed – 1 in 2 million.

- If you played all of The Beatles' singles and albums that came out between 1962 and 1970 back to back, it would only last for 10 hours and 33 minutes.

- Termites eat through wood twice as fast when listening to rock music.

- The *Apollo 11* only had twenty seconds of fuel left when it landed on the Moon.

- Thirteen people are killed each year by vending machines falling on them.

- There is 0.25lb (0.11kg) of salt in every gallon (4.5 litres) of seawater.

- About one-third of American adults are at least 20 per cent above their recommended weight.

- The average talker sprays about 300 microscopic saliva droplets per minute, or about 2.5 droplets per word.

- The average smell weighs 760 nanograms.

- The Earth experiences 50,000 earthquakes each year.

- Even on the hottest days, skin temperature does not go much above 35°C (95°F).

- In 1994, 314 Americans had buttock-lift surgery.

- Experts at Intel say that microprocessor speed will double every eighteen months for at least ten years.

- The Earth's revolution time increases 0.0001 seconds annually.

- The annual growth of Internet traffic is 314,000 per cent.

- Driving at 55mph (88km/h) instead of 65mph (105km/h) increases your car mileage by about 15 per cent.

- Airbags explode at 200mph (322km/h).

- A third of all cancers are sun-related.

- The average person flexes the joints in their fingers 24 million times during a lifetime.

- It would take 7 billion particles of fog to fill a teaspoon.

- Your brain weighs around 3lb (1.4kg) – all but 10oz (283.5g) is water.

- The average person makes about 1,140 telephone calls each year.

- The world record for rocking non-stop in a rocking chair is 440 hours.

- The world record distance for Wellington-boot tossing is 179ft 1.69in (54.6m).

- On average, Americans eat 18 acres (7.3 hectares) of pizza every day.

- Fingernails grow nearly four times faster than toenails.

- You blink more than 10,000,000 times a year.

- There are 1,525,000,000 miles (2,453,725,000km) of telephone wire strung across America.

- The average person laughs fifteen times a day...

- ... and spends about two years on the phone in a lifetime.

- A can of Spam is opened every four seconds.

10

THE UNIVERSE

- Venus spins the opposite way to the other planets.

- The brightest star in the night sky is Sirius. Also known as the Dog Star, it is 51 trillion miles (82 trillion km) from the Earth, or about 8.7 light-years away. The second brightest star is Canopus, which is only visible in the Southern Hemisphere.

- To reach outer space, you need to travel at least 50 miles (80km) from the Earth's surface.

- Mars was named after the Roman god of war.

- The largest asteroid on record is Ceres. It is so big it would stretch a distance of over 600 miles (966km)!

- Jupiter has no solid surface, only layers of gaseous clouds. It is composed mainly of hydrogen and helium.

- The average size of a meteor is no bigger than a grain of sand.

- The Earth spins faster on its axis in September than it does in March.

- The far side of the Moon was first photographed by a Russian satellite in 1959.

- The diameter of the Moon is 2,160 miles (3,476km).

- *Mariner 10* was the first spacecraft to fly by Mercury. In 1974, it sent back close-up pictures of a world that resembles our Moon.

- The surface temperature of Venus is hot enough to melt lead! Lead melts at 350°C (662°F) and the surface can reach temperatures of 462°C (864°F).

- Ninety-nine per cent of our solar system's mass is concentrated in the Sun.

- The Moon has about 3 trillion craters larger than 3ft (91cm) in diameter.

- It takes Jupiter almost twelve Earth years to orbit the Sun. The length of a day on Jupiter is 9 hours, 50 minutes, 30 seconds at the equator.

- Uranus is visible to the naked eye.

- The Moon orbits the Earth every 27.32 days.

- It takes 8.5 minutes for light to get from the Sun to the Earth.

- The Earth is the only planet not named after a god.

- On a clear night, over 2,000 stars are visible to the naked eye.

- The Sun's mass decreases by 4,000,000 tons (4,064,187 tonnes) per second due to conversion of hydrogen to helium by thermonuclear reaction; this conversion will continue for another 5,000 million years before the Sun's energy supply is exhausted.

- Due to gravitational effects, you weigh slightly less when the Moon is directly overhead.

- Uranus was only discovered 225 years ago, on 13 March 1781, by Sir William Herschel.

- The Milky Way galaxy contains 5 billion stars larger than our Sun.

- Our galaxy is 75,000 light-years in diameter and our Sun is 26,100 light-years from the centre.

- Based on various cosmological techniques, the universe is estimated at 10–18 gigayears old (1 gigayear = 1,000,000,000,000 years).

- The smallest star found to date is a neutron star, with a diameter of 37 miles (59km) but a mass of ten times that of our Sun. This star is more commonly known as a black hole.

- The Earth's average velocity orbiting the Sun is 66,623mph (107,220km/h).

- Driving at 75mph (121km/h), it would take 258 days to drive around one of Saturn's rings.

- The Sun has a core temperature of 154,000,000 Kelvin (277,199,540°F).

- Because of a large orbital eccentricity, Pluto was closer to the Sun than Neptune between January 1979 and March 1999.

- The Earth is the densest planet in the solar system.

- The Future's Museum in Sweden contains a scale model of the solar system. The Sun is 344ft (105m) in diameter and the planets range from 0.1in (3.5mm) to 3.7 miles (6km) from the Sun. This particular model also contains the nearest star, Proxima Centauri, still to scale, situated in the Museum of Victoria in Australia.

- The maximum possible duration of a solar eclipse is 7 minutes and 31 seconds.

- The Sun is 330,330 times larger than the Earth.

- In the 20th century, two objects hit the Earth's surface with enough force to destroy a medium-size city. By pure luck, both landed in sparsely populated Siberia. The generally agreed-upon theory is that on the morning of June 30, 1908, and then again in 1947, a meteorite, about 120 feet across, entered the atmosphere of Siberia and then detonated in the sky.

- Copernicus's book, which suggested that the Sun and not the Earth was the centre of the solar system, was officially banned by the papacy until 1835.

- Our own galaxy is minute compared to the radio galaxies being discovered at the edge of the universe.

- Scientists believe that hydrogen comprises approximately 90–99 per cent of all matter in the universe.

- Without using precision instruments, Eratosthenes measured the radius of the Earth in the 3rd century BC, and came within 1 per cent of the value determined by today's technology.

- Venus does not tilt as it goes around the Sun, so it has no seasons. On Mars, however, the seasons are more exaggerated and last much longer than on Earth.

- Venus is named after the Roman goddess of love.

- Scientists have determined that most rocks on the surface of the Moon are 3–4.6 billion years old.

- The point in a lunar orbit that is farthest from the Moon is called an apolune.

- Selenologists are those who study the Moon.

- The pressure at the centre of the Earth is 27,000 tons (274,332 tonnes) per in^2. At the centre of the giant planet Jupiter, the pressure is three times as great.

- The Sea of Tranquillity on the Moon is not a real sea, but a 'maria', one of the regions on the Moon that appear dark when you look at them.

- The star Alpha Herculis is twenty-five times larger than the circumference described by the Earth's revolution around the Sun.

- Uranus, the seventh planet from the Sun, is tipped on its side so that at any moment one pole is pointed at the Sun. The polar regions are warmer than the equator. At the poles, a day lasts for forty-two Earth years, followed by an equally long night.

- Pluto – once deemed the smallest planet in our solar system, though now regarded as a dwarf planet – is a little smaller than the Earth's Moon.

- The Sun gives off a stream of electrically charged particles called the solar wind. Every second, the Sun pumps more than a million tons of material into the solar wind.

- The solar wind flows past the Earth at 1,200 times the speed of sound.

- The smallest visible sunspots have an area of 500 million miles^2 (1,295 million km^2), about fifty times the size of Africa. The largest sunspots have an area of about 7,000 million miles^2 (18,130 million km^2).

- 'Ufology' is the study of UFOs, especially those thought to be from outer space.

- A brown dwarf is a very small dark object, with a mass less than one-tenth that of the Sun. They are 'failed stars' – globules of gas that have shrunk under gravity, but failed to ignite and shine as stars.

- A cosmic year is the amount of time it takes the Sun to revolve around the centre of the Milky Way, about 225 million years.

- The star Antares is 60,000 times larger than our Sun. If our Sun were the size of a softball, the star Antares would be as large as a house.

- A bucket filled with earth would weigh about five times more than the same bucket filled with the substance of the Sun. However, the force of gravity is so much greater on the Sun that a man weighing 150lb (68kg) on Earth would weigh 2 tons (2.03 tonnes) on the Sun.

- A car travelling at a constant speed of 60mph (96.6km/h) would take longer than 48 million years to reach the nearest star (other than our Sun), Proxima Centauri. This is about 685,000 average human lifetimes.

- The star known as LP 327-186, a so-called white dwarf, is smaller than the state of Texas, yet so dense that, if a cubic inch of it were brought to Earth, it would weigh more than 1.5 million tons (1.52 million tonnes).

- The star Sirius B is so dense, a handful of it weighs about 1 million lb (453,592kg).

- There are 100,000 million stars in our galaxy.

- The Sun contains over 99.8 per cent of the total mass in our solar system, while Jupiter contains most of the rest. The fractional percentage that is left is made up of our Earth and Moon and the remaining planets and asteroids.

- The discovery of Neptune was announced in 1846. But, when astronomers checked previous records, they found the record of an observation of the planet as far back as 1795 by astronomers who, believing it to be a star, recorded the position routinely.

- Since Neptune's discovery in 1846, it has made about three-quarters of one revolution of the Sun.

- The pressure at the centre of the Sun is about 700 million tons (711 million tonnes) per in². It's enough to smash atoms, expose the inner nuclei and allow them to smash into each other, interact and produce the radiation that gives off light and warmth.

- The reflecting power of a planet or satellite, expressed as a ratio of reflected light to the total amount falling on the surface, is called the albedo.

- The star Zeta Thaun, a supernova, was so bright when it exploded in 1054 that it could be seen during the day.

- The Sun is 93 million miles (150 million km) from Earth, yet it is 270,000 times closer than the next nearest star.

- A day on Mercury is twice as long as its year. Mercury rotates very slowly but revolves around the Sun in slightly less than eighty-eight days.

- A galaxy of typical size – about 100 billion suns – produces less energy than a single quasar.

- A solar day on Mercury, from sunrise to sunset, lasts about six Earth months.

- The Sun is about midway in the scale of star sizes, but most are smaller ones. Only 5 per cent of the stars in our galaxy are larger than the Sun. (That's still 5 billion larger stars.)

- A neutron star is the strongest magnet in the universe. The magnetic field of a neutron star is a million million times stronger than the Earth's magnetism.

- About twenty new stars are born in our galaxy each year.

- A pulsar is a small star that emits brief, sharp pulses of radio waves instead of the steady radiation associated with other natural sources. It is made up of neutrons so densely packed together that, if one the size of a 10-pence piece landed on Earth, it would weigh approximately 100 million tons (101.6 million tonnes).

- A space shuttle at lift-off develops more power than all the cars in England combined.

- A spectroheliokinematograph is a special camera used to film the Sun.

- Afternoon temperatures on Mars go up to about 27°C (80°F) in some areas, and down to -123°C (-190°F) at night.

- A sunbeam setting out through space at the rate of 186,000 miles (299,338km) a second would describe a gigantic circle and return to its origins after about 200 billion years.

- A typical nova explosion releases about as much energy as the Sun emits in 10,000 years, or as much as in 1,000,000,000,000,000,000,000,000 nuclear bombs.

- A white dwarf has a mass equal to that of the Sun, but a diameter only about that of the Earth. A cupful of white dwarf material weighs about 22 tons (22.4 tonnes), the same as five elephants.

- About forty novae erupt in our galaxy each year.

- Two of every three stars in the galaxy are binary, meaning pairs of stars are more common than single-star systems like our own.

- Gold exists on Mars, Mercury and Venus.

- All the coal, oil, gas and wood on Earth would only keep the Sun burning for a few days.

- All the planets in our solar system could be placed inside the planet Jupiter. Jupiter is two-and-a-half times larger than all the other planets, satellites, asteroids and comets of our solar system combined.

- If one were to capture and bottle a comet's 10,000-mile (16,093km) vapour trail, the amount of vapour actually present in the bottle would take up less than $1in^3$ (16.4cm^3) of space.

- Although the Sun is 400 times larger than the Moon, it appears the same size in the sky because it is 400 times further away.

- An area of the Sun's surface the size of a postage stamp shines with the power of 1,5 million candles.

- An estimated 10,000 million of the 100,000 million stars in our galaxy have died and produced white dwarfs.

- An object weighing 100lb (45kg) on Earth would weigh just 38lb (17kg) on Mars.

- If the Earth were the size of an apple, the atmospheric layer would be no thicker than the skin of the apple.

- If our whole galaxy were the size of a 10-pence piece, our solar system would be smaller than the size of a molecule. Other galaxies would be from 1ft to 1,000ft (0.3–305m) away.

- If the world were to become totally flat and the oceans distributed themselves evenly over the Earth's surface, the water would be approximately 2 miles (3.2km) deep at every point.

- Asteroids smaller than 600ft (183m) across entering the Earth's atmosphere burn away and lose most of their energy before hitting our planet. But even these smaller objects can cause devastation. A small asteroid exploded in the air in Siberia in 1908. The resulting shock wave flattened 800 miles^2 (2,072 km^2) of forest. The detonation's force was estimated to have been 1,000 times greater than the Hiroshima bomb.

- Ancient Chinese astronomers first observed sunspots about 2,000 years ago. Westerners took quite a while to catch up, first writing of the dark blotches 1,700 years later, and wrongly believing them to be small planets.

- Antarctica has been used as a testing laboratory for the joint United States–Soviet Union mission to Mars because it has much in common with the red planet.

- Aristarchus, a Greek astronomer living around 200 BC, was reportedly the first person to declare that the Earth revolved around the Sun. His theory was disregarded for hundreds of years.

- In 1959, Arthur C. Clarke made a bet that the first man to land on the Moon would do so by June 1969. US astronauts landed on 20 July 1969.

- At its centre, the Sun has a density of over 100 times that of water, and a temperature of 10–20 million degrees Celsius (18–36 million degrees Fahrenheit).

- If you travelled to Proxima Centauri, the star nearest to the Earth (outside our solar system), the Sun would appear to be a bright star in the constellation of Cassiopeia.

- In 1066, Halley's Comet appeared shortly before William the Conqueror invaded England. The Norman king took it as a good omen; his battle cry became 'A new star, a new king'.

- In 1937, the tiny asteroid Hermes passed uncomfortably close to the Earth, at a distance of less than twice that of the Moon.

- Astronomers believe Jupiter's moon, Europa, may have an ocean of liquid water beneath an ice cap.

- At the end of every nineteen years, the lunar phases repeat themselves. In effect, the tide tables for the next nineteen years will be approximately the same as those for the past nineteen years.

- Small satellites within a planet's rings are sometimes called 'mooms'.

- Some astronomers believe Pluto's strange and erratic orbit indicates that it was a moon of Neptune that somehow broke loose.

- In 1994, the comet Shoemaker-Levy 9 broke apart and plunged into Jupiter, ripping holes the size of Earth in the planet's atmosphere.

- Some neutron stars spin 600 times a second, which is as fast as a dentist's drill.

- Space dust particles are extremely small – smaller than a particle of smoke – and widely separated, with more than 320ft (97.5m) between particles.

- Statistically, UFO sightings are at their greatest number during those times when Mars is closest to the Earth.

- In the constellation Cygnus, there is a double star, one of whose components has such a high surface gravity that light cannot escape from it. Many astronomers believe Cygnus X-1 was the first 'black hole' to be detected.

- Temperature variations on Mercury are the most extreme in the solar system, ranging from 90°K to 700°K (-298°F to 800°F).

- In the 16th and 17th centuries, some people thought comets were the eggs or sperm of planetary systems.

- Barnard's star is approaching the Sun at a speed of 87 miles (140km) per second. By the year 11800, it will be the closest star to us.

- Because it is pouring energy out into space so rapidly, the Sun is shedding weight equivalent to that of a million elephants every second.

- Besides the Earth, only Jupiter, Saturn, Uranus and Neptune have known magnetic fields.

- By the year 14000, the new North Star will be Vega.

- Carbon dioxide makes up 97 per cent of Venus's atmosphere.

- Comets speed up as they approach the Sun – sometimes reaching speeds of over 1 million mph (1.6 million km/h). Far away from the Sun, speeds drop, perhaps down to as little as 700mph (1,127km/h).

- The Earth orbits the Sun at 18.5 miles (29.8km) a second.

- The atmosphere of Mars is relatively moist. However, because the atmosphere is thin, the total amount of water in the atmosphere is minimal. If all the water in the atmosphere of Mars was collected, it would probably only fill a small pond.

- The average meteor, though brilliantly visible in the night-time sky, is no larger than a grain of sand. Even the largest and brightest meteors, known as fireballs, rarely exceed the size of a pea.

- In the history of the solar system, 30 billion comets have been lost or destroyed. That amounts to only 30 per cent of the estimated number that remain.

- In the Middle Ages, millions of people believed that the stars were beams of light shining through the floor of heaven.

- The average surface temperature of the outer planets – Uranus, Neptune and the dwarf planet Pluto – is about -220°C (-364°F), eleven times colder than inside a home freezer.

- It has been estimated that at least a million meteors have hit the Earth's land surface, which is only 25 per cent of the planet. Every last trace of more than 99 per cent of the craters thus formed has vanished, erased by wind, water and living things.

- The brightest asteroid is called Vesta. It has a diameter of 335 miles (539km) and is the only asteroid visible to the unaided eye.

- It is estimated by scientists that the universe contains 0.000000000000000000000000000000001 grams of matter per cubic centimetre of space. It is also estimated that the universe is 35 billion light-years in size, or 210,000,000,000,000,000,000,000 miles (338,000,000,000,000,000,000,000km).

- Deimos, one of Mars's moons, rises and sets twice a day.

- It is estimated that, within the entire universe, there are more than a trillion galaxies.

- The brightness of a star is called its magnitude. The smaller the magnitude, the brighter the star.

- American physicist John Wheeler discovered the black holes of outer space, and named the phenomenon in 1967.

- The coldest place in the solar system is the surface of Neptune's largest moon, Triton, which has a temperature of -235°C (-391°F), only 20.5°C (69°F) above absolute zero.

- The dark spots on the moon that create the benevolent 'man in the moon' image are actually basins filled 1.8–5 miles (3–8km) deep with basalt, a dense mineral that causes immense gravitation variations.

- Jupiter is the largest planet, and it has the shortest day. Although Jupiter has a circumference of 280,000 miles (450,616km), compared with the Earth's 25,000 miles (40,233km), Jupiter manages to make one turn in 9 hours and 55 minutes. However, its years are twelve times as long as the Earth's.

- Jupiter is so big and has such a large atmosphere that many astronomers think it almost became a star.

- The Sun is nearly 600 times bigger than all the planets combined.

- The Sun isn't round. It is flattened on the top and the bottom.

- The Sun is so far from Neptune – 2,793,000,000 miles (4,494,897,792km) – that from there it would appear to be no more than a very bright star.

- The dense globules of gas from which stars are born are much larger than the stars they will form. In the Orion nebula, globules have been detected that are 500 times larger than the solar system.

The Sun produces more energy every minute than all the energy used on Earth in a whole year.

- The diameter of the star Betelgeuse is more than a quarter the size of our entire solar system.

- Every day the Sun provides our planet with 126,000,000,000,000 horsepower of energy. This means that 54,000 horsepower is delivered to every man, woman and child on Earth in each twenty-four-hour period.

- The distance around the Earth's equator is 24,920 miles (40,105km); it would take 33,000,000 people holding hands to reach across that distance.

- The diameter of Venus is only about 400 miles (644km) less than that of the Earth.

- The Sun's equator is 2,717,952 miles (4,374,120km) around; it would take 3,645,000,000 people holding hands to go around it.

- Jupiter spins faster than any other planet. A point on the equator of Jupiter spins around the centre of the planet at a speed of 28,273mph (45,500km/h). The speed of the spin makes the planet bulge slightly at its equator.

- The Sun's solar wind is so powerful that it has noticeable effects on the tails of comets, and scientists have determined that it even has measurable effects on the trajectories of spacecraft.

- The Sun's surface area is 12,000 times that of the Earth.

- The Earth's Moon has no global magnetic field.

- The Sun's total lifetime as a star capable of maintaining a life-bearing Earth is about 11 billion years, nearly half of which has passed.

- Jupiter's moon Adrastea is one of the smallest moons in our solar system. It measures about 12.4 miles (20km) in diameter.

- The Earth moves in its 585-million-mile (941-million-km) orbit around the Sun approximately eight times faster than a bullet travels.

- The Earth rotates on its axis more slowly in March than it does in September.

- Even though there were only six manned lunar landings, there are seven Apollo lunar landers on the moon. *Apollo X*, as part of its mission, dropped a lunar lander to test seismic equipment that had already been set up on a previous mission.

- Five times as many meteors can be seen after midnight as can be seen before.

- Four million tons (4,064,187 tonnes) of hydrogen dust are destroyed on the Sun every second.

- Because of its surface tension, free-moving liquid in outer space will form itself into a sphere.

- Galaxies come in many different shapes, which are determined by the effects of past gravitational encounters with other galaxies. Our Milky Way is a spiral-type galaxy.

- Neptune has eight known satellites.

- The surface of Venus is actually hotter than Mercury's, despite being nearly twice as far from the Sun.

- The Earth weighs nearly 6,588,000,000,000,000,000,000,000 tons (6,694, 000,000,000,000,000,000,000 tonnes).

- The surface temperature of a neutron star is about 999,980 degrees Celsius (1,800,000 degrees Fahrenheit).

- The energy released in an hour by a single sunspot is equal to all the electrical power that will be used in the USA over the next million years.

- The surface of Venus – millions of miles away and hidden by clouds of sulphuric acid – has been better mapped than the Earth's seabed.

- The tail of a comet can extend 90 million miles (145 million km) – nearly the distance between the Earth and the Sun.

- Less than 50 per cent of American adults understand that the Earth orbits the Sun yearly, according to a basic science survey.

- The final resting place for Dr Eugene Shoemaker is the Moon. The famed US Geological Survey astronomer had trained the Apollo mission astronauts about craters, but never made it into space. Dr Shoemaker had wanted to be an astronaut but was rejected because of a medical problem. His ashes were placed on board the *Lunar Prospector* spacecraft before it was launched on 6 January 1998. NASA crashed the probe into a crater on the Moon on 31 July 1999 in an attempt to learn if there is water there.

- The tails of comets generally point away from the Sun, whether the comet is approaching the Sun or whether it is receding.

- The first photo of the Earth taken from space was shot from the *Vanguard 2* in 1959.

- Light takes one-tenth of a second to travel from New York to London, 8 minutes to reach the Earth from the Sun and 4.3 years to reach the Earth from the nearest star.

- The Tarantula is the largest known nebula and is 160,000 light-years away. If it was as close to us as the Orion nebula, its light would cast shadows on Earth.

- The first pulsar, discovered in 1967, never varies in its timing by even as much as a hundred-millionth of a second. Its pulse is registered every 1.33730109 seconds.

- Light from the Moon takes about a second and a half to reach the Earth.

- The Tarantula nebula is thought to contain a huge star of over 1,000 times the mass of the Sun, ten times more massive than any star in the Milky Way.

- The first spacecraft to send back pictures of the far side of the Moon was *Luna 3* in October 1959. The photographs covered about 70 per cent of the far side.

- Liquid water was found inside a 4.5-billion-year-old meteorite in 1999, giving scientists their first look at extraterrestrial water.

- The telescope on Mount Palomar, California, can see a distance of 7,038,835,200,000,000,000,000 miles (1,132,790,719,600,000,000,000 km).

- The force of gravity is very strong on a neutron star because of its amazing density. Your weight on a neutron star would be 10,000 million times greater than on Earth.

- The temperature of the Earth's interior increases by 1 degree every 60ft (18.3m) down.

- The temperature on the Moon reaches 117°C (243°F) at midday on the lunar equator. During the night, the temperature falls to -163°C (-261°F).

- The footprints left by the Apollo astronauts will not erode since there is no wind or water on the Moon and they should last at least 10 million years.

- Mare Tranquillitatis, or Sea of Tranquillity, was the name of the first manned lunar landing.

- Galileo became totally blind shortly before his death, probably because of the damage done to his eyes during his many years of looking at the Sun through a telescope.

- Halley's Comet is named after Edmond G. Halley, who was the first person to suggest that comets were natural phenomena of our solar system, in orbit around the Sun.

- Maps showing the solar system published prior to 1979 had to be updated as Pluto (then regarded as a planet) was no longer the most distant planet from the Sun and it was Neptune instead. In its 248.8-year orbital revolution around the Sun, Pluto crossed Neptune's orbit in December 1978. Neptune and Pluto resumed their more familiar positions in March 1999 as Pluto journeyed to its farthest point from the Sun, over 4.5 billion miles (7.2 billion km) away.

- Ganymede, Jupiter's largest moon, is bigger than Mercury, the smallest planet. It is 3,275 miles (5,270km) in diameter.

- Giant flames called prominences shoot out from the Sun's surfaces for 310,000 miles (498,897km), more than the distance from the Earth to the Moon.

- The entire Earth could fit into one of these flames nearly forty times.

- Mars takes 1.88 years to orbit the Sun, so its seasons are about twice as long as those on Earth.

- If a pin were heated to the same temperature as the centre of the Sun, its heat would set alight everything within 60 miles (96.5km) of it.

- If a red giant star were the size of an ordinary living room, its energy-generating core would be the size of the full stop at the end of this sentence.

- The giant red star Betelgeuse – the red star in the shoulder of the constellation Orion – is 700 million miles (1,127 million km) across, about 800 times larger than the Sun. Light takes one hour to travel from one side of the giant star to the other.

- The Veil nebula was formed by an explosion that took place over 30,000 years ago, when the first people lived on Earth.

- If an astronaut tried to land on a neutron star, he or she would be crushed by the extremely strong force of gravity, and squashed into a thin layer less than an atom thick.

- The existence of Mercury has been known since about the 3rd millennium BC. The planet was given two names by the Greeks: Apollo, for its apparition as a morning star, and Hermes, as an evening star. Greek astronomers knew, however, that the two names referred to the same body.

- The universe is about 15,000 million years old. Put another way, if the years flashed by at a rate of one each second, the universe would already be nearly 47 years old.

- Halley's Comet, one of the most famous comets, returns to Earth every seventy-six years, and has been observed and recorded for more than 3,000 years.

- The winds of Venus blow steadily at 109mph (175km/h).

- Metis is the innermost of Jupiter's known satellites and was named after Metis, a Titaness who was the first wife of the Greek god Zeus, known later as Jupiter in Roman mythology.

- The gravitational pull of a black hole is so strong that, if a 2lb (0.9kg) book were brought within 20ft (6m) of a black hole, the book would weigh more than all the world's population combined.

- Millions of meteorites fall against the outer limits of the Earth's atmosphere every day and are burned away to nothing by the friction.

- The Venusian day is longer than the Venusian year. The planet spins on its axis once every 243 Earth days and orbits the Sun once every 224 Earth days.

- The Great Red Spot on Jupiter is a swirling hurricane of gases. The winds in the hurricane reach 21,700mph (34,922km/h).

- More than 100,000 asteroids lie in a belt between Mars and Jupiter.

- The weight of the Sun is 2 billion billion billion tons, about 333,420 times that of the Earth.

- The word 'comet' comes from the Greek *kométes*, meaning 'wearing long hair'.

- The heaviest meteorite known to have fallen to Earth – the Hoba West meteorite – lies where it fell in Africa. Weighing about 60 tons (61 tonnes), it is not likely to be moved.

- More than 20 million meteoroids enter the Earth's atmosphere every day, but most are no bigger than a speck of dust.

- The Hercules global cluster is the brightest cluster in the northern sky. It was discovered by English scientist Edmond Halley in 1714.

- The Hubble Space Telescope recently discovered a huge 295-mile (475km) crater on the asteroid Vesta. This is massive when compared to Vesta's 330-mile (531km) diameter. If the Earth had a crater of proportional size, it would fill most of the Pacific Ocean basin.

- The world is not round. It is an oblate spheroid, flattened at the poles and bulging at the equator.

- The huge halo of comets that surrounds our solar system is called the Oort Cloud.

- Neil Armstrong's spacesuit during his training brought in $178,500 at auction. This was more than double its pre-sale estimate.

- The jets of water vapour discharged by a comet have a rocket-like effect. They alter the comet's orbit enough to make its course unpredictable.

- Neptune is a maximum distance of 2.82 billion miles (4.54 billion km) from the Sun. The length of one of its days is 17 hours 6 minutes and the length of one of its years is 165 Earth days.

- Eighty-eight different constellations have been identified and named by astronomers.

- There are seven rings surrounding Saturn. Each of the rings is made up of thousands of ringlets, which are made up of billions of objects of varying sizes from 33ft-wide (10m) icebergs to pinhead-small ice specks.

- The largest crater that can be seen on the Moon is called Bailly, or the 'fields of ruin'. It covers an area of about 26,000 miles^2 (67,340km^2), about three times the size of Wales.

- There is a correspondence between the fluctuation of agricultural production and sunspot variations. Production of wheat, for example, reached high figures during sunspot maximums and low figures during sunspot minimums.

- There is now evidence that comets are propelled into the inner solar system by the tidal pull of the entire galaxy, rather than by the pull of passing stars, as many astronomers had believed. And just as the Moon pulls the Earth's oceans upwards on a regular, predictable timetable, the galaxy's pull on comets also follows a predictable pattern, causing greatly increased comet activity about once every 35 million years.

- The largest refracting telescope is the 40in (101cm) Yerkes telescope, built in 1897 and still in use. All larger telescopes are of the 'reflecting' variety, using mirrors instead of lenses.

- Neptune is so remote that light from the Sun – though travelling at 186,000 miles (299,338km) per second – takes more than four hours to reach the planet. By comparison, light from the Sun takes only eight minutes to reach the Earth.

- The Moon weighs 81 billion tons (83.3 billion tonnes).

- The largest volcano known is on Mars: Olympus Mons, 370 miles (595km) wide and 79,000ft (24,079km) high, is almost three times higher than Mount Everest.

- Three-quarters of the galaxies in the universe are spiral galaxies. There are three other types of galaxies: elliptical, irregular and lenticular.

- Venus is much brighter than any other planet or star.

- There may be a giant black hole at the centre of our galaxy, weighing up to 4 million times more than our Sun. The black hole may be capturing stars, gas and dust equivalent to the weight of three Earths every year.

- The layer of gas that spreads out from a nova explosion can be travelling at speeds of 5 million mph (8 million km/h).

- On 21 September 1978, two Soviet cosmonauts set a space endurance record of ninety-six days.

- Time slows down near a black hole; inside, it stops completely.

- The Moon is 238,330 miles (383,555km) away from the Earth.

- At that distance, the Moon is the Earth's closest neighbour.

- The Moon is about as wide as the United States: 2,160 miles (3,476km).

- On Venus, the Sun rises in the west and sets in the east, the opposite of the Earth. Venus rotates from east to west, not from west to east as the Earth and the other planets do.

- Titan, Saturn's largest moon, is the only moon in our solar system to have an atmosphere. However, it cannot support life as its atmosphere is made of nitrogen and methane gas.

- The Moon is one million times drier than the Gobi Desert.

- The Moon is always falling. It has a sideways motion of its own that balances its falling motion. It therefore stays in a closed orbit about the Earth, never falling altogether and never escaping altogether.

- To an observer standing on Pluto, the Sun would appear no brighter than Venus appears in our evening sky.

- Travelling at the speed of 186,000 miles (299,338km) per second, light takes six hours to travel from Pluto to the Earth.

- Triton, a moon of Neptune, is the coldest known place in the solar system. Its surface is 234°C below zero (-390°F).

- The most ancient report of a solar eclipse dates from records made in China. According to legend, the eclipse came without warning because the royal astronomers, Hsi and Ho, were too drunk to make the necessary computations. They were executed – the only astronomers known to have been killed for dereliction of duty.

- The largest number of telescopes in one city in the world is in Tucson, Arizona.

- The moons of Mars are called Phobos and Deimos after two mythical horses that drew the chariot of Mars, the Roman god of war.

- Our galaxy probably contains millions of old neutron stars that have stopped spinning, and so are undetectable.

- Until the mid-16th century, comets were believed to be not astronomical phenomena, but burning vapours that had arisen from distant swamps and were propelled across the sky by fire and light.

- Our solar system lies halfway along the Orion arm, about 24,000 light-years from the galactic centre.

- Venus has no magnetic field, perhaps because of its slow rotation. It also has no satellites.

- The most luminous star is probably Eta Carinae, which has a maximum luminosity of around 5 million times that of the Sun.

- Plenilune is an archaic term for a full moon.

- The multi-layered space suit worn by astronauts on the Apollo moon landings weighed 180lb (82kg) on Earth but 30lb (14kg) on the Moon, with the reduced lunar gravity.

- Phobos, one of the moons of Mars, is so close to its parent planet that it could not be seen by an observer standing at either of Mars's poles. Every day, Phobos makes three complete orbits around Mars.

- When astronauts first shaved in space, their weightless whiskers floated up to the ceiling. A special razor had to be developed for them, which drew the whiskers in like a vacuum cleaner.

- Physicists now believe the universe to be 3 billion years younger than previously thought. New information gathered by the Hipparcos satellite, combined with a re-analysis of other distance data, has enabled researchers to refine the lower age limit of the universe to 9.6 billion years.

- When the first pulsar signal was detected in 1967, it was thought that its signals might be a message from an alien civilisation deep in space. The signal was jokingly labelled 'LGM', for 'little green men'.

- At its brightest, the Moon can cast shadow, and can even be seen during the daytime.

- The nucleus of Halley's Comet is a peanut-shaped object, weighing about 100,000 million tons (101,600 million tonnes), and measuring about 9 x 5 miles (14.5 x 8km).

- Venus, the Earth's nearest planetary neighbour, at its closest to us is 105 times farther away than our Moon.

- Proxima Centauri is the closest star to the Earth (outside our solar system), but it is too small to be seen without a telescope.

- Pluto's one moon, Charon, is 12,200 miles (19,634km) from it and has a diameter of just 740 miles (1,190km). First seen from the Earth in 1978, tiny Charon is similar in size to Pluto. The two bodies orbit each other like a double planet, with the same sides permanently facing each other. Pluto and Charon are so close in proximity it is believed that they may share an atmosphere.

- Polaris, in the tail of the Little Bear constellation, is the closest visible star to true north and thus is referred to as the North Star. By about 2100, the wobble of the Earth's axis will slowly begin pointing the North Pole away from Polaris.

- The oldest features on Venus appear to be no older than 800 million years.

- Jupiter has sixteen moons, the largest of which is Ganymede, which looks like cracked eggshell.

- When the *Apollo 12* astronauts landed on the Moon, the impact caused the Moon's surface to vibrate for fifty-five minutes. The vibrations were picked up by laboratory instruments, leading geologists to theorise that the Moon's surface is composed of fragile layers of rock.

- Uranus has fifteen known satellites.

- Jupiter is named after the supreme god of the Romans. He was the god of the sky, the bringer of light, hurling lightning bolts down on the world when displeased.

- Quasars are amazingly bright objects. A quasar generates 100 times as much light as the whole of our galaxy in a space not much larger than our solar system.

- When we look at the farthest visible star, we are looking 4 billion years into the past – the light from that star, travelling at 186,000 miles (299,338km) a second, has taken that many years to reach us.

- Winds ten times stronger than a hurricane on Earth blow around Saturn's equator. Wind speeds can reach 1,100mph (1,770km/h).

- Pluto takes 248 Earth years to orbit the Sun. For twenty of those years, it is closer to the Sun than Neptune. The nature of its orbit, however, always prevents it from colliding with Neptune.

- Scientists are still finding new planets, but not in our solar system. Recently, a new planet was discovered orbiting the star Epsilon Eridani, which is only 10.5 light-years from the Earth.

- Saturn would float on water if there were an ocean large enough to accommodate it because of its density. However, Saturn is ninety-five times heavier than the Earth.

11

HISTORY

- The Aztec Indians of Mexico believed turquoise would protect them from physical harm, and so warriors used these green-and-blue stones to decorate their battle shields.

- More than 5,000 years ago, the Chinese discovered how to make silk from silkworm cocoons. For about 3,000 years, they kept this discovery a secret.

- Because poor people could not afford real silk, they tried to make other cloth look silky. Women would beat on cotton with sticks to soften the fibres. Then they rubbed it against a big stone to make it shiny. The shiny cotton was called 'chintz'. Because chintz was a cheaper copy of silk, calling something 'chintzy' means it is cheap and not of good quality.

- The pharaohs of Ancient Egypt wore garments made with thin threads of beaten gold. Some fabrics had up to 500 gold threads per inch of cloth.

- The Ancient Egyptians recommended mixing half an onion with beer foam as a way of warding off death.

- The Chinese, in olden days, used marijuana as a remedy for dysentery.

- In 1918, Captain Sarret made the first parachute jump in France from an airplane.

- *Scientific America* carried the first magazine automobile ad in 1898. The Winton Motor Car Company of Cleveland, Ohio invited readers to 'dispense with a horse'.

- The first paperback book was printed by Penguin Publishing in 1935.

- In 1956, the phrase 'In God We Trust' was adopted as the US national motto.

- Henry Ford flatly stated that history is 'bunk'.

- The first Eskimo bible was printed in Copenhagen in 1744.

- The last words spoken from the Moon were from Eugene Cernan, Commander of the Apollo 17 mission, on 11 December 1972. 'As we leave the Moon at Taurus-Littrow, we leave as we came, and, God willing, we shall return, with peace and hope for all mankind.'

- John Hancock was the only one of the fifty signatories of the Declaration of Independence who actually signed it on 4 July 1776.

- Virginia O'Hanlon Douglas was the 8-year-old girl who, in 1897, asked the staff of the *New York Sun* whether Santa Claus existed. In the now-famous editorial, Francis Church assured Virginia that yes, indeed, 'there is a Santa Claus'.

- The first dictionary of American English was published on 14 April 1828, by Noah Webster.

- No automobile made after 1924 should be designated as antique.

- The first US coast-to-coast airplane flight took place in 1911 and lasted forty-nine days.

- Escape maps, compasses and files were inserted into Monopoly game boards and smuggled into POW camps inside Germany during World War II; real money for escapees was slipped into the packs of Monopoly money.

- Incan soldiers invented the process of freeze-drying food. The process was primitive but effective – potatoes would be left outside to freeze overnight, then thawed and stamped on to remove excess water.

- False eyelashes were invented by the American film director D.W. Griffith while he was making his 1916 epic *Intolerance*. Griffith wanted actress Seena Owen to have lashes that brushed her cheeks, to make her eyes shine larger than life. A wigmaker wove human hair through fine gauze, which was then gummed to Owen's eyelids. *Intolerance* was critically acclaimed but flopped financially, leaving Griffith with huge debts that he might have been able to settle easily... had he only thought to patent the eyelashes.

- The Netherlands have many seas and many of their citizens wanted a shoe that kept their feet dry while working outside. The shoes were called 'klompen' and they were cut from one single piece of wood. Today the klompen – or clogs – are the favourite souvenir of people who visit the Netherlands.

- When airplanes were still a novel invention, seatbelts for pilots were installed only after the consequence of their absence was observed to be fatal – several pilots fell to their deaths while flying upside down.

- In 1893, Chicago hired its first policewoman, Marie Owens. While the city was progressive in its hiring practices, Chicago's female police officers were not allowed to wear uniforms until 1956.

- Limelight provided the means of lighting theatre stages before electricity was invented. Basically, illumination was produced by heating blocks of lime until they glowed.

- On 29 November 1941, the programme for the annual US Army–Navy football game carried a picture of the battleship *Arizona*, captioned: 'It is significant that despite the claims of air enthusiasts no battleship has yet been sunk by bombs.' Today you can visit the site – now a shrine – where Japanese dive bombers sunk the *Arizona* at Pearl Harbor only nine days later.

- Leonardo da Vinci could write with one hand and draw with the other at the same time.

- During the California Gold Rush of 1849, miners sent their laundry to Honolulu for washing and pressing. Due to the extremely high costs in California during these boom years, it was deemed more economic to send the shirts to Hawaii for servicing.

- According to the Greek historian Herodotus, Egyptian men never became bald. The reason for this, Herodotus claimed, was that as children Egyptian males had their heads shaved and their scalps were continually exposed to the health-giving rays of the sun.

12

Sayings and Omens

- You will have bad luck if you don't get out of bed on the same side that you got in.

- Wear a blue bead to protect yourself from witches.

- It is bad luck to place a hat on a bed.

- A necklace of amber beads protects against illness and colds.

- A bird entering the house is a sign of death.

- It is bad luck to take a broom with you when you move. Always throw out the old and buy a new one.

- If you see three butterflies together, it will bring you luck.

- Make a wish if you meet a chimney sweep by chance and it will come true.

- When cows lift their tails, it is a sign that rain is on the way.

- If you bid farewell to a friend while standing on a bridge, you will never see each other again.

- It is bad luck to turn a loaf of bread upside down once a slice has been removed.

- Leaving a house by a different door to the one you used on entry brings bad luck.

- If you dream of fish, then someone you know is pregnant.

- You can avoid headaches for the year to come by having your hair cut on Good Friday.

- Letting milk boil over brings bad luck.

- An itch in your right palm means you will soon be receiving money. However, an itch in the left palm means you will be soon paying money out.

- Saying the word 'pig' while fishing at sea brings bad luck.

- A major row with your best friend will follow if you spill pepper.

- If you catch a falling leaf in autumn, you won't get a cold all winter.

- Planting rosemary by the front door keeps witches away.

- If you drop a pair of scissors, then your lover is being unfaithful.

- Seeing an owl in sunlight is bad luck.

- Crossed knives on a table mean a quarrel.

- A wish made when you see a shooting star will come true.

- If you knit some of your own hairs into a garment, then the recipient will be bound to you.

- Mirrors should be covered during a thunderstorm, as they attract lightning.

- When three people are photographed together, the one in the middle will die first.

- When you sneeze, place a hand in front of your mouth to prevent your soul escaping.

- It is bad luck to open an umbrella indoors, especially if you put it over your head.

- If a dead person's eyes are left open, he will find someone to take with him.

- It is bad luck to count the cars in a funeral cortège.

- If you bite your tongue while eating, it shows you have recently told a lie.

- It is bad luck to wear opals unless you were born in October.

- All windows should be opened the moment someone dies so their soul can leave.

- If you dream of death it's a sign of birth, and if you dream of birth it's a sign of death.

- It is very bad luck to wear something new to a funeral, especially new shoes.

- To bring luck, the first gift a bride opens should be the first gift she uses.

- The person who gives the third wedding gift to be opened by a bride will soon have a baby.

- If the groom drops the wedding ring during the wedding ceremony, the marriage is doomed.

- Seeing a black cat or a chimney sweep on the way to a wedding is very lucky.

- If a girl sleeps with a piece of a friend's wedding cake under her pillow she will dream of her future husband.

- It is bad luck to let a flag touch the ground.

- An acorn carried in your pocket brings good luck and long life.

- Spitting on a new cricket bat before using it makes it lucky.

- If a swarm of bees nests in the roof, it means the house will burn down.

- If you sweep out the room occupied by an unwelcome guest, then it will prevent them returning.

- A black cat walking towards you brings good luck. Walking away from you, it takes the luck with it.

- It is bad luck to step on a crack in the pavement.

- Pulling out a grey or white hair will cause ten to grow in its place.

- Ivy on the walls of a house protects the occupants from witches and evil spirits.

- Dropping an umbrella on the floor means there will be a murder in the house.

- It is bad luck to spill salt, unless you throw a pinch of it over your left shoulder – into the face of the Devil, who is said to be waiting there.

- It is bad luck to kill a ladybird.

- You must hold your breath when walking past a cemetery or you will breathe in the spirit of someone who recently died.

- Thunder immediately following a funeral means the dead person's soul has reached heaven.

- An acorn on the windowsill will prevent lightning striking.

- It is unlucky to see your face in a mirror by candlelight.

- To know the number of children you will have, cut an apple in half and count the number of pips.

- When a bell rings, a new angel has received his wings.

- If the first butterfly you see in a year is white, then you will have good luck all year.

- If your right ear itches, someone is speaking well of you. If your left ear itches, they are speaking badly of you.

- A knife placed under the bed during childbirth will ease the pain of labour.

- A raw onion cut in half and placed under a sick person's bed will draw off fever and poisons.

- Use the same pencil for a test as you use to study for it, and it will remember the answers.

- Putting salt on the doorstep of a new house stops evil from entering.

- A woman buried in black will return to haunt the family.

- Mirrors in a house with a corpse should be covered or the person who sees himself will die next.

- Seeing an ambulance is very unlucky, unless you hold your breath or pinch your nose until you see a black or brown dog.

- Starting a trip on a Friday means you will meet misfortune.

13

SCIENCE AND NATURE

- A Boeing 747 jumbo jet weighs fifty-five times the weight of an average African elephant.

- The catfish has more taste buds than any other creature, totalling over 27,000.

- A cubic mile (4km³) of ordinary fog contains less than a gallon (4.5 litres) of water.

- A US-backed government study found that pigs can become alcoholics.

- Sound waves move 1,100ft (335m) per second in the air.

- A lightning bolt generates temperatures five times hotter than those found at the Sun's surface.

- The name of the statuette atop the hood of every Rolls-Royce car is 'The Spirit of Ecstasy'.

- A manned rocket reaches the Moon in less time than it once took a stagecoach to travel the length of Britain.

- A one-day weather forecast requires about 10 billion mathematical calculations.

- The 'sound of the seashore' inside large seashells is caused by the shell echoing surrounding sounds, jumbling and amplifying them.

- A balloon released into the jet stream would take two weeks to travel around the globe.

- All the land mass of the Earth, plus some, could fit into the Pacific Ocean.

- A car with manual gears gets 2 miles (3km) more per gallon (4.5 litres) of petrol than a car with automatic gears.

- During the typical growing season, a sizeable oak tree gives off 28,000 gallons (127,288 litres) of moisture.

- A typical lightning bolt is only 2–4in (5–10cm) wide, but 2 miles (3km) long.

- An average toilet uses 5–7 gallons (23–32 litres) of water every time it is flushed. A single leaky toilet can waste more than 50 gallons (227 litres) a day, amounting to 18,000 gallons (81,830 litres) a year.

- A mile on the ocean and a mile on land are not the same distance. On the ocean, a nautical mile measures 6,080ft (1,853m), while a land or statute mile is 5,280ft (1,609m).

- Crystals grow by reproducing themselves, making them the nearest to being 'alive' of all members of the mineral kingdom.

- Assuming a rate of one drop per second, a leaking tap wastes about 900 gallons (4,091 litres) of water a year.

- Glass can be made so strong that a pressure of 350 tons (356 tonnes) is required to crush a 2in (5cm) cube, and it can be made so fragile that the breath will break a drinking glass.

- It takes a ton (1,016.05kg) of ore to produce one gold wedding ring.

- Bamboo can grow by the height of a two-year-old child a day. That's a daily distance of 36in (91cm)!

- Lightning is more likely than not to strike twice in the same place. Like all electric currents or discharges, lightning follows the path of least resistance.

- It takes as much heat to turn 1oz (30ml) of snow to water as it does to make 1oz of soup boil at room temperature.

- It takes glass 1 million years to decompose, which means it never wears out and can be recycled an infinite amount of times.

- It has been estimated that the deep seas may contain as many as 10 million species that have yet to be discovered.

- Air pressure at sea level is roughly equal to the weight of an elephant spread over a small coffee table.

- It is estimated that 60 per cent of home smoke detectors in use do not work because they don't have a battery in them or the battery in the detector no longer has any potency.

- Avocado trees have collapsed under the weight of their fruit.

- Granite conducts sound ten times faster than air.

- It takes 3,000 seeds from the Giant Sequoia tree to weigh one ounce (around 28g).

- It would take eighty Moons to equal the weight of the Earth.

- It would take a car travelling at 100mph (160km/h) nearly 30 million years to reach our nearest star.

- Fleas can accelerate fifty times faster than the Space Shuttle.

- The science of determining characteristic traits by examining a person's shoes is called 'scarpology'.

- Laptop computers get bumped around too much, which makes them around 30 per cent more likely to fail than a computer that stays in one place.

- For every person on earth, there are 200 million insects.

- The skins of turkeys are tanned and used to make items like cowboy boots, belts and other accessories.

- The hardness of ice is similar to that of concrete.

- If hot water is suddenly poured into a glass, that glass is more apt to break if it is thick than if it is thin. This is why test tubes are made of thin glass.

- A total of 7.5 million toothpicks can be produced from one cord of wood.

- Small animals like bats and shrews consume up to one-and-a-half times their bodyweight in food every day. For an adult male, this would be like eating 1,000 quarter-pound cheeseburgers a day, every day, or about fifty Christmas dinners daily.

- Tobacco grows from seeds so small that it takes 350,000 seeds to make an ounce (around 28g).

- If all the gold suspended in the world's seawater were mined, each person on Earth would receive about 10lb (4.5kg).

- It's possible to lead a cow upstairs but not downstairs.

- The structure of an igloo is so well insulated that it is possible to sit inside without a coat, while the outside temperature is as low as -40°C (-40°F).

- It takes the Saguaro cactus thirty years to grow one branch.

- One ounce (around 28g) of gold can be drawn out to 43 miles (69 km).

- Ninety-nine per cent of all life forms that have existed on Earth are now extinct.

- More than 1,500 new species have been discovered in Australian waters in the past ten years.

- In a moderate-size office with room for twenty-five employees, the air can weigh nearly as much as the staff.

- The world consumes 1 billion gallons (4,546,000,000 litres) of petroleum a day.

- Telecom provider Telewest Broadband is testing a device that hooks up to your PC and wafts a scent when certain emails arrive.

- The Air Force's F-117 fighter uses aerodynamics discovered during research into how bumblebees fly.

- illy Putty was 'discovered' as the residue left behind after the first latex condoms were produced. It's not widely publicised, for obvious reasons.

- The Mars Rover 'Spirit' is powered by six small motors the size of 'C' batteries. It has a top speed of 0.1mph (0.16km/h).

- The largest thing ever built was the Grand Coulee dam. Three times the bulk of the Boulder dam and four times the volume of the Great Pyramid, nearly a mile (1.6km) long and 550ft (167m) high. Its 30-acre (12-hectare) base was 500ft (152m) wide and held back the Columbia River. It consumed 12 million yd³ (9.2 million m³) of concrete.

- Bulletproof vests, fire escapes, windshield wipers and laser printers were all invented by women.

- The Oblivion ride at Alton Towers has a G-force of 5. That's higher than the G-force of an average NASA take-off!

- It took approximately 2.5 million blocks to build the Pyramid of Giza, which is one of the Great Pyramids.

- Each year, 16 million gallons (72.7 million litres) of oil run off pavements into streams, rivers and eventually oceans in the United States. This is more oil than was spilled by the *Exxon Valdez*.

- The Earth is turning to desert at a rate of 40 miles² (104km²) per day.

- Orthodox rabbis have warned that New York City drinking water might not be kosher; it contains harmless micro-organisms that are technically shellfish.

- There are more stars than all of the grains of sand on Earth.

- The Netherlands has built 800 miles (1,287km) of massive dykes and sea walls to hold back the sea.

- Twenty per cent of the Earth's surface is permanently frozen.

- The rain in New York carries so much acid from pollution that it has killed all the fish in 200 lakes in the Adirondack State Park.

- All humans are 99.9 per cent genetically identical and 98.4 per cent of human genes are the same as the genes of a chimpanzee.

- Natural gas has no odour. The smell is added artificially so that leaks can be detected.

- The magnetic North Pole shifts by about 23ft (7m) a day.

- In 1783, an Icelandic eruption threw up enough dust to temporarily block out the Sun over Europe.

- A huge underground river runs underneath the Nile, with six times more water than the river above.

- Mexico City sinks about 10in (25cm) a year.

- An estimated 2–4 million tons (2.03–4.06 million tonnes) of oil leak into the Soviet water table every year from the Siberian pipeline.

- The dioxin 2,3,7,8-tetrachlorodibenzo-p-dioxin is 150,000 times deadlier than cyanide.

- Some large clouds store enough water for 500,000 showers.

- There is an average of two earthquakes every minute in the world.

- After billions of years, black holes become white holes and they spit out all the things they sucked up.

- Siberia contains more than 25 per cent of the world's forests.

- The world's windiest place is Commonwealth Bay, Antarctica.

- Half of all forest fires are started by lightning.

- It is said the average person speaks only ten minutes a day.

- The only rock that floats in water is pumice.

- The most abundant metal in the Earth's crust is aluminium.

- Plants that are not cared for will cry for help; a thirsty plant will make a high-pitched sound that is too high for us to hear.

- Seawater, loaded with mineral salts, weighs about 1.5lb (0.7kg) more per cubic foot than fresh water at the same temperature.

- If you were to count off 1 billion seconds, it would take you 31.7 years.

- If you disassembled the Great Pyramid of Cheops, you would get enough stones to encircle the earth with a brick wall 20in (51cm) high.

- Electricity doesn't move through a wire but through a field around the wire.

- Six of the seven continents can grow pumpkins – even Alaska can. Antarctica is the only continent where they won't grow.

- It can take up to fifteen years for a Christmas tree to grow, but on average, it takes about seven years.

- Myrrh is a plant oil used when burying the dead and is a symbol of mortality.

- The size of a raindrop is around 0.5mm–2.5mm; raindrops fall from the sky on average at a speed of 21ft (6.4m) per second.

- Sound carries so well in the Arctic that, on a calm day, a conversation can be heard from 1.8 miles (2.9km) away.

- Sleet is a form of snow that begins to fall but melts on its way down.

- The large number of reflecting surfaces of the crystal makes snow appear white.

- Partly melted ice crystals usually cling together to form snowflakes, which may in rare cases grow in size up to 3–4in (7.6–10.2cm) in diameter.

- If a person were to ask what is the most northern point in the United States, the most southern point in the United States, and so on, three of the four compass directions are located in Alaska: north, east and west.

- A small child could crawl through a blue whale's major arteries.

- After the Krakatoa volcano eruption in 1883 in Indonesia, many people reported that, because of the dust, the sunset appeared green and the moon blue.

- If you are standing on a mountain top and the conditions are just right, you can see a lit match from 50 miles (80.5km) away.

- A 'gnomon' is the thing that casts the shadow on a sundial.

- The biggest crystals in the world are found in a silver mine in Mexico, The Cave of Crystals. They are made of gypsum and some of them are 39ft (12m) long.

- The Cullinan Diamond is the largest gem-quality diamond ever discovered. Found in 1905, the original 3,100 carats were cut to make jewels for the British Crown Jewels and the British Royal family's collection.

- The fastest shooting stars travel at 150,000mph (241,402km/h).

- When you look at the full moon, what you see is only one-fifth the size of the continent of Africa.

- A coalmine fire in Haas Canyon, Colorado, was ignited by spontaneous combustion in 1916 and withstood all efforts to put it out. The 900–1700-degree fire was eventually quenched by a heat-resistant foam mixed with grout in 2000.

- In November 2004, an iceberg the size of Long Island, New York, broke off Antarctica and blocked sea lanes used by both ships and penguins.

- The winter of 1932 was so cold that Niagara Falls froze completely solid.

- In 2003, there were eighty-six days of below-freezing weather in Hell, Michigan.

- Plants can suffer from jet lag.

- The Eiffel Tower shrinks 6in (15.2cm) in winter.

- A snowflake can take up to an hour to fall from the cloud to the surface of the Earth.

- Only 5 per cent of the ocean floor has been mapped in as much detail as the surface of Mars.

- Urea is found in human urine and Dalmatian dogs and nowhere else.

- Humans have dammed up over 10 trillion gallons of water over the last four decades.

- In spring, the melting dome of an igloo is replaced with a covering of animal skins to form a between-season dwelling called a 'qarmaq'.

- One per cent of the land area in the USA has been hit by tornadoes in the last 100 years.

- It is estimated that 10,000,000,000,000,000,000,000,000,000,000,000 snowflakes have fallen to the Earth since it was formed.

- In Gabon, there are several 1.8 billion-year-old natural nuclear reactors.

- Lightning strikes about 6,000 times per minute on this planet.

- In Montana, in 1887, the largest snowflakes on record fell. Each snowflake was 15in (38.1cm) in diameter.

14

THE WIT AND WISDOM
OF OSCAR WILDE

- 'It is a very sad thing that nowadays there is so little useless information.'

- 'A cynic is a man who knows the price of everything but the value of nothing.'

- 'A gentleman is one who never hurts anyone's feelings unintentionally.'

- 'A little sincerity is a dangerous thing, and a great deal of it is absolutely fatal.'

- 'A man can't be too careful in the choice of his enemies.'

- 'A man's face is his autobiography. A woman's face is her work of fiction.'

- 'A poet can survive everything but a misprint.'

- 'A thing is not necessarily true because a man dies for it.'

- 'A true friend stabs you in the front.'

- 'A work of art is the unique result of a unique temperament.'

- 'Women are made to be loved, not understood.'

- 'Alas, I am dying beyond my means.'

- 'All bad poetry springs from genuine feeling.'

- 'All that I desire to point out is the general principle that life imitates art far more than art imitates life.'

- 'All women become like their mothers. That is their tragedy. No man does. That's his.'

- 'Work is the curse of the drinking classes.'

- 'Always forgive your enemies – nothing annoys them so much.'

- 'Ambition is the germ from which all growth of nobleness proceeds.'

- 'Ambition is the last refuge of the failure.'

- 'America is the only country that went from barbarism to decadence without civilisation in between.'

- 'An idea that is not dangerous is unworthy of being called an idea at all.'

- 'Arguments are extremely vulgar, for everyone in good society holds exactly the same opinion.'

- 'Arguments are to be avoided: they are always vulgar and often convincing.'

- 'When the gods wish to punish us they answer our prayers.'

- 'As long as a woman can look ten years younger than her own daughter, she is perfectly satisfied.'

- 'As long as war is regarded as wicked, it will always have its fascination. When it is looked upon as vulgar, it will cease to be popular.'

- 'As yet, Bernard Shaw hasn't become prominent enough to have any enemies, but none of his friends like him.'

- 'At forty-six, one must be a miser; only have time for essentials.'

- 'Bigamy is having one wife too many. Monogamy is the same.'

- 'Yet each man kills the thing he loves, by each let this be heard, some do it with a bitter look, some with a flattering word. The coward does it with a kiss, the brave man with a sword!'

- 'Children begin by loving their parents; after a time they judge them; rarely, if ever, do they forgive them.'

- 'Biography lends to death a new terror.'

- 'Between men and women there is no friendship possible. There is passion, enmity, worship, love, but no friendship.'

- 'Between the optimist and the pessimist, the difference is droll. The optimist sees the doughnut; the pessimist the hole!'

- 'Charity creates a multitude of sins.'

- 'Why was I born with such contemporaries?'

- 'Woman begins by resisting a man's advances and ends by blocking his retreat.'

- 'Conscience and cowardice are really the same things. Conscience is the trade-name of the firm. That is all.'

- 'Conversation about the weather is the last refuge of the unimaginative.'

- 'Deceiving others. That is what the world calls a romance.'

- 'Whenever people agree with me I always feel I must be wrong.'

- 'Democracy means simply the bludgeoning of the people by the people for the people.'

- 'Do you really think it is weakness that yields to temptation? I tell you that there are terrible temptations which it requires strength, strength and courage to yield to.'

- 'Each class preaches the importance of those virtues it need not exercise. The rich harp on the value of thrift, the idle grow eloquent over the dignity of labour.'

- 'Education is an admirable thing, but it is well to remember from time to time that nothing that is worth knowing can be taught.'

- 'Every portrait that is painted with feeling is a portrait of the artist, not of the sitter.'

- 'Every saint has a past and every sinner has a future.'

- 'When good Americans die they go to Paris.'

- 'When I was young I thought that money was the most important thing in life; now that I am old I know that it is.'

- 'Experience is simply the name we give our mistakes.'

- 'Hatred is blind, as well as love.'

- 'He hadn't a single redeeming vice.'

- 'He has no enemies, but is intensely disliked by his friends.'

- 'He lives the poetry that he cannot write. The others write the poetry that they dare not realise.'

- 'He must have a truly romantic nature, for he weeps when there is nothing at all to weep about.'

- 'He was always late on principle, his principle being that punctuality is the thief of time.'

- 'Fashion is a form of ugliness so intolerable that we have to alter it every six months.'

- 'Fathers should be neither seen nor heard. That is the only proper basis for family life.'

- 'How can a woman be expected to be happy with a man who insists on treating her as if she were a perfectly normal human being?'

- 'How marriage ruins a man! It is as demoralising as cigarettes, and far more expensive.'

- 'How strange a thing this is! The Priest telleth me that the Soul is worth all the gold in the world, and the merchants say that it is not worth a clipped piece of silver.'

- 'I always pass on good advice. It is the only thing to do with it. It is never of any use to oneself.'

- 'I never travel without my diary. One should always have something sensational to read in the train.'

- 'I am not young enough to know everything.'

- 'I can resist everything except temptation.'

- 'I choose my friends for their good looks, my acquaintances for their good characters, and my enemies for their intellects.'

- 'I have nothing to declare except my genius.'

- 'I have the simplest tastes. I am always satisfied with the best.'

- 'I hope you have not been leading a double life, pretending to be wicked and being really good all the time. That would be hypocrisy.'

- 'I put all my genius into my life; I put only my talent into my works.'

- 'When a woman marries again it is because she detested her first husband. When a man marries again, it is because he adored his first wife. Women try their luck; men risk theirs.'

- 'I see when men love women. They give them but a little of their lives. But women when they love give everything.'

- 'I sometimes think that God in creating man somewhat overestimated his ability.'

- 'If one cannot enjoy reading a book over and over again, there is no use in reading it at all.'

- 'I suppose society is wonderfully delightful. To be in it is merely a bore. But to be out of it is simply a tragedy.'

- 'I want my food dead. Not sick, not dying, dead.'

- 'If one could only teach the English how to talk, and the Irish how to listen, society here would be quite civilised.'

- 'If one plays good music, people don't listen and if one plays bad music, people don't talk.'

- 'If there was less sympathy in the world, there would be less trouble in the world.'

- 'If you are not too long, I will wait here for you all my life.'

- 'What we have to do, what at any rate it is our duty to do, is to revive the old art of Lying.'

- 'If you pretend to be good, the world takes you very seriously. If you pretend to be bad, it doesn't. Such is the astounding stupidity of optimism.'

- 'In America the young are always ready to give to those who are older than themselves the full benefits of their inexperience.'

- 'In America the President reigns for four years, and Journalism governs forever and ever.'

- 'In all matters of opinion, our adversaries are insane.'

- 'In England people actually try to be brilliant at breakfast. That is so dreadful of them! Only dull people are brilliant at breakfast.'

- 'In every first novel the hero is the author as Christ or Faust.'

- 'It is absurd to divide people into good and bad. People are either charming or tedious.'

- 'It is an odd thing, but everyone who disappears is said to be seen at San Francisco. It must be a delightful city, and possess all the attractions of the next world.'

- 'It is better to be beautiful than to be good. But... it is better to be good than to be ugly.'

- 'Its failings notwithstanding, there is much to be said in favour of journalism in that, by giving us the opinion of the uneducated, it keeps us in touch with the ignorance of the community.'

- 'It is better to have a permanent income than to be fascinating.'

- 'In married life three is company and two none.'

- 'Illusion is the first of all pleasures.'

- 'It is only an auctioneer who can equally and impartially admire all schools of art.'

- 'It is through art, and through art only, that we can realise our perfection.'

- 'It is perfectly monstrous the way people go about, nowadays, saying things against one behind one's back that are absolutely and entirely true.'

- 'Women are never disarmed by compliments. Men always are. That is the difference between the sexes.'

- 'Laughter is not at all a bad beginning for a friendship, and it is far the best ending for one.'

- 'Life is far too important a thing ever to talk seriously about.'

- 'Life is never fair, and perhaps it is a good thing for most of us that it is not.'

- 'When a man has once loved a woman he will do anything for her except continue to love her.'

- 'Man is least himself when he talks in his own person. Give him a mask, and he will tell you the truth.'

- 'Memory... is the diary that we all carry about with us.'

- 'Men always want to be a woman's first love – women like to be a man's last romance.'

- 'Mere colour, unspoiled by meaning, and unallied with definite form, can speak to the soul in a thousand different ways.'

- 'Moderation is a fatal thing. Nothing succeeds like excess.'

- 'Morality is simply the attitude we adopt towards people whom we personally dislike.'

- 'Most modern calendars mar the sweet simplicity of our lives by reminding us that each day that passes is the anniversary of some perfectly uninteresting event.'

- 'Most people are other people. Their thoughts are someone else's opinions, their lives a mimicry, their passions a quotation.'

- 'Most people die of a sort of creeping common sense, and discover when it is too late that the only things one never regrets are one's mistakes.'

- 'Nothing is so aggravating as calmness.'

- 'No woman should ever be quite accurate about her age. It looks so calculating.'

- 'No man is rich enough to buy back his past.'

- 'Music makes one feel so romantic – at least it always gets on one's nerves, which is the same thing nowadays.'

- 'My great mistake, the fault for which I can't forgive myself, is that one day I ceased my obstinate pursuit of my own individuality.'

- 'No great artist ever sees things as they really are. If he did, he would cease to be an artist.'

- 'No object is so beautiful that, under certain conditions, it will not look ugly.'

- 'Now that the House of Commons is trying to become useful, it does a great deal of harm.'

- 'Nowadays to be intelligible is to be found out.'

- 'Of course America had often been discovered before Columbus, but it had always been hushed up.'

- 'Of course I have played outdoor games. I once played dominoes in an open-air café in Paris.'

- 'One of the many lessons that one learns in prison is that things are what they are and will be what they will be.'

- 'One can survive everything, nowadays, except death, and live down everything except a good reputation.'

- 'One should always be in love. That is the reason one should never marry.'

- 'One should always play fairly when one has the winning cards.'

- 'One's past is what one is. It is the only way by which people should be judged.'

- 'We are all in the gutter, but some of us are looking at the stars.'

- 'Only the shallow know themselves.'

- 'Ordinary riches can be stolen; real riches cannot. In your soul are infinitely precious things that cannot be taken from you.'

- 'Patriotism is the virtue of the vicious.'

- 'Self-denial is the shining sore on the leprous body of Christianity.'

- 'Our ambition should be to rule ourselves, the true kingdom for each one of us; and true progress is to know more, and be more, and to do more.'

- 'Perhaps, after all, America never has been discovered. I myself would say that it had merely been detected.'

- 'Pessimist: one who, when he has the choice of two evils, chooses both.'

- 'Questions are never indiscreet, answers sometimes are.'

- 'Relations are simply a tedious pack of people, who haven't got the remotest knowledge of how to live, nor the smallest instinct about when to die.'

- 'Selfishness is not living as one wishes to live, it is asking others to live as one wishes to live.'

- 'Seriousness is the only refuge of the shallow.'

- 'She wore far too much rouge last night and not quite enough clothes. That is always a sign of despair in a woman.'

- 'The basis of optimism is sheer terror.'

- 'Some cause happiness wherever they go; others whenever they go.'

- 'Some of these people need ten years of therapy – ten sentences of mine do not equal ten years of therapy.'

- 'Success is a science; if you have the conditions, you get the result.'

- 'The books that the world calls immoral are books that show the world its own shame.'

- 'The difference between literature and journalism is that journalism is unreadable and literature is not read.'

- 'The English country gentleman galloping after a fox: the unspeakable in full pursuit of the uneatable.'

- 'The imagination imitates. It is the critical spirit that creates.'

- 'The man who can dominate a London dinner table can dominate the world.'

- 'The liar at any rate recognises that recreation, not instruction, is the aim of conversation, and is a far more civilised being than the blockhead who loudly expresses his disbelief in a story which is told simply for the amusement of the company.'

- 'The moment you think you understand a great work of art, it's dead for you.'

- 'The old believe everything, the middle-aged suspect everything, the young know everything.'

- 'The one charm about marriage is that it makes a life of deception absolutely necessary for both parties.'

- 'The past is of no importance. The present is of no importance. It is with the future that we have to deal. For the past is what man should not have been. The present is what man ought not to be. The future is what artists are.'

- 'The public have an insatiable curiosity to know everything. Except what is worth knowing. Journalism, conscious of this, and having tradesman-like habits, supplies their demands.'

- 'The public is wonderfully tolerant. It forgives everything except genius.'

- 'The pure and simple truth is rarely pure and never simple.'

- 'The salesman knows nothing of what he is selling save that he is charging a great deal too much for it.'

- 'The typewriting machine, when played with expression, is no more annoying than the piano when played by a sister or near relation.'

- 'The true mystery of the world is the visible, not the invisible.'

- 'The security of society lies in custom and unconscious instinct, and the basis of the stability of society, as a healthy organism, is the complete absence of any intelligence amongst its members.'

- 'The world has grown suspicious of anything that looks like a happily married life.'

- 'The world is divided into two classes: those who believe the incredible and those who do the improbable.'

- 'There are only two kinds of people who are really fascinating – people who know absolutely everything, and people who know absolutely nothing.'

- 'There are only two tragedies in life: one is not getting what one wants, and the other is getting it.'

- 'There are two ways of disliking poetry; one way is to dislike it, the other is to read Pope.'

- 'This suspense is terrible. I hope it will last.'

- 'There is no such thing as a moral or an immoral book. Books are well written, or badly written.'

- 'To expect the unexpected shows a thoroughly modern intellect.'

- 'There is no such thing as an omen. Destiny does not send us heralds. She is too wise or too cruel for that.'

- 'To lose one parent may be regarded as a misfortune; to lose both looks like carelessness.'

- 'They afterwards took me to a dancing saloon where I saw the only rational method of art criticism I have ever come across. Over the piano was printed a notice "Please do not shoot the pianist. He is doing his best." '

- 'Those whom the gods love grow young.'

- 'There is no sin except stupidity.'

15

RELIGION

- The tradition of Peter being the first Bishop of Rome only surfaced in the 4th century.

- Scholars estimate that the sixty-six books of the King James version of the Bible were written by some fifty different authors.

- Almonds and pistachios are the only nuts mentioned in the Bible.

- Seven suicides are recorded in the Bible.

- Some biblical scholars believe that Aramaic (the language of the ancient Bible) did not contain an easy way to say 'many things' and used a term that has come down to us as 'forty'. This means that when the Bible – in many places – refers to 'forty days', the words 'many days' were actually intended.

- The Bible devotes some 500 verses to prayer, fewer than 500 verses to faith, but over 2,000 verses to money and possessions.

- In the 9th century, Pope Nicholas I decreed that a cockerel would be displayed from every church steeple as a weather vane. The cockerel was used to remind all parishioners of Peter's three denials of Christ before the cock crowed, to keep them from this sin.

- St Augustine was the first major proponent of the 'missionary' position.

- The books of the Bible were chosen, after a bit of haggling, by the Catholic Council of Carthage in AD 397 – more than 350 years after the time of Jesus. This collection is broken into two major sections: the Old Testament, which consists of thirty-nine books, and the New Testament, which consists of twenty-seven books. (Catholic bibles include an additional twelve books known as the Apocrypha.)

- The gospels for the New Testament were chosen from a huge selection. Many were discarded or destroyed because they did not agree with the then accepted version of Christianity. The church that came out on top simply preserved texts in its favour and destroyed or let vanish opposing documents. In some of these other gospels, we find women in very different positions – as disciples, as apostles, as teachers – from the way they are depicted in the gospels of the New Testament.

- The Red Sea is not mentioned in the Bible.

- Constantine changed the date of Jesus's birthday from spring to 25 December, feast of Dies Natalis Invicti, which was the birthday of the Roman pagan god Mithra and the biggest day of the year for the sun-worshipping pagans.

- Cardinal John Henry Newman (1801–90), one of the authorities most respected by Rome, wrote in his book *The Development of the Christian Religion*: 'Temples, incense, candles, votive offerings, holy water, holidays, and seasons of devotions, processions, blessing of fields, sacerdotal vestments, priests, monks and nuns are all of pagan origin.'

- Pope Alexander VI, a Spaniard, fathered children both before and after he bribed his way into the papacy in 1492, the same year Christopher Columbus 'discovered' America.

- Pope Alexander VI was born Rodrigo de Borja y Borja in 1431 and was made a cardinal at the age of 25 by his uncle, Pope Callistus III, who reigned from 1455 to 1458. Once pope, Alexander VI named his own 18-year-old son a cardinal, along with the brother of a papal mistress.

- There are forty-nine different foods mentioned in the Bible.

- The first Patriarch of Rome to bear the title of pope was Pope Boniface III in AD 607, the first Bishop of Rome to assume the title of 'universal Bishop' by decree of Emperor Phocas.

- At least four popes have had illegitimate children.

- Pope John XII (955–64) is remembered as possibly the most morally corrupt pontiff. He was accused by some of turning Rome's Lateran Palace into a brothel.

- Long ago, when many people were unable to read the Bible, pictures were put in stained-glass windows to remind them of the stories.

- Gabriel, Michael and Lucifer are the three angels mentioned by name in the Bible.

- At least five popes were sons of priests, including at least one pope (maybe two) who was the son of another pope! Some of these priests may have been married but left their families to become priests.

- The Immaculate Conception of Mary protected her from the first instant of her existence, or conception in her mother's womb, so as to be free from the corrupt nature that original sin brings. This is a different concept from that of her being a virgin when she conceived Jesus.

- Bethlehem, which was selected by the early Christians as the scene of the birth of Jesus, was an early shrine of the pagan god Adonis. It was believed that this god suffered a cruel death, after which he descended into hell, rose again and then ascended into heaven. Each year, there was a great festival in commemoration of his resurrection.

- Many customs of the Catholic Church did not begin until sometimes centuries after the death of Christ. These are just some of them:

- The daily mass was first practised in AD 394.

- There is no record of any exaltation of the Virgin Mary until the 5th century, when she was first called the 'Mother of God'.

- Prayers to the Virgin, Queen of Heaven commenced in AD 600.

- The first pope (Boniface III) was appointed in AD 610.

- The practice of kissing the pope's foot began in AD 709.

- The temporal power of the pope was declared in AD 750.

- The worship of images, relics and the cross started in AD 788.

- Holy water, blessed by a priest, was introduced in AD 850.

- The canonisation of dead saints began with Pope John XV in AD 995.

- Lent and Good Friday began in AD 998.

- The mass first declared to be a sacrifice of Christ took place in 1050.

- Celibacy for the priesthood and nuns was inaugurated in 1079.

- The rosary was introduced by Peter the Hermit in 1090.

- Selling indulgences began in 1190.

- The confession of sins to a priest started in 1215.

- The adoration of the water was first practised by Pope Honorius in 1220.

- The concept that interpretation of the Bible was forbidden to laity arose in 1229.

- The superstitions of the Ave Maria arose with Pope Sextus V in 1508.

- The belief that tradition was established as infallible authority started in 1545.

- Apocryphal books were added to the Bible in 1546.

- The concept of the Immaculate Conception of the Virgin Mary arose in 1854.

- The infallibility of the pope was officially declared in 1870. It was decided by a majority vote of cardinals and means that the pope cannot be in error; his pronouncements on matters of doctrine and morals are infallible and are binding upon all Roman Catholics, who are commanded to accept the decrees of the pope without questioning them.

- Mary was declared to be the Mother of God in 1931.

- There was a time when the pope excommunicated members of the Church for praying to the Virgin Mary. The worship of Mary, today acclaimed as an infallible dogma, was once condemned by the same 'infallible' Church as a deadly sin.

- 'Sensible men are all of the same religion.'
  'Pray, what is that?'
  'Sensible men never tell.'

  Benjamin Disraeli

- 'To become a popular religion, it is only necessary for a superstition to enslave a philosophy.'

  William Ralph Inge

- 'Prisons are built with stones of law, brothels with blocks of religion.'

  William Blake

- 'I can't talk religion to a man with bodily hunger in his eyes.'

  George Bernard Shaw

- 'It is a mistake to suppose that God is only, or even chiefly, concerned with religion.'

  William Temple

- 'Every dictator uses religion as a prop to keep himself in power.'

  Benazir Bhutto

- 'In matters of religion and matrimony, I never give any advice, because I will not have anybody's torments in this world or the next laid to my charge.'

  Lord Chesterfield

- 'Superstition is the religion of feeble minds.'

  Edmund Burke

- 'Conservatives do not believe that political struggle is the most important thing in life... The simplest of them prefer fox-hunting; the wisest... religion.'

  Lord Hailsham

- 'We have just enough religion to make us hate, but not enough to make us love one another.'

  Jonathan Swift

- 'What a pity it is that we have no amusements in England but vice and religion.'

  Sydney Smith

- 'Science without religion is lame, religion without science is blind.'

  Albert Einstein

- 'The Revised Prayer Book: a sort of attempt to suppress burglary by legalising petty larceny.'

  Dean Inge

- 'The spirituality of man is most apparent when he is eating a hearty dinner.'

  W. Somerset Maugham

- 'Puritanism. The haunting fear that someone, somewhere, may be happy.'

  H.L. Mencken

- 'There is only one religion, though there are a hundred versions of it.'

  George Bernard Shaw

- 'People may say what they like about the decay of Christianity; the religious system that produced green Chartreuse can never really die.'

  Saki

- 'God is a man, so it must be all rot.'

  Nancy Nicholson

- 'Baptists are only funny under water.'

  Neil Simon

- 'There's no reason to bring religion into it. I think we ought to have as great a regard for religion as we can, so as to keep it out of as many things as possible.'

  Sean O'Casey

- 'How can what an Englishman believes be heresy? It is a contradiction in terms.'

  George Bernard Shaw

- 'Every reformation must have its victims. You can't expect the fatted calf to share the enthusiasm of the angels over the prodigal's return.'

  Saki

- 'Protestant women must keep taking the pill; Roman Catholic women must keep taking *The Tablet* [largest-circulation Catholic newspaper].'

  Eileen Thomas

- A survey disclosed that 12 per cent of Americans believe that Joan of Arc was Noah's wife.

- Portions of the Bible have been printed in 2,212 languages. A complete Bible exists in 366 languages; an additional 928 languages have a New Testament; and 918 have at least one book of the Bible.

- More than 95 per cent of the population of Greece belong to the Greek Orthodox Church.

- Studies show that Protestants and Jews married to Catholics have sex more frequently than those married to members of their own faith, or those in intermarriages of Protestants and Jews.

- The Roman Catholic population of the world is larger than that of all other Christian sects combined.

- There are many patron saints for human physical afflictions, including St Teresa of Avila and St Denis, Bishop of Paris, who are the patron saints of headaches; St James the Greater, patron saint of rheumatoid sufferers; St Apollonia, patron saint of toothaches and dentists; and St Genevieve (Genofeva), patron saint of fevers.

- The Ancient Egyptians worshipped a sky goddess called Nut.

16

ALCOHOL

- Alcohol is derived from the Arabic *al kohl*, meaning 'the essence'.

- The Sumerians were the first to brew beer, and all the brewers were women.

- There is one bar in Paris that serves only bottled and canned water.

- A pub in London's West End, the Fox and Grapes, serves no spirits.

- A raisin dropped in a glass of fresh champagne will bounce up and down continually from the bottom of the glass to the top.

- To determine the percentage of alcohol in a bottle of liquor, divide the proof by two.

- In old English pubs, ale is ordered by pints and quarts. So, when customers in old England got unruly, the bartender would yell at them to mind their own pints and quarts, and settle down. This is where we get the phrase 'Mind your Ps and Qs'.

- In the state of Queensland, Australia, it is still constitutional law that all pubs must have a railing outside for patrons to tie up their horses.

- Many years ago in England, pub-goers had a whistle baked into the rim or handle of their ceramic cups. When they needed a refill, they used the whistle to get some service, which inspired the phrase 'Wet your whistle'.

- Unlike wines, most beers should be stored upright to minimise oxidation and metal or plastic contamination from the cap. High-alcohol ales, however, which continue to ferment in their corked bottles, should be stored on their sides.

- Studying the experimentally induced intoxicated behaviour of ants in 1888, naturalist John Lubbock noticed that the insects that had too much to drink were picked up by nest mates and carried home. Conversely, drunken stranger ants were summarily tossed in a ditch.

- In Bavaria, beer isn't considered an alcoholic drink but rather a staple food.

- Despite the month implied by its name, Munich's annual sixteen-day Oktoberfest actually begins in mid-September and ends on the first Sunday in October.

- There are nineteen different versions of Guinness.

- The familiar Bass symbol, a red triangle, was registered in 1876 and is the world's oldest trademark.

- According to a journal entry from 1636, farm workers in the colony of Quebec not only received an allowance of flour, lard, oil, vinegar and codfish, but were also given 'a chopine of cider a day or a quart of beer'.

- Beck's is not only Germany's top export beer, it also accounts for 85 per cent of all German beer exports to the United States.

- Pennsylvania has had more breweries in its history than any other state. In 1910 alone, 119 of the state's towns had at least one licensed beer-maker.

- Gilroy, USA, home of the Coast Range Brewing Company since 1995, is also the self-proclaimed 'garlic capital of the world'.

- Beer and video games have a long association. Tapper, originally a 1983 arcade game and now a computer one, tests players' skills by challenging them to co-ordinate the movements of beers, a bartender, empty mugs and patrons.

- Beer-advertising matchbook covers have become sought-after collectibles on Internet auction sites. A 1916 matchbook promoting Brehm's Brewery in Baltimore brought $43, while a 1930s cover promoting Eastside Beer from Los Angeles went for $36.

- An eighteen-year study by the US National Institute on Aging found that 50-plus men who consumed a drink a day during middle age scored significantly better on cognitive tests later in life than non-drinkers did.

- In Ancient Babylon, female brewers also assumed the role of temple priestesses. The goddess Siris was the patron of beer.

- Nine people in St Giles, England, were killed and two houses destroyed on 17 October 1814 when a brewery tank containing 3,500 barrels of beer ruptured and created a giant wave.

- According to a diary entry from a passenger on the *Mayflower*, the pilgrims made their landing at Plymouth Rock, rather than continuing to their destination in Virginia, due to a lack of beer.

- In the USA, a barrel contains 31 gallons (141 litres) of beer.

- In 1788, ale was proclaimed 'the proper drink for Americans' at a parade in New York City.

- George Washington had his own brewery in the grounds of Mount Vernon.

- Bottle caps, or 'crowns', were invented in Baltimore in 1892 by William Painter. He proved his invention's worth when he convinced a local brewer to ship a few hundred cases of beer to South America and back: they returned without a leak.

- After consuming a bucket or two of vibrant brew they called 'aul', or ale, the Vikings would head fearlessly into battle, often without armour or even shirts. In fact, 'berserk' means 'bare shirt' in Norse, and eventually came to be used as a term to describe their wild battles.

- The Budweiser Clydesdale horses weigh up to 2,300lb (1,043kg) and stand nearly 6ft (1.83m) at the shoulder.

- Twelve ounces (0.3kg) of a typical American pale lager actually has fewer calories than 2% milk or apple juice.

- In Utah it is illegal to swallow wine served at wine tastings.

- Adding a miniature onion to a martini turns it into a Gibson.

- In 1926, Montana became the first state to repeal its enforcement of Prohibition (Prohibition lasted from 1920 to 1933).

- The longest bar in the world is 684ft (208.5m) long and is located at the New Bulldog in Rock Island, Illinois.

- Christopher Columbus introduced sherry to the New World.

- The space in the New York City building that once housed the National Temperance Society is now a bar.

- Each molecule of alcohol is less than a billionth of a metre long and consists of a few atoms of oxygen, carbon and hydrogen.

- Outfitting his ship to sail around the world in 1519, Magellan spent more on sherry than on weapons.

- The founder of US campaign MADD (Mothers Against Drunk Driving) resigned after the campaign became increasingly anti-alcohol rather than simply anti-drunk-driving.

- New York State's exclusive Vassar College was established and funded by a brewer.

- Franklin D. Roosevelt was elected president of the USA in 1932 on a pledge to end National Prohibition.

- The consumption of alcohol was so widespread throughout history that it has been called 'a universal language'.

- A 'tequini' is a martini made with tequila instead of dry gin.

- Shochu, a beverage distilled from barley, was the favourite beverage of the world's longest-living man, Shigechiyo Izumi of Japan, who lived for 120 years and 237 days.

- Bourbon is the official spirit of the United States, by act of Congress.

- One glass of milk can give a person a 0.02 blood alcohol concentration on a breathalyser test, enough in some US states for persons under the age of 21 to lose their driver's licence or be fined.

- Fermentation within the body is essential for human life to exist.

- Fermentation is involved in the production of many foods, including bread (bread 'rises' as it ferments), sauerkraut, coffee, black tea, cheese, yogurt, buttermilk, pickles, cottage cheese, chocolate, vanilla, ginger, ketchup, mustard, soy sauce and many more.

- The US Marines' first recruiting station was in a bar.

- The first US First Lady, Martha Washington, enjoyed daily toddies.

- In the 1790s, 'happy hour' began at 3pm and cocktails continued until dinner.

- Hollywood stars Tom Arnold, Sandra Bullock, Chevy Chase, Bill Cosby, Kris Kristofferson and Bruce Willis are all former bartenders.

- Frederick the Great of Prussia tried to ban the consumption of coffee and demanded the populace drink alcohol instead.

- When informed that General Grant drank whiskey while leading his troops, President Lincoln reportedly replied, 'Find out the name of the brand so I can give it to my other generals.'

- Being intoxicated had desirable spiritual significance for the Ancient Egyptians. They often gave their children names such as 'How Drunk is Cheops' or 'How Intoxicated is Hathor'.

- The bill for a celebration party for the fifty-five drafters of the US Constitution was for fifty-four bottles of Madeira, sixty bottles of claret, eight bottles of whiskey, twenty-two bottles of port, eight bottles of hard cider, twelve beers and seven bowls of alcohol punch large enough that 'ducks could swim in them'.

- During the reign of William III, a garden fountain was once used as a giant punch bowl. The recipe included 560 gallons (2,546 litres) of brandy, 1,200lb (544kg) of sugar, 25,000 lemons, 20 gallons (91 litres) of lime juice and 5lb (2.3kg) of nutmeg. The bartender rowed around in a small boat filling up guests' punch cups.

- The Manhattan cocktail (whisky and sweet vermouth) was invented by Winston Churchill's mother.

- *I Love Lucy* star Desi Arnaz, Jr's grandfather was one of the founders of the largest rum distillery in the world.

- Among the Lepcha people of Tibet, alcohol is considered the only proper payment for teachers.

- The national anthem of the USA, 'The Star-Spangled Banner', was written to the tune of a drinking song.

- In the 17th century, thermometers were filled with brandy instead of mercury.

- If a young Tiriki man offers beer to a woman and she spits some of it into his mouth, they are engaged to be married.

- Among the Bagonda people of Uganda, the several widows of a recently deceased king have the distinctive honour of drinking the beer in which his entrails have been cleaned.

- The Chagga people of Tanzania believe that a liar will be poisoned if he or she consumes beer mixed with the blood of a recently sacrificed goat.

- Beer is mixed with saliva and blood for a drink that is shared when two men of the Chagga tribe in Tanzania become blood brothers.

- The shallow champagne glass originated with Marie Antoinette. It was first formed from wax moulds taken from her breasts.

- As late as the mid-17th century, French winemakers did not use corks. Instead, they stuffed the necks of bottles with oil-soaked rags.

- The corkscrew was invented in 1860.

- The bubbles in Guinness sink to the bottom rather than float to the top as in other beers.

- The longest recorded champagne cork flight was 177ft 9in (54.2m), 4ft (1.2m) from level ground at Woodbury Vineyards in New York State.

- In the 19th century, rum was considered excellent for cleaning hair and keeping it healthy.

- Brandy was believed to strengthen hair roots.

- The purpose of the indentation at the bottom of a wine bottle is not for the wine waiter to place his fingers there, but to strengthen the structure of the bottle.

- Bubbles in champagne were seen by early winemakers as a highly undesirable defect to be prevented.

- Liquor stores in the USA are called 'package stores' and sell 'package goods' because of laws requiring that alcohol containers be concealed in public by being placed in paper bags or 'packages'.

- Alcohol consumption decreases during the time of the full moon.

- Methyphobia is fear of alcohol.

- The term 'brand name' originated among American distillers, who branded their names and emblems on their kegs before shipment.

- The region of the USA that consumes the least alcohol (commonly known as the 'Bible Belt') is also known by many doctors as 'Stroke Alley'.

- 'The quick brown fox jumps over the lazy dog' is commonly believed to be the only English sentence devised to include all the letters of the alphabet. Drinkers prefer, 'Pack my box with five dozen liquor jugs'.

- The word 'toast', meaning a wish of good health, started in Ancient Rome, where a piece of toasted bread was dropped into wine.

- Do you like *isyammitilka* or *ksikonewiw*? Those are the words for alcohol beverages among the Alabama and the Maliseet-Passamaquoddy tribes of American Indians.

- The first canned beer was created on 24 January 1935. It was called Krueger Cream Ale and was sold by the Kruger Brewing Company of Richmond, Virginia.

- Drinking lowers rather than raises the body temperature.

- Rhode Island never ratified the 18th Amendment establishing Prohibition.

- In West Virginia, bars can advertise alcohol-beverage prices, but not brand names.

- There is a cloud of alcohol in outer space with enough alcohol to make 4 trillion trillion drinks. It's free for the taking... but it's 10,000 light-years away from the Earth.

- In the 19th century, people believed that gin could cure stomach problems.

- The *Mayflower*, well known for bringing the Pilgrims to the New World, ordinarily transported alcohol beverages between Spain and England.

- Wine has about the same number of calories as an equal amount of grape juice.

- During World War II, a group of alpine soldiers who were stranded in mountain snows survived for an entire month on one cask of sherry.

- Johnny Appleseed probably distributed apple seeds across the American frontier so that people could make fermented apple juice ('hard' cider) rather than eat apples.

- There are eighty-three 'dry' towns and villages in Alaska.

- White wine gets darker as it ages, while red wine becomes lighter.

- 'White lightning' is a name for illegally distilled spirits. All spirits are clear, or 'white', until aged in charred oak barrels.

- The letters VVSOP on a cognac bottle stand for Very Very Superior Old Pale.

- It is estimated that the US Government takes in fourteen times more in taxes on distilled spirits than producers of the products earn making them. That does not include what states and localities additionally take in taxes on the same products.

- 'Whisky' is the international aviation word used to represent the letter 'w'.

- Most vegetable, and virtually all fruit, juices contain alcohol.

- Temperance activists, who strongly opposed the consumption of alcohol, typically consumed patent medicines that, just like whisky, generally contained 40 per cent alcohol!

- US president Thomas Jefferson was the nation's first wine expert.

- US president Jimmy Carter's mother once said, 'I'm a Christian, but that doesn't mean I'm a long-faced square. I like a little bourbon.'

- It's impossible to create a beverage of over 18 per cent alcohol by fermentation alone.

- In Malaysia, drunk drivers are jailed and so are their spouses.

- The word 'liquor' is prohibited on storefronts in some states of the USA.

- Drinking alcohol in moderation reduces the risk of heart disease by an average of about 40 per cent.

- US president Abraham Lincoln once stated, 'It has long been recognised that the problems with alcohol relate not to the use of a bad thing, but to the abuse of a good thing.'

- The wine district of the Napa Valley has replaced Disneyland as California's number-one tourist destination, with 5.5 million visitors per year.

- A labeorphilist is a collector of beer bottles.

- British men are twice as likely to know the price of beer as their partner's bra size. A poll by *Prima* magazine found that 77 per cent of males knew how much their beer cost, but only 38 per cent knew the correct size of their partner's bra.

- A restaurant liquor licence in Philadelphia costs $35,000. It's a bargain compared to obtaining one in Evesham Township (New Jersey) at over $475,000 or one in Mount Laurel (New Jersey) at over $675,000.

- One brand of Chinese beer reportedly includes in its recipe 'ground-up dog parts'.

- In Bangladesh, $5 will buy a beer... or a first-class train ticket for a cross-country trip.

- It takes an average of 600 grapes to make a bottle of wine.

- Gin and tonic can help relieve cramps.

- Paul Domenech, aged 34, was arrested for drink-driving, but was found innocent of the charge when he proved before a jury in Tampa, Florida, that the alcohol officers had smelled on his breath was from the mixture of rubbing alcohol and gasoline that he had just used in his performance as a professional fire-eater.

- The largest cork tree in the world is in Portugal. It averages over a ton (1.02 tonnes) of raw cork per harvest, enough to cork 100,000 bottles.

- The pressure in a bottle of champagne is about 90lb per in^2 (620.5 kilonewtons per m^2). That's about three times the pressure in car tyres.

- The soil of one famous vineyard in France is considered so precious that vineyard workers are required to scrape it from their shoes before they leave for home each night.

- Gin is a mild diuretic, which helps rid the body of excessive fluid. Thus, it can reduce problems such as menstrual bloating.

- Adolf Hitler was one of the world's best-known teetotallers, while his English counterpart, Sir Winston Churchill, was one of the world's best-known heavy drinkers.

- In Pennsylvania, the tax on wine and spirits is called the Jamestown Flood tax because it was imposed in 1936 to raise funds to help the city recover from a devastating flood. The city was quickly rebuilt but the tax continues, costing the state taxpayers over $160 million each year.

- Regardless of sex, age or weight, it takes an hour for 0.015 per cent of blood alcohol content (BAC) to leave the body. It takes ten hours for a person with a BAC of 0.15 to become completely sober. Giving a drunk coffee will merely produce a wide-awake drunk.

- Every person produces alcohol normally in the body for twenty-four hours, each and every day from birth until death. Therefore, we always have alcohol in our bodies.

- The Soviet Bolsheviks (communists) imposed national prohibition following the Russian Revolution.

- The top ten alcohol-consuming countries are:
  Portugal
  Luxembourg
  France
  Hungary
  Spain
  Czech Republic
  Denmark
  Germany
  Austria
  Switzerland

- Of Texas's 254 counties, seventy-nine are still completely 'dry' seven decades after the repeal of Prohibition. Many of the remaining counties are 'moist' or 'partially dry'.

- There is no worm in tequila. It's in *mescal*, a spirit beverage distilled from a different plant. And it's not actually a worm, but a butterfly caterpillar (*Hipopta agavis*) called a gurano.

- Vikings used the skulls of their enemies as drinking vessels.

- The production of *chicha*, an alcohol beverage that has been made for thousands of years in Central and South America, begins with people chewing grain and spitting into a vat. An enzyme in saliva changes the starch in the grain to sugar, which then ferments.

- In 1989, William Sokolin paid $519,750 for a bottle of 1787 vintage wine, which supposedly had been owned by US president Thomas Jefferson. Later, he accidentally knocked it over, breaking it and spilling the precious contents on the floor.

- Of all the countries that had armies stationed in Bosnia, only the USA forbade its soldiers to consume alcohol.

- An award-winning adaptation of Little Red Riding Hood was withdrawn from a recommended reading list by the school board in Culver City, California, simply because the heroine had included a bottle of wine in the basket she brought to her grandmother.

- McDonald's restaurants in some European countries serve alcohol because otherwise parents would be less willing to take their children to them.

- The entire production of kosher wine, including cultivation of the grapes, must be performed by Sabbath-observant Jews and it remains kosher only if opened and poured by an orthodox Jew.

- Thousands of waxwing birds in Sweden became intoxicated by gorging on fermenting berries. About fifty lost their lives by flying into nearby windows.

- Early recipes for beer included such ingredients as poppy seeds, mushrooms, aromatics, honey, sugar, bay leaves, butter and breadcrumbs.

- Men in the USA who drink alcohol receive around 7 per cent higher wages than do abstainers, according to data from the National Household Survey on Drug Abuse (United States Department of Health and Human Services).

- Women who drink receive about 3.5 per cent higher wages than those who abstain.

- The USA has the strictest youth drinking laws in Western civilisation.

- In some countries, the penalty for driving while intoxicated can be death.

- Then again, in Uruguay, intoxication is a legal excuse for having an accident while driving.

- In Utah, it's illegal to advertise drink prices, alcohol brands, to show a 'drinking scene', to promote happy hour, to advertise free food or for restaurants to furnish alcohol beverage lists unless a customer specifically requests one.

- The USA has the highest minimum drinking age in the entire world.

- Among the Abipone people of Paraguay, individuals who abstain from alcohol are thought to be 'cowardly, degenerate and stupid'.

- Kinpaku-iri *sake* contains flakes of real gold. While this adds a touch of extravagance, it doesn't affect the flavour at all.

- The Uape Indians of the Upper Amazon in Brazil mix the ashes of their cremated dead with *casiri*, the local alcohol beverage. The deceased's family, young and old, then drink the beverage with great reverence and fond memories.

- The Aztecs of Mexico used a 'rabbit scale' to describe degrees of intoxication. It ranged from very mild intoxication (a few rabbits) to heavy drunkenness (400 rabbits).

- The highest price ever paid for distilled spirits at auction was $79,552 for a fifty-year-old bottle of Glenfiddich whisky in 1992.

- 'Fat Bastard Chardonnay' is a French wine label.

- The more educated people are, the more likely they are to drink.

- Research evidence from around the world generally shows that countries with higher alcohol consumption have fewer drinking problems than those where consumption is relatively low.

- Beer is believed to have been a staple before bread.

- The world's oldest known recipe is for beer.

- Early Egyptian writings urged mothers to send their children to school with plenty of bread and beer for their lunch.

- Alcoholic beverages have been produced for at least 12,000 years.

- Our early ancestors probably began farming not so much to grow food, which they could usually find easily, as to ensure a steady supply of ingredients needed to make alcoholic beverages.

- In Ancient Egypt, 'bread and beer' was a common greeting.

- Every year, Bavarians and their guests drink 1.2 million gallons (5.5 million litres) of beer during Oktoberfest. The first Oktoberfest was in 1810 and celebrated the marriage of King Ludwig I of Bavaria.

- The Romans drank a wine containing seawater, pitch, rosin and turpentine.

- A Chinese imperial edict of about 1116 BC asserted that the use of alcohol in moderation was required by heaven.

- To the pre-Christian Anglo-Saxons, heaven was not a place to play harps, but somewhere to visit with other departed souls and enjoy alcoholic beverages.

- Drinking liqueurs was compulsory at all treaty signings during the Middle Ages.

- The word 'symposium' originally referred to a gathering of men in Ancient Greece for an evening of conversation and drinking.

- Jesus drank alcohol (Luke 7:33–35) and approved of its moderate consumption (1 Timothy 5:23).

- The early Church declared that alcohol was an inherently good gift of God to be used and enjoyed. While individuals might choose not to drink, to despise alcohol was heresy.

- During the Middle Ages, it was mainly the monasteries that maintained the knowledge and skills necessary to produce quality alcoholic beverages.

- Distillation was developed during the Middle Ages and the resulting alcohol was called 'aqua vitae' or 'water of life'.

- The adulteration of alcoholic beverages was punishable by death in medieval Scotland.

- Rye was the first distinctly American whiskey. It is distilled from a combination of corn, barley malt and at least 51 per cent rye.

- Mai Tai means 'out of this world' in Tahitian.

- 'Whiskey' and 'whisky' both refer to alcohol distilled from grain. 'Whiskey' is the usual American spelling, especially for beverages distilled in the USA and Ireland. 'Whisky' is the spelling for Canadian and Scottish distilled beverages.

- Bourbon takes its name from Bourbon County in Kentucky, where it was first produced in 1789 by a Baptist minister, although Bourbon County no longer produces bourbon.

- Gin is spirit alcohol flavoured from juniper berries. First made by the Dutch, it was called *junever*, the Dutch word for 'juniper'. The French called it *genièvre*, which the English changed to 'geneva' and then modified to gin.

- Sloe gin is not gin at all but a liqueur made with sloe berries (blackthorn bush berries).

- *Vodka* ('little water') is the Russian name for grain spirits without added flavour.

- The word 'Brandy' comes from the Dutch brandewijn, meaning burned (or distilled) wine.

- Vermouth is a white appetiser wine flavoured with a maximum of up to fifty different berries, herbs, roots, seeds and flowers, and takes about a year to make.

- Scotch whisky's distinctive smoky flavour comes from drying malted barley over peat fires.

- Writer H.L. Mencken worked out that 17,864,392,788 different cocktails could be made from the ingredients in a well-stocked bar.

- Although the origins of the martini are obscure, it actually began as a sweet drink.

- Colonial New Englanders often put barrels of cider outdoors in cold weather, then removed the ice to increase the alcoholic content of the remaining beverage.

- The Mint Julep was once a very popular everyday drink, the 'Coca-Cola of its time'.

- Most European grapevines are planted on American grape rootstock.

- Mead is a beverage made of a fermented honey and water mixture.

- Poor soil tends to produce better wines.

- 'Cocktails for Hitler' weren't drinks at all. During World War II, distillers shifted all production to industrial alcohol for the war effort. Hence, they were making 'cocktails for Hitler'.

- White wine is usually produced from red grapes.

- No government health warning is permitted on wine imported into any country in the European Union.

- One of every five glasses of wine consumed in the world is *sake*.

- In a martini competition in Chicago in 1951, the winner was a martini made with an anchovy-stuffed olive that was served in a glass rinsed with Cointreau liqueur.

- In Europe and North America, lower-status people tend to prefer beer, whereas upper-status people tend to prefer wine and distilled spirits. In Latin American and Africa, lower-class people tend to drink homebrew, middle-class people bottled beer and upper-class people distilled spirits.

- There are an estimated 49 million bubbles in a bottle of champagne.

- 'Muscatel' means 'wine with flies in it' in Italian.

- For over twenty-five years, vodka has been the largest-selling distilled spirit in the USA and one out of every four alcoholic drinks consumed in the world is vodka or vodka-based.

- All thirteen minerals necessary for human life can be found in alcoholic beverages.

- In Welsh, the word for beer is *cwrw*, pronounced 'koo-roo'.

- From 1651 until 1970, rum was issued daily to every sailor in the British Navy.

- The strongest that any alcohol beverage can be is 190 per cent proof (or 95 per cent alcohol). At higher proof, the beverage draws moisture from the air and self-dilutes.

- Foot-treading of grapes is still used in producing a small quantity of the best port wines.

- A *trokenbeerenauslese* is a type of German wine made from vine-dried grapes so rare that it can take a skilled picker a day to gather enough for just one bottle.

- One popular drink used during the Middle Ages to soothe those who were sick and to heal them was called a 'caudle'. It was an alcoholic drink containing eggs, bread, sugar and spices.

- Most wines do not improve with age.

- Champagne is bottled in eight sizes: a Bottle, Magnum (two bottles), Jeroboam (four bottles), Rehoboam (six bottles), Methuselah (eight bottles), Salamanca (twelve bottles), Balthazar (sixteen bottles) and Nebuchadnezzar (twenty bottles).

- The most popular gift in Eastern Europe is a bottle of vodka.

- The Asian cordial *kumiss* is made of fermented cow's milk.

- Drinking chocolate mixed with beverage alcohol was fashionable at European social events in the 17th century.

- L'Esprit de Courvoisier, a cognac made from brandies distilled between 1802 and 1931, sells for around £300 a shot.

- The alcohol content of the typical bottle of beer, glass of wine and mixed drink are equivalent.

- Vintage port can take forty years to reach maturity.

- British wine is different to English wine. British wine is made from imported grapes; English wine is not.

- The indentation at the bottom of some wine bottles is called a 'kick' or a 'punt'.

- Distilled spirits (whisky, brandy, rum, tequila, gin, etc) contain no carbohydrates, no fats of any kind and no cholesterol.

- Some people in Malaysia wash their babies in beer to protect them from diseases.

- Over half of the hospitals in the largest sixty-five metropolitan areas in the USA have reported that they offer an alcohol-beverage service to their patients.

- A mixed drink containing carbonated beverage is absorbed into the body more quickly than straight shots are.

- The alcohol in drinks of either low alcohol content (below 15 per cent) or high alcohol content (over 30 per cent) tend to be absorbed into the body more slowly.

- Armstrong County in Texas has the most driving-while-intoxicated (DWI) arrests among young drivers, yet it is 'dry' – that is, it prohibits the sale of alcohol.

- The moderate consumption of alcohol is often associated with improved cognitive functioning. One can limit the effect of alcohol by eating and by not consuming more than one drink per hour. High-protein foods, such as cheese and peanuts, help slow the absorption of alcohol into the body, though eventually it is all absorbed.

- The Ancient Greeks thought that eating cabbage would cure a hangover and the Ancient Romans considered that eating fried canaries would do the same.

17

ASSASSINATED PRESIDENTS

- Abraham Lincoln was elected to Congress in 1846.

- John F. Kennedy was elected to Congress in 1946.

- Abraham Lincoln was elected president in 1860.

- John F. Kennedy was elected president in 1960.

- Both were particularly concerned with civil rights.

- Both presidents' wives lost children while living in the White House.

- Both men were shot on a Friday.

- Both were shot in the head.

- Lincoln's secretary was named Kennedy.

- Kennedy's secretary was named Lincoln.

- Both were assassinated by Southerners.

- Both were succeeded by Southerners named Johnson.

- Andrew Johnson, who succeeded Lincoln, was born in 1808.

- Lyndon Johnson, who succeeded Kennedy, was born in 1908.

- John Wilkes Booth, who assassinated Lincoln, was born in 1839.

- Lee Harvey Oswald, who assassinated Kennedy, was born in 1939.

- Both assassins were known by their three names.

- Both names are composed of fifteen letters.

- Lincoln was shot at the theatre named 'Ford'.

- Kennedy was shot in a car called 'Lincoln' made by Ford.

- Booth ran from the theatre and was caught in a warehouse.

- Oswald ran from a warehouse and was caught in a theatre.

- Booth and Oswald were both assassinated before their trials.

- A week before Lincoln was shot, he was in Monroe, Maryland.

- A week before Kennedy was shot, he was with Marilyn Monroe.

18

ADVERTISING

- General Motors was puzzled when their new model Nova car failed to sell as well as expected in Central and South America, until it was pointed out that *No va*, in Spanish, means 'it doesn't go'. In its Spanish markets, the company renamed the car the 'Caribe'.

- The Dairy Association's huge success with the campaign 'Got milk?' prompted them to expand advertising to Mexico. Then they discovered the Spanish translation read, 'Are you lactating?'

- Coors translated its slogan 'Turn it loose' into Spanish, where it was read as 'Suffer from diarrhoea'.

- Scandinavian vacuum manufacturer Electrolux used the following advertisement in an American campaign: 'Nothing sucks like an Electrolux'.

● Clairol introduced the 'Mist Stick', a curling iron, into Germany only to find out that *mist* is slang for 'manure'. Not too many people had use for the 'Manure Stick'.

● American chicken-man Frank Purdue's slogan, 'It takes a tough man to make a tender chicken', got terribly mangled in a Spanish translation. A photo of Purdue with one of his birds appeared on billboards all over Mexico with the caption, 'It takes a hard man to make a chicken aroused'.

● When Gerber started selling baby food in Africa, they used the same packaging as in the US, with a smiling baby on the label. Later, they learned that in Africa companies routinely put pictures of what's inside on the labels since many people can't read.

● When American Airlines wanted to advertise its new first-class leather seats in the Mexican market, it translated its 'Fly in leather' campaign literally, which meant 'Fly naked' (*Vuela en cuero*) in Spanish.

● Colgate introduced a toothpaste in France called 'Cue', the name of a notorious porno magazine.

● An American T-shirt maker in Miami printed shirts for the Spanish market promoting the pope's visit but, instead of 'I saw the Pope' (*el Papa*), the shirts read, 'I Saw the Potato' (*la papa*).

● Pepsi's 'Come alive with the Pepsi generation' translated into 'Pepsi brings your ancestors back from the grave' in Chinese.

- The Coca-Cola name in China was first read as *kekoukela*, meaning 'bite the wax tadpole' or 'female horse stuffed with wax', depending on the dialect. The company then researched 40,000 characters to find a phonetic equivalent – *kokou kole* – which translated as 'happiness in the mouth'.

- When Parker Pen marketed a ballpoint pen in Mexico, its ads were supposed to have read, 'It won't leak in your pocket and embarrass you'. The company mistranslated the word 'embarrass' as *embarazar* ('to impregnate'), so the ad read: 'It won't leak in your pocket and make you pregnant'!

- Toyota renamed their MR2 model 'MR' in France because they feared that, if the French pronounced MR2 quickly, it could sound like '*Toyota merdeux*'.

- The American slogan for Salem cigarettes 'Salem – feeling free' was translated in the Japanese market as 'When smoking Salem, you feel so refreshed that your mind seems to be free and empty'.

- In Italy, a campaign for Schweppes Tonic Water translated the name into Schweppes Toilet Water!

- Ford had a problem in Brazil when the Pinto car flopped. When the company found out that *Pinto* was Brazilian slang for 'tiny male genitals', they prised the nameplates off and substituted *Corcel*, which means 'horse'.

- When Vicks first introduced its cough drops to the German market, they were irritated to learn that the German pronunciation of 'v' is 'f' – meaning that in Germany their name sounded like the guttural equivalent of 'sexual penetration'.

- Not to be outdone, Puffs tissues tried to introduce its product in Germany, only to learn that in German *puff* is a colloquial term for a whorehouse.

- For beer commercials, liquid detergent is added to the beer to make it foam more.

- Personal ads seen in America:
  Auto Repair Service. Free pick-up and delivery. Try us once, you'll never go anywhere again.
  Our experienced mom will care for your child. Fenced yard, meals and smacks included.
  Dog for sale: eats anything and is fond of children.
  Man wanted to work in dynamite factory. Must be willing to travel.
  Three-year-old teacher needed for pre-school. Experience preferred.
  Mixing bowl set designed to please a cook with round bottom for efficient beating.
  Girl wanted to assist magician in cutting-off-head illusion. Blue Cross and salary.
  Dinner Special – Turkey $2.35; Chicken or Beef $2.25; Children $2.00

- Chrysler Corp built a compact Plymouth a few years ago, which they named the 'Volare', presumably a reference to the verb 'to fly' in Italian, as it was the title of a popular song at the time. Someone in the body-styling division decided, without consultation apparently, that an accent mark looked good on the 'e'. With that change, in Spanish, *volaré* could mean 'I will fly' but it could also be translated as 'I will explode.'

- Seen on an American Airlines packet of nuts: INSTRUCTIONS – OPEN PACKET, EAT NUTS.

- Bacardi concocted a fruity drink with the name Pavian to suggest French chic... but *pavian* means baboon in German.

- On the label of Boots' children's cough medicine – DO NOT DRIVE A CAR OR OPERATE MACHINERY.

- When Otis Engineering took part in an exhibition in Moscow, a translator somehow managed to render a 'completion equipment' sign into 'equipment for orgasms'.

- 'Body by Fisher' boasted the auto giant General Motors. 'Corpse by Fisher' was how the Belgians read it.

- In Chinese, the Kentucky Fried Chicken slogan 'Finger-lickin' good' translated as 'Eat your fingers off'.

- Label on a Marks & Spencer's bread pudding – PRODUCT WILL BE HOT AFTER HEATING.

- On the label of the Nytol sleeping aid – WARNING: MAY CAUSE DROWSINESS.

- On a packet of Sainsbury's peanuts – WARNING: CONTAINS NUTS.

- On a Sears' hairdryer – DO NOT USE WHILE SLEEPING.

- On a packet of Sunmaid raisins – WHY NOT TRY TOSSING OVER YOUR FAVOURITE BREAKFAST CEREAL?

- On a Swann frozen dinner – SERVING SUGGESTION: DEFROST.

- Jolly Green Giant Sweetcorn translated into Arabic means 'Intimidating Green Ogre'.

- Printed on the bottom of the box of Tesco's Tiramisu dessert – DO NOT TURN UPSIDE DOWN.

- A famous drug company marketed a new remedy in the United Arab Emirates and used pictures to avoid any mistakes. The first picture was of someone ill, the next showed the person taking the medication, and the last one showed them looking well. What they forgot is that in the Arab world people read from right to left...

- Japan's second-largest tourist agency was mystified when it entered English-speaking markets and began receiving requests for unusual sex tours. When they found out why, the owners of Kinki Nippon Tourist Company changed its name.

- Microsoft Mouse was translated into Italian as 'Micro tender rat' on the instruction sheet for a Taiwanese Microsoft-compatible mouse.

- In an effort to boost orange-juice sales in England, a campaign was devised to extol the drink's eye-opening, pick-me-up qualities. Hence, the slogan, 'Orange juice. It gets your pecker up'.

19

SPORTS AND GAMES

- A Formula 1 tyre costs approximately £850.

- The first set of ice hockey rules was drawn up in 1865.

- The New York Mets' baseball manager Bobby Valentine received a two-match ban when he attempted to retake his seat on the bench in a game against the Toronto Blue Jays having been sent off for arguing too fiercely. He disguised himself in a cap, sunglasses and false moustache but was spotted by TV cameras.

- Sumner, Bramich and McKee are all types of hares used in greyhound racing.

- Cricketer Sachin Tendulkar scored seven Test centuries before his 21st birthday.

- A fan at the 1999 Phoenix Golf Open was arrested for carrying a gun.

- Only eight players have scored a total of ten or more goals in World Cup Finals tournaments.

- A rubber cube was originally used instead of a ball in hockey.

- The Swedes pioneered orienteering.

- The original basket in basketball, as invented by James Naismith in 1891, was a peach basket.

- Mark and Steve Waugh were the first twins to play Test cricket.

- Cricketer Imran Khan studied at Keble College, Oxford.

- The 1977 League Cup Final was replayed twice.

- Margaret Thatcher is Honorary Vice-President of Blackburn Rovers.

- Rocky Marciano is the only world-heavyweight-boxing champion to remain undefeated throughout his entire professional career.

- The standard size of a clay pigeon is 120mm (4.7in) in diameter with a 26mm (1in) breadth.

- British tennis rivals Tim Henman and Greg Rusedski share the same birthday.

- *Escrima* is a Philippine martial art using sticks, knives and hands.

- The official width of a cricket bat is 4in (10cm).

- The ancient Olympic Games started in 776 BC.

- Octopush is an underwater hockey game played between two teams of eight.

- The first Grand Prix World Championship was held in 1950.

- Cricketer Denis Compton also won an FA Cup winner's medal with Arsenal.

- Olympic double-winning marathon runner Abebe Bikila won one race barefoot, the other in shoes.

- Numbers on the backs of FA Cup shirts were first in evidence in 1933.

- Amateur baseball players are called sandlotters.

- The ancient Olympic Games ended in 395 BC, when Olympia was destroyed by an earthquake.

- Putting on the green is called the 'game within a game'.

- Bruce, Danforth and Meon are all types of anchor.

- Torquay United banned pre-match kickabout shots aimed at the goal, fearing legal action from fans hit by misses.

- The Boston Marathon is the world's oldest annual race. It started in 1897.

- West Ham's Paolo Futre exited Highbury before a game with Arsenal because he wasn't allowed to wear the number 10 shirt.

- When the first tennis racquets appeared in the 1920s, the strings were made from piano wire.

- Cricketer Ian Botham's son Liam played county cricket for Hampshire.

- George Ligowsky invented the clay pigeon in the 1880s.

- British father and son Donald and Michael Campbell both held the land speed record.

- The line from behind which the darts are thrown is called the 'hockey'.

- Synchronised swimming was introduced to the Olympics in 1984.

- The US race meeting Breeders Cup Day is the richest day's sport in the world.

- The Virginia Slims tennis championship is the only tournament in which women play the best of five sets.

- Yorker, googly and chinaman are styles of bowling in cricket.

- A badminton racquet was once known as a 'battledore'.

- Two is the lowest possible score to conclude a game of darts.

- Dutch and German immigrants introduced ninepin bowling to the USA.

- The horizontal lines on a chessboard are called ranks.

- The FA Cup Final was replayed in successive years from 1981 to 1983.

- Cricketer Ian Botham also played football for Scunthorpe United.

- Snooker was invented in India.

- David Beckham's father missed his son's home debut for Real Madrid after losing his passport.

- The 'huddle' in American football was formed because of a deaf football player who used sign language to communicate. His team didn't want the opposition to see the signals he used and in turn huddled around him.

- When a male skier falls down, he tends to fall on his face. A woman skier tends to fall on her back.

- Tiger Woods is the only person to hold all four major golf championships at one time, although it did not happen in the calendar year. He also currently holds the scoring record for all four majors.

- Tony Hawk has made more money from video games and TV commercials than from skateboarding.

- David Beckham wears a new pair of football boots for every game he plays at an estimated cost of £300 a pair.

- Men are much more streamlined than women for swimming, because female mammaries create a lot of drag. So much so, in fact, that racing suits have been developed with tiny pegs above the breasts to cause disturbance, which decreases the drag.

- Steven Gerrard's fiancée arrived in Portugal not knowing who England were playing in their first match of Euro 2004.

- Sainsbury's minted Euro 2004 medals engraved with the names and pictures of three players not in the England squad.

- 'Vaimonkanto' or 'wife carrying' is a sports event. The championship games are held annually in Sonkajarvi, Finland.

- Enthusiasts of a 'sport' called extreme ironing are trying to get Olympic recognition by going to the USA to show off their skills by ironing in 'extreme' places such as Times Square and Mount Rushmore.

- David Beckham's weekly wage is reported to be £145,000.

- Around 18 million more text messages than normal were sent on the day England clinched victory against Australia in the Rugby World Cup final.

- In the 1870s, William Russell Frisbie opened a bakery called the Frisbie Pie Company in Bridgeport, Connecticut. His lightweight pie tins were embossed with the family name. In the mid-1940s, students at Yale University began tossing the empty pie tins as a game.

- In the United States, more Frisbee discs are sold each year than baseballs, basketballs and footballs combined.

- Ernie Els's real name is Theodore.

- Go-karting started in the mid-1950s and was originally considered to be a fad.

- 'Hot cockles' was a popular game at Christmas in medieval times. Players took turns striking a blindfolded player, who had to guess the name of the person delivering each blow.

- There are more recreational golfers per capita in Canada than any other country in the world.

- On 21 February 2004, over 1,500 minor hockey players gathered along Ottawa's 4.8-mile (7.8km) Rideau Canal for 110 simultaneous games of hockey.

- Daniele Carassai, manager of semi-professional football side Gotico, lost his post via a text message that stated simply: 'You're sacked'.

- Scarborough goalie Leigh Walker said he was 'sickened' after his mother washed a Chelsea shirt that had been signed by all the team.

- Brazilian soccer star Ronaldinho smashed a window at a 12th-century cathedral after fluffing an overhead kick while filming an advert.

- Camden playground in Janesville, Wisconsin, is the largest disabled-accessible playground in the world.

- Aged 101, Larry Lewis ran the 100yd dash (91.5m) in 17.8 seconds, setting a new world record for runners 100 years old or older.

- A helicopter installed the world's largest Olympic torch on top of the Calgary tower. The flame was visible for up 12.4 miles (20km) and required 30,000 feet^3 (849m^3) of natural gas per hour.

- Johnny Plessey batted .331 for the Cleveland Spiders in 1891, even though he spent the entire season batting with a rolled-up, lacquered copy of the *Toledo Post-Dispatch*.

- The average IQ of a WWF fan is 83, roughly 17 points below the national average.

- When the golf ball was introduced in 1848, it was called a 'gutta-percha'.

- To bulk up, sumo wrestlers eat huge portions of protein-rich stews called *chankonabe*, packed with fish or meat and vegetables, plus vast quantities of less healthy foods, including fast food. They often force themselves to eat when they are full, and they have a nap after lunch, thus acquiring flab on top of their strong muscles, which helps to keep their centre of gravity low.

- The chances of making two holes-in-one in a round of golf are 1 in 67 million.

- If placed end-to-end, all Lego sets sold during the past ten years would stretch from London to Perth, Australia.

- In 1974, Bob Chandler built the first monster truck – *Bigfoot* – his dream truck, a four-wheel drive Ford F-250 with a jacked-up suspension and oversized tyres.

- In 1988, the heaviest sumo wrestler ever recorded weighed in at a thundering 560lb (254kg).

- Table tennis was originally played with balls made from champagne corks and paddles made from cigar-box lids.

20

LONDON

- The tomb of Elizabethan poet Edmund Spenser in Westminster Abbey is said to contain unpublished works by his contemporaries, including works from William Shakespeare, who threw manuscripts into his grave to honour his genius.

- 'One, London' is the postal address of Apsley House, the Duke of Wellington's former residence at Hyde Park Corner.

- The 'Old Lady of Threadneedle Street' is the nickname for the Bank of England, located near the Tower of London.

- St Thomas' Hospital used to have seven buildings, one for each day of the week. Supposedly, this was so staff knew on which day patients has been admitted. Only two of the buildings remain.

- Signs on Albert Bridge order troops to break step while marching over it; this is to avoid damaging the structure with the resonating vibrations.

- Before the 17ft (5.2m) statue of Admiral Lord Nelson was erected on top of the Trafalgar Square column in 1842, fourteen stonemasons held a dinner on top of the 170ft-high (51.8m) pedestal.

- The exact centre of London is marked by a plaque in the church of St Martin-in-the-Fields overlooking Trafalgar Square, but the actual point is on the corner of Strand and Charing Cross Road, near the statue of Charles I. There is even a plaque on a nearby wall confirming this.

- The Monument, built to commemorate the Great Fire of London that devastated the original walled city in September 1666, is the tallest isolated stone monument in the world. It is 205ft (62.5m) high, and is said to be 205ft west of where the fire started in a baker's house, on Pudding Lane.

- Brixton Market was the first electrified market in the country and stands, as a result, on Electric Avenue.

- Dr Samuel Johnson once owned seventeen properties in London, only one of which still survives: Dr Johnson's Memorial House in Gough Square, which contains a brick from the Great Wall of China, donated to the museum in 1822.

- The annual Notting Hill Carnival is the second largest carnival in the world after Rio de Janeiro.

- The Monument to the Great Fire of London was intended to be used as a fixed telescope to study the motion of a single star by Robert Hooke, who designed the structure with Sir Christopher Wren.

- Postman's Park, behind Bart's hospital, is one of London's great hidden contemplative spots. It is full of memorials to 'ordinary people' who have committed acts of heroism.

- The tiered design of St Bride's Church off Fleet Street is said to have inspired the traditional shape of wedding cakes.

- The nursery rhyme 'Pop Goes the Weasel' refers to the act of pawning one's suit after spending all of one's cash in the pubs of Clerkenwell.

- Oxford Street is the busiest shopping street in Europe, having over 300 shops and receiving in excess of 200 million visitors a year, with an annual turnover of approximately £5 billion.

- The Piccadilly Circus statue known as Eros was originally intended as an angel of mercy but renamed after the Greek god of love. It was actually meant to depict the Angel of Christian Charity, and is part of a memorial to the Seventh Earl of Shaftesbury. Its stance, aiming an arrow up Shaftesbury Avenue, is thought to be a coarse visual pun.

- Contrary to a famous scene in the movie *Help!*, the only true home shared by all four Beatles was a flat at 57 Green Street near Hyde Park, where they lived in the autumn of 1963.

- The gravestone of the famous Elizabethan actor Richard Burbage in the graveyard of St Leonard's, Shoreditch, reads simply 'Exit Burbage'.

- London was the first city to reach a population of more than a million people, in 1811. It remained the largest city in the world until it was overtaken by Tokyo in 1957.

- The Dome, the focus of the Millennium celebrations in London, is the largest structure of its kind in the world. It is big enough to house the Great Pyramid of Giza or the Statue of Liberty.

- Only six people died in the Great Fire of London, but seven people died by falling or jumping from the Monument, which commemorates it, before a safety rail was built.

- 'Pearly Kings and Queens' – so named because of the clothes they wear, which are studded with countless pearl buttons – were originally the 'aristocracy' of the representatives of east London's traders.

- Mayfair is named after a fair that used to be held in the area every May.

- Covent Garden is actually a spelling mistake! The area used to be the market garden for what is now Westminster Abbey monastery and convent.

- London's smallest house is only 3ft 6in (1.1m) wide, and forms part of the Tyburn Convent in Hyde Park Place, where twenty nuns live. These nuns have taken a vow of silence and still pray for the souls of those who lost their lives on the 'Tyburn Tree', London's main execution spot until 1783, where about 50,000 people were executed. There is a plaque at the junction of Edgware Road and Marble Arch marking the site.

- Inside Marble Arch is a tiny office that once used to be a police station.

- Harrods, London's most famous department store, had its beginnings in 1849 when Charles Henry Harrod opened a small grocery shop nearby on Brompton Road.

- The Houses of Parliament has 1,000 rooms, 100 staircases, eleven courtyards, eight bars, and six restaurants – none of them open to the public. The Palace of Westminster was sited by the river so it could not be totally surrounded by a mob.

- The architect of the Oxo Tower originally wanted to use electric lighting to advertise the meat-extract product, but permission was refused so he redesigned it with windows set out to spell the word 'OXO' on all four sides, through which the advertising message could shine. The building now houses restaurants, design shops and galleries.

- There is a 19th-century time capsule under the base of Cleopatra's Needle, the 68ft (20.7m), 3,450-year-old obelisk on the Embankment. It contains a set of British currency, a railway guide, a bible and twelve portraits of 'the prettiest English ladies'.

- Piccadilly is named after a kind of stiff collar made by a tailor who lived in the area in the 17th century.

- The Tower of London's most celebrated residents are a colony of seven ravens. It is not known when they first settled there, but there is a legend that, should they ever desert the Tower, the kingdom and monarchy will fall.

- Only one British prime minister out of the fifty-one who have held the office since 1751 has ever been assassinated; Spencer Perceval was shot in the House of Commons in 1812.

- In 1881, the Savoy Theatre became the first theatre to be lit by electricity.

- The oldest surviving bridge on the Thames Path, now the longest riverside walk, is the Clattern Bridge at Kingston, dating back to the 12th century. Richmond Bridge is the oldest surviving Thames bridge, built in 1774.

- Police are sometimes called the 'fuzz' because London police used to wear fuzzy helmets.

- Beefeaters at the Tower of London are struggling to get home contents insurance because they are judged too much of a risk. Most insurers won't give the thirty-eight Beefeaters, who look after the Crown Jewels and live within the Tower walls, a policy.

- The inner and outer dome of St Paul's Cathedral is the second largest dome in the world, standing at 360ft (110m) high; St Peter's in Rome is the largest.

- The sculpture on top of Wellington Arch, by Adrian Jones, was added in 1912, and it is said that, before it was installed, Jones seated eight people for dinner in the body of one of the horses.

- England's first printing press was set up in Fleet Street in the 15th century by William Caxton's assistant. The area remained a centre of London's publishing industry well into the late 20th century.

- The London Eye used 1,673 tons (1,700 tonnes) of steel in its construction and is heavier than 250 double-decker buses.

- Hungerford Bridge, built in 1864, is the only bridge crossing the Thames that was built to carry both trains and pedestrians to Charing Cross.

- With a population of 7.3 million, London is the largest city in Europe. The average household size is 2.3 people.

- London contains 143 registered parks and gardens, which account for 30 per cent of all of London's open spaces.

- There are over 300 languages spoken in the Greater London area and almost half of Britain's black and ethnic-minority residents live there, with resident communities from over ninety different countries. More than a third of Londoners belong to an ethnic-minority community.

- London is currently home to four World Heritage Sites: the Palace of Westminster, the Tower of London, Maritime Greenwich and Kew Gardens.

- Big Ben, which most people think of as the name of the four-faced clock tower of the Houses of Parliament, actually refers to the resonant bell on which the hours are struck. It was named after Sir Benjamin Hall, Chief Commissioner of Works when the bell was hung in 1858. Cast in Whitechapel, it was the second giant bell made for the clock, after the first became cracked during a test ringing.

21

FIRSTS

- The first sheets of toilet paper, each measuring 2 x 3ft (0.6 x 0.9m), and for use by the emperors, were introduced in China in 1391.

- The first toilet paper rolls were marketed by the Scott Paper Company in Philadelphia in 1879.

- The first child born to American colonists, on what is now Roanoke Island, North Carolina, was Virginia Dare in 1587.

- The first published American woman writer was Anne Bradstreet with *The Tenth Muse Lately Sprung Up* in America in 1650.

- The first woman newspaper editor was Ann Franklin, in 1762, of the *Newport Mercury* in Newport, Rhode Island.

- The first (and the only unanimously elected) US president was George Washington in 1789.

- The first US First Lady was Martha Washington.

- The first magician to perform the trick of sawing a woman in half was Count de Grisley in 1799.

- The first person to cross the Antarctic Circle was James Cook in 1773.

- The first humans to fly, and who were airborne in a hot-air balloon for 20 minutes, in Paris on 21 November 1783, were the Marquis d'Arlandes and Pilatre de Rozier.

- The first parachute jump, in 1797, was made by André-Jacques Garnerin, who was dropped from about 6,500ft (1,981m) over a Paris park, in a 23ft-diameter (7m) parachute, made of white canvas with a basket attached.

- The first grapefruit trees in Florida, around Tampa Bay, were planted by Frenchman Count Odette Phillipe in 1823. Today, Florida produces more grapefruit than the rest of the world combined.

- The first known person to survive the jump off the Niagara Falls was Sam Patch in 1829.

- The first indicted bank robber in the USA was Edward Smith in 1831. He was sentenced to five years' hard labour on the rock pile at Sing Sing Prison.

- The first monarch to live in London's Buckingham Palace was Queen Victoria in 1837.

- The first American woman ordained a minister by a recognised denomination (Congregational) was Antoinette Brown Blackwell in 1853.

- The first person to cross the Niagara Falls on a tightrope was Jean François 'Blondin' Gravelet in 1859.

- The first US president to die in office was William Harrison in 1841. At thirty-two days, his was also the shortest term in office.

- The first rubber band was made, and patented, in 1845.

- The first flying trapeze circus act in the world, performed at the Cirque Napoléon in Paris without safety nets, was by Jules Leotard in 1859.

- The first recognised boxing (fisticuffs) champion was Tim Hyer in 1841.

- The first US train robbery was committed on 6 October 1866 by the Reno brothers (Frank, Simeon and William), who boarded an eastbound train in Indiana wearing masks and toting guns. After clearing out one safe, they tossed another out the window and jumped off the train before making an easy getaway.

- The first woman to successfully climb the Matterhorn in Switzerland was Lucy Walker in 1871.

- The first woman to run for president of the USA was Victoria Woodhall in 1872.

- The first known person to swim across the English Channel was Matthew Webb in 1875. (He drowned in 1883 after unsuccessfully trying to swim across the whirlpools and rapids beneath the Niagara Falls.)

- The first woman to swim across the English Channel in each direction was Florence Chadwick in 1951.

- The first world chess champion was Wilhelm Steinitz in 1886.

- The first criminal to be executed in the electric chair (in Auburn Prison, Auburn, NY) was William Kemmler in 1890.

- The first skyscraper, the ten-storey Wainwright Building, Grover, Cleveland, was designed by Louis Henry Sullivan in 1891.

- The first immigrant to pass through Ellis Island was Annie Moore in 1892. She was 15 years old and from County Cork, Ireland.

- The first woman to appear on a US postage stamp was Queen Isabella of Spain in 1893.

- The first woman to go over the Niagara Falls in a barrel was Annie Taylor in 1901. She was aged 64 years at the time.

- The first bottled Coca-Cola appeared in 1899 in Chattanooga, Tennessee.

- The first woman in the British Empire to run for a national office was Vida Goldstein in 1902. She ran for the Australian Senate when women there got the right to vote in all federal elections.

- The first successful heavier-than-air machine flight was on 17 December 1903, at Kitty Hawk, NC, when Orville Wright crawled to his prone position between the wings of *Flyer I*, the biplane he and his brother Wilbur had built. The 12-horsepower engine covered 120ft (36.6m) in twelve seconds. Later that day, in one of four flights, Wilbur stayed up fifty-nine seconds and covered 852ft (260m).

- The first winner of the Tour de France was Maurice Garin in 1903.

- The first land speed record in car racing was set in 1903 by Alexander Winton, at Daytona Beach. His speed was 68.18mph (109.73km/h).

- The first Tsar of Russia was Ivan IV (the Terrible) in 1547.

- The first American woman to win the ladies singles tennis championship at Wimbledon was May Sutton Brandy in 1904.

- The first winner of the Grand Prix held at Le Mans, France, was Romanian driver Ferenc Szisz in 1906. He drove a Renault.

- Australia's first prime minister was Edmund Barton, in 1900.

- The first airplane fatality was Thomas Selfridge, a lieutenant in the US Army Signal Corps, who was in a group evaluating the Wright brothers' plane at Fort Myer, in 1908. He was up 75ft (22.9m) with Orville Wright when the propeller hit a bracing wire and was broken, throwing the plane out of control. Selfridge was killed and Wright seriously injured.

- The first licensed female pilot was Baroness Raymonde de la Roche of France, who learned to fly in 1909, and received ticket No. 36 on 8 March 1910.

- The first reigning Queen of England was Queen Mary I in 1553.

- The first policewoman in the USA was Alice Wells in 1910. She was hired by the Los Angeles Police Department and was allowed to design her own uniform.

- The first winner of the Miss World beauty pageant, at the age of 17, was Alice Hyde in 1911.

- The first man to reach the South Pole, beating an expedition led by Robert F. Scott, was Roald Amundsen, the Norwegian explorer, in 1911.

- The first US black female pilot was Bessie Coleman in 1921. She was killed on 30 April 1926 in a flying accident.

- The first aerial combat was in August 1914, when Allied and German pilots and observers started shooting at each other using pistols and rifles – with negligible results.

- The first Miss America was Margaret Gorman, who was 16 years old and 30-25-32, in 1921.

- The first person to have his diabetes successfully treated was a 14-year-old Canadian boy named Leonard Thompson, who was injected with Banting and Best's new discovery, insulin, at Toronto General Hospital in 1922.

- The first person to star in a talking motion picture was Al Jolson in 1927 in *The Jazz Singer*.

- The first man to fly solo across the Atlantic was Charles Lindbergh in 1927.

- The first Scrabble game was played in 1931.

- The first footprints at Grauman's Chinese Theater (now Mann's Chinese Theater) were made by Norma Talmadge in 1927.

- The first Oscar winner for Best Actor was Emil Jannings in 1928.

- The first Oscar winner for Best Actress was Janet Gaynor in 1928.

- The first airline hostess was Ellen Church in 1930. She served passengers flying between San Francisco, California and Cheyenne, Wyoming on United Airlines.

- The first transatlantic solo flight by a woman was by Amelia Earhart in 1932. She travelled from Harbor Grace, Newfoundland, to Ireland in approximately fifteen hours.

- The first woman to win an Olympic Gold Medal (for tennis) was Charlotte Cooper in 1900.

- The first big band, which started the swing era on radio, was that of Benny Goodman, which was heard on NBC's *Let's Dance* in 1934.

- The first telephone call made around the world was in 1935.

- The first quintuplets to survive infancy were Marie, Cecile, Yvonne, Emilie and Annette Dionne, who were born near Callender, Ontario, to Oliva and Elzire Dionne in 1934.

- The first winner of the US Masters Golf Tournament, at Augusta National in Georgia, was Horton Smith in 1934.

- The first television service, showing three hours a day, was started by the BBC in 1936.

- The first gold record ever awarded to a recording artist was to Glenn Miller in 1941.

- The first around-the-world commercial flight was made by Pan American airlines in January 1942.

- The first canonised American saint was Mother Frances Xavier Cabrini in 1946.

- The first person to break the sound barrier by flying faster than the speed of sound was Chuck Yeager, who flew a Bell X-1 rocket at 670mph (1,078km/h) in level flight on 14 October 1947.

- The first sex-change operation was performed on George (Christine) Jorgenson in 1952.

- The first monarch to have a televised coronation was Queen Elizabeth II in 1953.

- The first recorded climb of Mount Everest was by Sir Edmund Hillary in 1953.

- The first professional woman bullfighter was Patricia McCormick, who fought two bulls in Ciudad Juarez, Mexico, in 1952.

- The first TV guide, in April 1953, had Desi Arnaz, Jr, and Lucille Ball on the cover.

- The first woman to fly faster than the speed of sound was Jacqueline Cochrane in 1953. She piloted an F-86 Sabrejet over California at an average speed of 652.337mph (1,049.835km/h).

- The first recorded person to run a mile race in under four minutes was Sir Roger Bannister on 6 May 1954. He broke the four-minute barrier at Imey Road, Oxford, in a time of 3 minutes 59.4 seconds.

- The first breasts to be exposed on television were those of film star Jayne Mansfield, who exhaled at the 1957 Academy Awards and accidentally let it all hang out.

- The first living creature to orbit the Earth was Laika, the dog, in 1957, aboard the Soviet satellite *Sputnik 2*.

- The first human in space, and to orbit the Earth, was Yuri Alekseyevich Gagarin in 1961.

- The first woman in space was Russian cosmonaut Valentina Vladimirovna Tereshkova in 1963.

- The first woman to be elected a head of state was Sirimavo Bandaraneike, who became president of Sri Lanka in 1960.

- The first Jewish female prime minister, and Israel's first prime minister, was Golda Meir in 1964.

- The first around-the-world solo flight by a woman was by Jerrie Mock in 1964.

- The first male to appear on the cover of *Playboy* magazine was Peter Sellers in 1964.

- The first human to walk in space was Alexei Arkhovich Leonov in 1965.

- The first-ever nude centrefold girl was Amber Dean Smith who, in 1965, at the age of 19, was crowned 'Pet Of The Year' by *Penthouse* magazine.

- The first human heart transplant was performed in 1967 by South African heart surgeon Christiaan Barnard.

- The first artist on the cover of *Rolling Stone* magazine was John Lennon on 9 November 1967.

- The first time the word 'hell' was used on television was in 1967 in *Star Trek*, when Jim Kirk said, 'Let's get the hell out of here'.

- The first woman to be placed on the FBI's Most Wanted List, for kidnapping, extortion and other crimes, was Ruth Eisemann-Schier in 1968.

- The first woman to set foot on the North Pole was Fran Phillips on 5 April 1971.

- The first athlete to win seven Olympic gold medals was US swimmer Mark Spitz in 1972.

- The first female commercial airline pilot in the US was Emily Warner on Frontier Airlines in 1973.

- The first *People* magazine cover was of Mia Farrow in 1974.

- The first rape scene on television was in the controversial TV movie *Born Innocent*, starring Linda Blair, on the NBC network on 10 September 1974.

- The first woman to reach the summit of Mount Everest was Junko Tabei in 1975.

- The first time the word 'bastard' was used on television was when Meg called her son Ben a 'bastard' in the soap opera *Love of Life* in 1974.

- The first and only US president to resign from office was Richard Milhaus Nixon in 1974.

- The first actor to portray an openly gay main character in a TV show was Billy Crystal, who played Jodie Dallas on ABC's *Soap*, which aired from 1977 to 1981.

- The first woman to qualify and race at the Indianapolis 500 was Janet Guthrie in 1977.

- The first test-tube baby was Louise Brown from Lancashire, born in 1978.

- The first Pole to become pope was John Paul II, Karol Wojtyla, in 1978.

- The first woman chief of a major American Indian tribe was Wilma Mankiller. She was elected Principal Chief of the Cherokee Nation in 1985.

- The first recipient of a permanent artificial heart was Barney Clark on 2 December 1982. He lived until 23 March 1983.

- The first black man in space was Guion Stewart Bluford, Jr, in 1983.

- The first female prime minister of Great Britain was Margaret Thatcher in 1979.

- The first female artist inducted into the Rock & Roll Hall of Fame was Aretha Franklin in 1987.

- The first figure skater to land a quadruple jump in competition was Kurt Browning in 1988.

- The first athlete in a team sport to 'come out' during his athletic career and admit that he was gay was British football player Justin Fashanu in 1988.

- The first woman film director to have a film take in more than $100 million at the box office was Penny Marshall, with *Big*, in 1988.

- The first lesbian kiss on television was the *LA Law* kiss between Amanda Donohoe and Michelle Green in 1991.

- The first black woman in space was Mae Carol Jemison on the *Endeavor* in 1992.

- The first woman to pilot Concorde was Barbara Harmer on 25 March 1993.

- The first female serial killer in America was Aileen Wuornos. In 1992, she was charged with killing five middle-aged men she met on highways while hitchhiking. She was later executed.

- The first cloned mammal was Dolly, the lamb, in 1996.

- The first person to break the sound barrier in a car was Craig Breedlove, with a speed of over 760mph (1,223km/h), at Lake Bonneville, Utah, in 1998.

- The first female combat pilot to bomb an enemy target was Lt Kendra Williams of the US Navy, who bombed enemy targets over Iraq during Operation Desert Fox in 1998.

- The first balloonist to fly solo around the world was Steve Fossett, who landed in Australia on 4 July 2002.

22

THE UNDERGROUND

- There are only two Tube station names that have all five vowels in them – Mansion House and South Ealing. Chancery Lane has the shortest escalator on the system – fifty steps.

- The shortest distance between Tube stations is Leicester Square to Covent Garden on the Piccadilly line – 0.16 miles (0.26km).

- The most popular route for tourists is Leicester Square to Covent Garden on the Piccadilly line. It is quicker to walk this distance than travel on the Tube.

- The only Tube station that shares the name of a well-known pop group is All Saints.

- The phrase 'Mind the Gap' originated on the Northern line.

- The Jubilee line was originally going to be called the Fleet line.

- Northfields station on the Piccadilly line was the first to use kestrels and hawks to kill pigeons and stop them setting up homes in stations.

- The Central line covers the longest route – from West Ruislip to Epping, you will travel 34 miles (54.7km) without changing.

- The Waterloo and City line covers the shortest route – 1.2 miles (2km).

- The oldest Tube line in the world is the Metropolitan line. It opened on 10 January 1863.

- Tube carriages originally had no windows and buttoned upholstery and were nicknamed 'padded cells'.

- More of the London Underground is in open air than in tunnels.

- Bank has more escalators than any other station on the Tube – fifteen, plus two moving walkways.

- Out of the 287 Tube stations, only twenty-nine are south of the river Thames.

- One of the female automated voice announcers is called Sonia.

- Edward Johnston designed the text font used for the London Underground in 1916.

- The peak hour for Tube suicides is 11am.

- People who commit suicide by throwing themselves under Tube trains are called 'one-unders'. In New York, they are known as 'track pizza'.

- The Jubilee line extension was the most expensive railway line ever built. It cost £173 million per kilometre.

- All 409 Tube escalators combined do the equivalent of two round-the-world trips every week.

- Amersham is not only the most westerly station on the Tube but also the highest – it's 492ft (150m) above sea level.

- People were smaller when Tube carriages were built in the 1860s – which is one of the reasons why you'll find your journey so uncomfortable today.

- Harry Beck, designer of the Tube map in 1933, was only paid five guineas for his original job. His design is still the basis of today's Tube map. Had he taken royalties, he would have become a very rich man.

- William Gladstone and Dr Barnado were the only people to ever have their coffins transported by Tube.

- The first escalator was introduced at Earl's Court in 1911.

- Not only were the early escalators made of wood, but also the legs of the people who demonstrated them. Wooden-legged 'Bumper' Harris was employed to travel up and down the Tube's first escalator to prove that it was safe.

- Angel has Western Europe's longest escalator — 318 steps.

- Mosquitoes that live in the Underground have evolved into a completely different species, one that appears separated from the above-ground mozzie by over a thousand years.

- Regent's Park, Piccadilly Circus, Hyde Park Corner and Bank stations do not have an above-ground station building.

- The air in the underground is on average 10°C hotter than the air on the surface.

- Pigeons regularly travel from West Ham in east London to central London on the Tube in order to get more food.

- Green grapes cause more accidents on the London Underground than banana skins.

- The best places to spot mice running around the tracks of the Underground are Waterloo station (northbound on the Bakerloo line) and any platform at Oxford Circus.

- Anthea Turner and her sister Wendy have written a series of children's books about mice living on the London Underground.

- Only one person was ever born in a Tube carriage and her name is Thelma Ursula Beatrice Eleanor. She was born in 1924 on a Bakerloo line train at Elephant & Castle, and her initials spell TUBE.

- An advertising campaign that wafted the aroma of almond liqueur through the London Underground has been dropped because the smell is similar to cyanide gas.

- Victoria and King's Cross record the highest number of Tube suicides each year. This isn't surprising, as Victoria is the Tube's busiest station, with 85 million passengers each year, and King's Cross has 70 million passengers each year.

- Aldwych station (now closed) is featured on level 12 in the *Tomb Raider* game with Lara Croft killing rats.

- Christopher Lee and Donald Pleasance starred in a 1970s horror film called *Death Line* (aka *Raw Meat*), in which man-eating troglodytes terrorise people on the London Underground.

- The Cadbury's Whole Nut chocolate bar is the biggest seller in the chocolate machines at Tube stations.

- A fragrance called 'Madeleine' was introduced at St James's Park, Euston and Piccadilly stations in an effort to make the Tube smell better on 23 March 2001. It was taken out of action on 24 March 2001, as it was making people feel sick.

- The sexiest film scene featuring the London Underground is in *The Wings of the Dove*. Helena Bonham Carter and Linus Roache travel in a 19th-century carriage together before getting off to make love in a lift.

23

ABOUT THE SEXES

- A team of medical experts in Virginia contends that you're more likely to catch the common cold virus by shaking hands than by kissing.

- It is a matter of record that romantic Canadian porcupines kiss one another on the lips.

- Matrimonial pollsters contend that a man who kisses his wife goodbye when he leaves for work every morning averages a higher income than a man who doesn't. Husbands who exercise the rituals of affection tend to be more painstaking, more stable, more methodical and, thus, higher earners, it's believed.

- It has also been documented that men who kiss their wives before leaving home in the morning live five years longer than those who do not.

- In medieval Italy, kisses weren't taken – or given – lightly; if a man and a woman were seen embracing in public they could be forced to marry.

- The longest kiss listed in *Guinness World Records* lasted an incredible 30 hours 45 minutes.

- Women can talk longer with less effort than men, as the vocal cords of women are shorter than those of men and so release less air through them to carry the sound. It's all a matter of breathing.

- The German language contains thirty words referring to the act of kissing. There is even a word, *Nachkuss*, for all the kisses that haven't yet been named.

- The average woman uses up approximately her own height in lipstick every five years.

- On the island of Trobriand, a lover customarily bites off his lady friend's eyelashes. But he would never take her out to dinner unless they were married. To share a meal with her would disgrace her.

- Porn star Annie Sprinkle claims to have had sex with 3,000 men.

- Studies by Dr Karl F. Robinson of Northwestern University reportedly prove that men change their minds two or three times more often than women.

- Women in nudist camps tend to use more make-up than women elsewhere.

- The first nipple rings, called 'bosom rings', appeared in Victorian Europe in the 1890s. They became fashionable among women, who often wore them joined together by a small gold chain.

- Approximately 3 million women in the USA sport tattoos.

- Until recently, among some tribes in New Guinea it was the custom for a young fighting man to give his girlfriend a finger cut from the hand of his opponent. She wore the finger on a string around her neck. Some elderly natives there still have missing fingers.

- Recent research indicates about 9,000 romantic couples each year take out marriage licences, then fail to use them.

- There are more 20-year-old virgins now than there were in the late 1950s.

- Both women and men are most likely to have their first orgasm alone.

- The USA has more laws governing sexual behaviour than every country in Europe combined.

- According to a 1996 study, homophobic men demonstrate a higher arousal rate when shown gay porn than men with ambivalent attitudes towards homosexuals.

- Among transsexuals who choose sex-change operations, females who elect to become male are reportedly happier and better adjusted after the procedures than males who elect to become female.

- Beau Brummell started the craze for ultra-tight men's trousers in the early 19th century. Because they were so tight, the penis needed to be held to one side so as not to create an unsightly bulge. To accomplish this, some men had their penis pierced to allow it to be held by a hook on the inside of the trousers at the time. This piercing was called a 'dressing ring' because tailors would ask if a gentleman dressed to the left or the right and tailor the trousers accordingly. To this day tailors will ask if you dress to the left or right.

- A 'buckle bunny' is a woman who goes to rodeos with the express intent of having sex with a rodeo cowboy.

- In Ancient Babylon, all women were required to serve as prostitutes in the temple before getting married. Some unattractive women sometimes had to serve three or four years before finally being chosen.

- A condom will last about a month in a wallet before the rubber gets worn down by friction, making it more likely to break.

- Black women are 50 per cent more likely than white women to have an orgasm when they have sex.

- Empress Wu Hu of the T'ang Dynasty (AD 683–705) insisted that all visiting dignitaries perform oral sex on her to pay her homage.

- In Oxford, Ohio, it's illegal for a woman to strip off her clothes in front of a man's picture.

- The most female orgasms per hour on record are a staggering 134. The most male orgasms per hour are just sixteen.

- Jews and atheists tend to have more sex partners than Catholics or Protestants.

- In 1869, Dr George Taylor invented the world's first vibrator, called 'the manipulator'. It was powered by steam and was intended as a cure for just about any medical problem a woman had.

- Oculolinctus is a fetish whereby people are sexually aroused by licking a partner's eyeball.

- The most successful X-rated movie of all time is *Deep Throat* (1972). It cost less than $50,000 to make and has earned more than $100 million to date.

- In Washington State there is a law against having sex with a virgin under any circumstances (including the wedding night).

- The only acceptable sexual position in Washington, DC, is the missionary position. Any other sexual position is considered illegal.

- The usual result of ingesting Spanish Fly is vomiting.

- In Maryland, it is illegal to sell condoms from vending machines with one exception – prophylactics may be dispensed from a vending machine only 'in places where alcoholic beverages are sold for consumption on the premises'.

- The left testicle usually hangs lower than the right for right-handed men. For lefties, the opposite is true.

- In North Carolina, it is illegal to have sex with a drunken fish.

- The first sperm banks opened in 1964 in Tokyo and Iowa City.

- Impotence is grounds for divorce in twenty-four American states.

- In Mississippi, S&M is against the law, specifically, 'The depiction or description of flagellation or torture by or upon a person who is nude or in undergarments or in a bizarre or revealing costume for the purpose of sexual gratification'.

- In the state of Utah, sex with an animal – unless performed for profit – is not considered sodomy and is therefore legal.

- The average male member in all its glory is 6in (15.2cm) long and 5in (12.7cm) in circumference.

- In Ancient Greece, young aristocratic women were deflowered by having their hymens pierced by a stone penis before marrying.

- King Richard the Lionheart, J. Edgar Hoover, Oscar Wilde, Chief Crazy Horse, Leonard Bernstein, Alexander the Great, Sigmund Freud, Lawrence of Arabia, Plato, Peter Tchaikovsky and Florence Nightingale were all gay or bisexual.

- The least expensive prostitutes in the world are the Petrapole people, who live on the border of Bangladesh. They charge as little as 10 rupees, which is the equivalent of 17 pence.

- The earliest breast implants were done in the 1940s by Japanese prostitutes hoping to entice American GIs. They injected their breasts with liquid silicon.

- Twenty-five per cent of sexually active people engage in anal sex.

- Humans are the only species on Earth to have face-to-face sex.

- In Cali, Colombia, a woman may only have sex with her husband when accompanied by her mother.

- In the 1940s, Dr Walter J. Freeman began prescribing, in widespread fashion, a cure for homosexuality. He 'cured', to an arguable degree of success, mostly institutionalised patients. By 1955 more than 19,000 American 'deviants' had received this treatment – a lobotomy.

- Semen contains small amounts of more than thirty elements, including fructose, ascorbic acid, cholesterol, creatine, citric acid, lactic acid, nitrogen, vitamin B12, and various salts and enzymes.

- Exhibitionists are most likely to be married men.

- Women who went to college are more likely to enjoy both the giving and receiving of oral sex than high-school dropouts are.

- According to statistics, Australian women are most likely to have sex on the first date.

- The male foetus is capable of attaining an erection during the last trimester.

- The anus is approximately 4 degrees warmer than the vagina and has over eight working muscles.

- Around the world people are having sex an average of 103 times a year. In terms of consistency, the French get it on an average of 137 times a year. The Greeks come a close second at 133 times and the Hungarians third at 131 times per year. The UK gets it 119 times, beating the USA at an average of only 111 times a year. In Hong Kong and Singapore, they manage only seventy-nine times, and Japan comes in last, managing just forty-six times a year.

- According to CNN, a new study performed by Anthony Bogaert – a psychologist and human sexuality expert at Brock University in St Catherine's, Ontario – revealed that about 1 in 100 people are completely asexual, having no interest in sex at all.

- An excerpt from Kentucky state legislation: 'No female shall appear in a bathing suit on any highway within this state unless she be escorted by at least two officers or unless she be armed with a club.'

- When asked, white women and women with a college degree said they were more receptive to anal sex than women of other races or without college educations.

- For every 'normal' webpage, there are five porn pages.

- A medical study conducted in Pennsylvania showed that people who have sex once or twice a week slightly boost their immune systems.

- Women are most likely to want to have sex when they are ovulating.

- Over 11,000 people are injured every year trying out new sexual positions.

- The smallest erect penis on record was 0.4in (1cm) long.

- 'Ithyphallophobia' is a morbid fear of seeing, thinking about or having an erect penis.

- In the Aztec culture, avocados were considered so sexually powerful that virgins were restricted from contact with them.

- Marilyn Monroe, the most celebrated sex icon of the 20th century, confessed to a friend that, despite her three husbands and a parade of lovers, she had never had an orgasm. So, apparently blondes don't always have more fun.

- According to a US market research firm, the most popular American bra size is currently 36C, up from 1991 when it was 34B.

- The female bedbug has no sexual opening. To get around this dilemma, the male uses his curved penis to drill a vagina into the female.

- Male bats have a higher rate of homosexuality than any other mammal.

- A law in Oblong, Illinois, makes it a crime to make love while fishing or hunting on your wedding day.

- Humans and dolphins are the only species to have sex for pleasure.

- Hotel owners in Hastings, Nebraska, are required by law to provide a clean white cotton nightshirt to each guest. According to the law, no couple may have sex unless they are wearing the nightshirts.

- A man's penis not only shrinks during cold weather but also from non-sexual excitement such as when his favourite football team scores a goal, etc.

- Seventy per cent of women would rather have chocolate than sex, according to a poll taken in a 1995 popular women's magazine.

- A parthenologist is someone who specialises in the study of virgins and virginity.

24

WAYS TO GO

- Every day, 155,000 people die.

- Clara Blandick, the actress who played Auntie Em in *The Wizard of Oz*, killed herself in 1962 by taking sleeping pills and placing a plastic bag tied over her head. She was 81 years old and suffering from crippling arthritis.

- Talk-show host Ray Combs hanged himself on the night of 2 June 1996 with bed sheets in his hospital room, while on a seventy-two-hour 'suicide watch'.

- Poet Hart Crane committed suicide by drowning in 1932. While on a steamship, he bid his fellow passengers farewell and jumped overboard.

- Eighty per cent of deaths in US casinos are caused by sudden heart attacks.

- Thich Quang Duc was the Buddhist monk who famously set himself on fire on the streets of Saigon to protest against government persecution of Buddhists in 1963.

- By January 1987, Pennsylvanian politician R. Budd Dwyer had been convicted of bribery and conspiracy in federal court and was about to be sentenced. He called a press conference and, in front of spectators and TV cameras, he shot himself in the mouth.

- Lillian Millicent Entwistle, actress, committed suicide in 1932 by jumping from the 'H' of the HOLLYWOOD sign.

- Joseph Goebbels, the Nazi politician, killed himself along with his wife and six children by poisoning while at Hitler's Berlin bunker in the final days of World War II.

- Another Nazi politician, Hermann Goering, poisoned himself hours before he was to be executed in 1946.

- Thirty people a year in Canada, and 300 people a year in the USA, are killed by trains.

- In 1998, more fast-food employees were murdered on the job than police officers.

- Singer Donny Hathaway committed suicide in 1979 by jumping from his room on the fifteenth floor of New York's Essex House Hotel.

- Amusement-park attendance goes up after a fatal accident. It seems many people want to travel on the same ride that killed someone.

- Rudolf Hess, the last surviving member of Adolf Hitler's inner circle, strangled himself in 1987 with an electrical cord aged 93 while he was the only prisoner in Spandau Prison, Berlin.

- Newscaster Chris Chubbuck shot herself in the head during a prime-time news broadcast on Florida TV station WXLT-TV in 1974. She died fourteen hours later.

- Michael Hutchence, INXS band member, hanged himself with a belt in his room in the Ritz-Carlton Hotel, in Sydney, Australia, in November 1997.

- Writer Eugene Izzi hanged himself from an eleventh-floor window on Michigan Avenue, Chicago, in 1996. It was possibly an accident brought about while he was researching a scene for a book.

- Jim Jones, the leader of a religious cult known as the People's Temple, killed himself in 1978 after watching more than 900 of his followers die from the ingestion of Flavor Aid laced with cyanide.

- Jesse William Lazear, a US physician, voluntarily infected himself with and died of yellow fever as part of Walter Reed's research in 1900.

- More people in the United States die during the first week of the month than during the last, an increase that may be a result of the abuse of substances purchased with benefit cheques that come at the beginning of each month.

- In 1933, student Kiyoko Matsumoto died by leaping into the 1,000ft (305m) crater of a volcano on the island of Oshima, Japan. Disturbingly, over the following few months 300 children emulated her act.

- The Japanese writer Yukio Mishima committed suicide in 1979 by disembowelment and decapitation in a protest against the westernisation of Japan. He killed himself in front of an assembly of all of the students that he was teaching at a university at that time.

- Former French president Francois Maurice Marie Mitterrand died in 1996 by intentionally terminating his treatment for prostate cancer.

- Roman Emperor Claudius Drusus Germanicus Nero stabbed himself with a sword in AD 68.

- Poet Sylvia Plath committed suicide in 1963 by inhaling gas from her oven.

- Margaret Mary Ray, a celebrity stalker, ended her life by kneeling in front of an oncoming train in 1998.

- In 399 BC, Socrates was required to drink hemlock to end his life after being found guilty of corrupting the youth of Athens.

- an Gogh shot himself in 1890 and died two days later.

- Horace Wells, who pioneered the use of anaesthesia in the 1840s, was arrested for spraying two women with sulphuric acid; he anaesthetised himself with chloroform and slashed his thigh open with a razor in 1848.

- Japanese and Chinese people die on the 4th of the month more often than any other date. The reason may be that they are 'scared to death' by the number four. The words 'four' and 'death' sound alike both in Chinese and Japanese.

- People with initials that spell out GOD or ACE are likely to live longer than people whose initials spell out words like APE, PIG, or RAT.

- Virginia Woolf committed suicide by drowning in 1941.

- In 1978, actor Gig Young shot and killed his wife of three weeks, Kim Schmidt, then shot himself.

- In 1941, writer Sherwood Anderson swallowed a toothpick at a cocktail party on an ocean liner bound for Brazil. He died of peritonitis.

- John Jacob Astor drowned with the 'unsinkable' *Titanic*.

- Attila the Hun bled to death from a nosebleed on his wedding night in AD 453.

- Alexander I of Greece died from blood poisoning in 1920 after being bitten by his gardener's pet monkey.

- Alexander II, Tsar of Russia from 1855 to 1881, was assassinated by a bomb that tore off his legs, ripped open his belly and mutilated his face.

- Jane Austen died of Addison's disease in 1817.

- Sir Francis Bacon died of pneumonia caught while he was experimenting with freezing a chicken by stuffing it with snow in 1626.

- In 1984, Velma Barfield became the first woman executed in the USA since the restoration of the death penalty in 1977.

- Thomas a Becket, Archbishop of Canterbury, was murdered in Canterbury cathedral in 1170 by four knights, supposedly on the orders of Henry II.

- Ludwig van Beethoven died in 1827 of cirrhosis of the liver.

- Actor John Belushi died of a drug overdose in 1982.

- Rainey Bethea was the last publicly executed criminal in the USA, and was hanged in 1936.

- Bridget Bishop was the first of the supposed witches hanged in Salem, Massachusetts. She was executed on 10 June 1692.

- Salvatore 'Sonny' Bono crashed into a tree while skiing in 1998.

- In 1982, Charles Brooks, Jr, became the first criminal to be executed in the USA by lethal injection.

- Calamity Jane died in 1903 from pneumonia following a bout of heavy drinking.

- Al Capone died of syphilis in 1947.

- Singer Karen Carpenter passed away from heart failure, caused by anorexia nervosa, at age 32 in 1983.

- Actor Jack Cassidy died in a fire, while asleep on the couch in his apartment, in 1976.

- In 1796, Catherine the Great, Empress of Russia, had a fatal stroke while going to the bathroom.

- Romanian president Nicolae Ceausescu was executed in 1989 by firing squad, on live television, along with his wife.

- Diver Sergei Chalibashvili attempted a three-and-a-half reverse somersault in the tuck position during the World University Games in 1983. On the way down, he smashed his head on the board and was knocked unconscious. He died after being in a coma for a week.

- Cleveland Indians baseball player Raymond Johnson Chapman died in 1920 after being struck on the head by a baseball pitch, becoming the only player ever killed as a result of a major-league baseball game.

- Conor Clapton, son of musician Eric Clapton, fell out of a fifty-third-floor window at the age of four in 1991.

- Cleopatra committed suicide by poison, supposedly from the bite of a venomous snake called an asp, in 30 BC.

- Nat 'King' Cole died of complications following surgery for lung cancer in 1965.

- Explorer Christopher Columbus died in 1506 from rheumatic heart disease.

- Actor Bob Crane was murdered in his hotel room in 1978.

- Singer Jim Croce perished in a plane crash in 1973. The plane crashed into a tree 200yd (183m) past the end of the runway while taking off from Natchitoches, Louisiana, Municipal Airport.

- Marie Curie, the chemist who discovered Radium, died of leukaemia, caused by exposure to radiation, in 1934.

- Mass murderer Jeffrey Dahmer was beaten to death with a broomstick by a fellow inmate at the Columbia Correctional Institute in 1994.

- Albert Dekker, actor and California legislator, was found dead, having suffocated by hanging from a shower curtain rod while being handcuffed and wearing women's lingerie, in 1968.

- According to a British law passed in 1845, attempting to commit suicide was a capital offence. Offenders could be hanged for trying.

- Edward Despard (and his six fellow conspirators) was the last criminal to be sentenced to be hung, drawn and quartered in England, in 1803. However his sentence was commuted to hanging and beheading.

- Trombonist Tommy Dorsey choked to death in his sleep in 1956, because of food that had lodged in his windpipe.

- Philanthropist Anthony J. Drexel III shot himself accidentally while showing off a new gun in his collection to his friends in 1893.

- Jessica Dubroff died aged 7 in 1996 in a plane crash, while attempting to become the youngest pilot to fly cross-country.

- Actress Isadora Duncan was killed in 1927 by accidental strangulation when her trademark long scarf caught in a car wheel.

- Singer Nelson Eddy suffered a stroke in 1965 while entertaining on stage in Miami Beach. He died the next day.

- Colombian footballer Andres Escobar was murdered by unknown assailants in 1994. It's possible that he was killed because of a goal he had accidentally scored for the USA in the World Cup.

- Jim Fixx, who helped to popularise jogging, died of a heart attack in 1984 after jogging.

- Actor Eric Fleming drowned in 1966 when his canoe capsized during the filming of a movie near the headwaters of the Amazon in the Haullaga River, Peru.

- Rajiv Gandhi, Prime Minister of India from 1984 until 1989, was assassinated in 1991 by a bomb hidden in a bouquet of flowers, which exploded in his hand.

- Judy Garland died from an overdose of barbiturates in 1969.

- Marvin Gaye was murdered on his birthday in 1984 by his father.

- John Glasscock, bassist with rock group Jethro Tull, died of a heart infection caused by an abscessed tooth in 1979.

- Russian figure skater Sergei Grinkov died of a heart attack during skating practice in 1995.

- American Henry Gunther was the last soldier killed in World War I.

- Alexander Hamilton, former US treasury secretary, was shot in 1804 by Vice-President Aaron Burr in a pistol duel near Weehawken, New Jersey.

- World War I spy Mata Hari was executed by firing squad in 1917; she refused a blindfold and threw a kiss to the executioners.

- Leslie Harvey, lead guitarist of the Glasgow band Stone the Crows, died after being electrocuted on stage at Swansea's Top Rank Ballroom on 3 May 1972.

- WWF wrestler Owen Hart died in 1999, while performing a stunt in the wrestling ring. He was being lowered into the ring by a cable, when he fell 70ft (21.3m) to his death, snapping his neck.

- In 1987, actress Elizabeth Hartman fell to her death from a fifth-floor window in a bizarre echo of the fate of a character in her 1966 movie *The Group*.

- Jockey Frank Hayes died from a heart attack during a race in New York in 1923. His horse, Sweet Kiss, won the race with Hayes still in the saddle, making him the only deceased jockey to win a race.

- Ernest Miller Hemingway committed suicide with a shotgun in 1961.

- Margaux Hemingway committed suicide in 1996 with an overdose of a sedative. She was the fifth person in her family to take their own life.

- Actor Jon-Erik Hexum playfully shot himself with a blank-loaded pistol on the set of TV spy show *Cover Up* in 1984. The concussion forced a chunk of his skull into his brain; he died six days later.

- Actor William Holden was found dead in his apartment in 1981. He had been drinking, and apparently fell, struck his head on an end table and bled to death.

- John C. Holmes, porn film star, died through complications arising from AIDS in 1988.

- Harry Houdini died of a ruptured appendix. He died on Halloween, 1926.

- Actor Leslie Howard (Ashley Wilkes in *Gone With the Wind*) was killed when his civilian plane was shot down by German fighter planes during World War II.

- Rock Hudson died of AIDS in 1985. He was the first major public figure to announce he had the disease.

- William Huskisson was the first person killed by a train. His death occurred in 1830 when he was attending the opening of the Liverpool–Manchester Railway. As he stepped on the track to meet the Duke of Wellington, Stephenson's *Rocket* hit him. He died later that day.

- Hal Mark Irish was killed in a leap from a hot-air balloon in what was believed to be the first US death from the thrill sport of bungee jumping. Irish fell more than 60ft (18.3m) to his death on 29 October 1991, after breaking loose from his bungee cord during a demonstration.

- German spy Josef Jakobs was the last person to be executed in the Tower of London, in 1941.

- Thomas Jefferson died of dysentery in 1826. He died on the fiftieth anniversary of the signing of The Declaration of Independence, and on the same day as John Adams.

- Olympic cyclist Knut Jensen died of a fractured skull during the 1960 Olympics in Rome. In the 93° heat, he collapsed from sunstroke and hit his head. He was one of only two athletes to die as a result of Olympic competition.

- Brian Jones, musician and one-time Rolling Stone, drowned in his swimming pool in 1969.

- Spanish bullfighter Joselito was fatally gored fighting his last bull in 1920.

- In 1967, cosmonaut Vladimir Komarov became the first person to die in space.

- Mary Jo Kopechne drowned when the car in which she was a passenger, driven by Senator Edward Kennedy, plunged off a bridge in 1969.

- Olympic runner Francisco Lázaro collapsed and died towards the end of the 1912 Olympic marathon in Stockholm.

- Brandon Lee was shot by a gun firing blanks, while filming the movie *The Crow* in 1993, and died later. His missing scenes were later filled in by computer animation.

- Bruce Lee died suddenly in 1973 from a swollen brain.

- Actress Jayne Mansfield died in a car accident in 1967. Her wig flew off in the impact, leading to rumours that she had been decapitated.

- In 1964, Mark Maples became the first person to be killed on a ride in Disneyland. He stood up while riding the Matterhorn Bobsleds and was thrown to his death.

- Bill Masterton, hockey player for Minnesota North Stars, fell over backwards and hit his head on the ice after being checked during a game against the Oakland Seals in 1968. His is the only death in pro-hockey during the modern era.

- Kenneth Allen McDuff is thought to be the only person ever freed from death row and then put back on it after killing again. He was executed by injection on 17 November 1998, in Huntsville, Texas.

- William McKinley, twenty-fifth US president, died of gangrene in 1901. He was shot by an assassin and his wounds were not properly dressed.

- Margaret Mitchell, author of *Gone With the Wind*, was crossing an Atlanta street on her way to the theatre in 1949 when she was hit by a speeding vehicle. She died of her injuries five days later.

- Actor Vic Morrow died in a helicopter accident on the set of *Twilight Zone – The Movie* in 1982.

- Laura Patterson, professional bungee jumper, was killed during rehearsals for the Super Bowl at the New Orleans Superdome in 1997. She died of massive head injuries.

- French highwayman Nicolas Jacques Pelletier was the first person beheaded with the guillotine, on 25 April 1792.

- Pope Johann XII was beaten to death in AD 963, aged 18, by the husband of a woman with whom he was having an affair.

- Grigory Rasputin was assassinated in 1916. He had been poisoned (with cyanide), shot (four times) and thrown into a river.

- John Augustus Roebling, designer of the Brooklyn Bridge, died of a tetanus infection in 1869 after having his leg crushed by a ferryboat while working on the bridge.

- Julius and Ethel Rosenberg were executed in the electric chair on 19 June 1953. They were the first husband-and-wife team executed in the USA and had been charged with espionage.

- Singer Selena was shot by the president of her fan club in 1995.

- Fencer Vladimir Smirnov died of brain damage. During a fencing match against Matthias Behr in 1982, Behr's foil snapped, pierced Smirnov's mask, penetrated his eyeball and entered his brain. Smirnov died nine days later.

- Actor Yoshiuki Takada died in 1985. The Sankai Juku Dance Company of Toyko had been performing *The Dance Of Birth And Death* on the side of Seattle's Mutual Life building when Takada's rope broke and he plunged six storeys to his death.

- Musician Tommy Tucker died of carbon tetrachloride poisoning sustained while he was finishing floors in his home in 1982.

- Sir William Wallace, Scottish rebel, was executed in 1305 by being hanged for a short time, taken down still breathing and having his bowels torn out and burned. His head was then struck off, and his body divided into quarters, in the punishment known as 'hanged, drawn and quartered'.

- In 1983, playwright Tennessee Williams choked to death on an eye-drop bottle cap that accidentally dropped into his mouth while he was using the spray.

25

LANGUAGE AND LITERATURE

- George Bernard Shaw was 29 years old when he lost his virginity to an elderly widow. This event traumatised him so much that he didn't have sex for another fifteen years.

- D.H. Lawrence was a prude and would only make love in the dark.

- Hans Christian Andersen was so terrified of being killed in a fire that he always carried a piece of rope with him so that he could escape any building that was alight.

- During the Chinese Cultural Revolution, all literary works by Charles Dickens and William Shakespeare were banned.

- At one time, Chinese books had the footnotes printed at the top of the page.

- Samuel Pepys loved to play the recorder.

- Playwright Richard Brinsley Sheridan was such a compulsive drinker that he would drink eau de cologne.

- When the British painter and poet Rossetti's wife died, he decided to bury his book of poems with her. Seven years later, however, he changed his mind and decided that he wanted them back, so he arranged for the grave to be opened, removed the book of poems and had them disinfected. They were later published to great acclaim.

- In Shakespeare's *Julius Caesar* there is a reference to a clock striking, but clocks did not appear until at least a thousand years after Caesar's death.

- Dostoyevsky and F. Scott Fitzgerald were both foot fetishists.

- John Milton received just £10 for *Paradise Lost* during his entire lifetime.

- American author Truman Capote would only ever write on yellow paper.

- William Prynne, the British pamphleteer, had his ears cut off because of his inflammatory publications.

- Anthony Trollope invented the pillar box.

- Jane Austen's book *Northanger Abbey* was originally called 'Susan'.

- William Ireland once forged a new version of *King Lear* and various other documents supposedly written by Shakespeare. He then wrote a story called 'Voltigern', which he claimed was a lost Shakespearean play. Many scholars examined the documents and declared them to be authentic, but when it was performed on stage it was so terrible that it was booed off.

- Charles Dickens would work himself up so much when he performed his own works on stage that he sometimes fainted.

- The *New York Times* once published an apology to a professor forty-nine years after his theories about travelling into space, which the paper had scoffed at, were proved to be correct.

- Winston Churchill wrote his book *The History of the English Speaking Peoples* when he was 82 years old.

- In Shakespeare's *The Winter's Tale*, he writes about a ship that has been wrecked off the coast of Bohemia, yet Bohemia has never had a coastline.

- Books that are made in the present day only have a life expectancy of about 100 years because the sulphuric acid in the wood-pulp paper rots rapidly.

- William Shakespeare's signature is worth millions of pounds, as there are only seven known specimens in the entire world.

- Robert Louis Stevenson was inspired by a real-life man, Deacon William Brodie, in devising his story *Dr Jekyll and Mr Hyde*. Brodie, a man who by day was a respected man of society and the Deacon of Edinburgh, and at night had a gambling habit, kept mistresses and took up burglary. He was hanged for his wrongdoings, but just beforehand he managed to slip a tube in his throat to prevent his neck from snapping. After the hanging, he was cut from the gallows and rushed to his home, where a private doctor attempted to revive him. However he could not be revived, although witnesses reported seeing him in Paris after his death.

- Ben Jonson was buried upright in Westminster Abbey's Poets' Corner because he died in debt and couldn't afford a proper gravesite.

- *Catch 22*, by Joseph Heller, was originally entitled 'Catch 18'.

- Robert Browning used Chianti to help wean his wife, Elizabeth Barrett Browning, from her addiction to laudanum.

- The first issue of *The Lady* magazine gave its readers detailed instructions on how to take a bath properly. Although *The Lady* was a woman's magazine, however, the article was illustrated with pictures of a man instead of a woman because of decency.

- There are more than 13,000 existing towns and cities in Great Britain that can claim to have been mentioned in the Domesday Book.

- Lord Byron, considered one of the most dashing and attractive men of his time, was overweight and had a club foot.

- There is approximately one library book for each and every person on Earth.

- After the death of her husband, poet Percy Shelley, Mary Shelley kept his heart wrapped up in silk until she died.

- Henrik Ibsen always had a picture of his arch-rival August Strindberg hanging over his desk so that it would make him work harder.

- In 1975, Indian poet Sri Chinmoy wrote 843 different poems in a single day.

- In Denmark, an author who wrote a book criticising the Swedes, who were at that time occupying his country, was arrested and then given the choice of either being beheaded or of eating his own words. He opted to eat his own words by boiling his book in broth and making a soup out of it.

- Charles Dickens' knowledge of Victorian life in London was mainly due to the fact that he would walk as much as 20 miles (32km) a night around the streets of London to cure his insomnia.

- The very first newspaper to use a perfumed page was the *Washington Daily News*, in 1937.

- Lord Byron had four pet geese that he took everywhere with him, even to social gatherings.

- George Orwell worked as a policeman before turning to a writing career.

- More books have been written about Jack the Ripper than any other murderer in the world.

- Charles Darwin thought that the 1,250 first-run copies of his book *The Origin of Species* were too many, but they sold out the first day of publication.

- *The Great Gatsby* was originally entitled 'Incident at West Egg'.

- Edgar Rice Burroughs wrote twenty-six Tarzan books without ever visiting Africa.

- Beatrix Potter, famous for writing and illustrating the Peter Rabbit children's books, actually had a squirrel shot to death in order to provide a model for the character Nutkin, and had a rabbit killed with chloroform to provide the model for Peter Rabbit. When she needed a model for a fox character, she had a recently killed fox skinned and boiled and the skeleton rebuilt.

- There is no living descendant of William Shakespeare.

- There have been copies made of the Holy Bible and the Koran that are small enough to fit in a walnut shell.

- In Turkey, during the 19th century, newspapers were severely censored, to such an extent that when the King and Queen of Turkey were murdered it was reported that they had both died of indigestion.

- The poet Shelley hated cats so much that he once tied one to the string of a kite during a thunderstorm to see if it would be electrocuted.

- Rudyard Kipling was fired as a reporter for the *San Francisco Examiner*. His dismissal letter stated, 'I'm sorry, Mr Kipling, but you just don't know how to use the English language. This isn't a kindergarten for amateur writers.'

- John Grisham is a sixteenth cousin of President Bill Clinton.

- John Ruskin was so appalled by the sight of his wife's pubic hair on their wedding night that he totally gave up sex.

- In literature, the average length of a sentence is around thirty-five words.

- *Don Quixote* has been translated into more languages than any book apart from the Bible.

- It is believed that the Greek poet Aeschylus was killed when a bird flying overhead dropped a tortoise and struck him on the head. The bird had mistaken his bald head for a rock that would crack the tortoise's shell on impact.

- There really was a Cyrano de Bergerac. He lived from about 1620 to 1655, had a big nose and duelled. He was also a science-fiction writer who was the first person in history to suggest that a rocket could carry someone into space.

- James Joyce suffered from stomach ulcers most of his life and believed that the key to good health was defecation, and if he didn't get to do so at least three times a day he would fret. He was so fascinated by stools that he once asked his wife, Nora, to go on a piece of paper while he lay down underneath her and observed her in the act.

- Ernest Hemingway drove an ambulance during World War I.

- After reading *Alice in Wonderland*, Queen Victoria sent a letter to author Lewis Carroll asking for another of his books to read. Carroll, who was also a brilliant mathematician, sent her a book on algebra.

- The young Charles Dickens wanted to be an actor.

- D.H. Lawrence enjoyed taking off his clothes and climbing mulberry trees.

- Emile Zola had two families with his wife and his mistress, and they all lived in the same house together.

- Leo Tolstoy's wife had to copy his manuscript of *War and Peace* by hand seven times.

- In the 17th century, there once lived a real-life Victor Frankenstein. Physician Konrad Johann Dippel set up a laboratory at Frankenstein Castle, near Darmstat, Germany, where he could pursue his hobby of alchemy. Like Victor Frankenstein of the novel, Dippel was also interested in the possibility of immortality through scientific means, and exhumed corpses from Frankenstein's cemetery to experiment on. When the townspeople started to suspect him of stealing corpses, he turned to trying the experiments on himself, and died drinking one of these formulas.

- A Sunday edition of the *New York Times* uses the equivalent of 63,000 trees.

- Wilfred Owen's brother found himself inexplicably depressed amid a ship's celebrations at the end of the World War I. He went down to his cabin and saw Wilfred sitting in his chair with a characteristic expression that turned to a broad smile before he disappeared. The poet had been killed on the last day of the war.

- The only other word with the same number of letters as pneumonoultramicroscopicsilicovolcanoconiosis is its plural.

- The longest place name currently in use is Taumatawhakatangihangakoauauotamateaturipukakapikimaungahoronukupokaiwhenuakitanatahu, a hill in New Zealand.

- Donald Duck's middle name is Fauntleroy.

- Steely Dan got their name from a sexual device depicted in William Burroughs's *The Naked Lunch*.

- The Ramses-brand condom is named after the great pharaoh Ramses II, who fathered over 160 children.

- The letters KGB stand for Komitet Gosudarstvennoi Bezopasnosti.

- Can you score 3 in this quiz?
  1. How long did the Hundred Years War last?
  2. Which country makes Panama hats?
  3. From which animals do we get catgut?
  4. In which month do Russians celebrate the October Revolution?
  5. What is a camel's hair brush made of?
  6. The Canary Islands in the Pacific are named after which animal?
  7. What was King George VI's first name?
  8. What colour is a purple finch?

  Now check your answers...
  1. 116 years.
  2. Ecuador.
  3. A range of animals including sheep and horse but NOT cats.
  4. November.
  5. A range of animals including squirrels, but NOT camels.
  6. Dogs (Canines).
  7. Albert.
  8. Crimson.

- Facetious and abstemious contain all the vowels in the correct order, as does arsenious, meaning 'containing arsenic'.

- To 'testify' was based on men in the Roman court swearing to a statement on their testicles.

- 'Strengths' is the longest word in the English language with just one vowel.

- Can you name three consecutive days without using the words Monday, Tuesday, Wednesday, Thursday, Friday, Saturday or Sunday?
  Yesterday, today and tomorrow.

- Quick eye exam... Count the number of 'f's in the following text:
  Finished files are the result of years of scientific study combined with the experience of years.

  How many? Three?
  Wrong, there are six. The brain cannot process the word 'of'.

- The first episode of *Joanie Loves Chachi* was the highest-rated US programme in the history of Korean television. 'Chachi' is Korean for 'penis'.

- 'Stewardesses' is the longest word that is typed with only the left hand.

- A 'blue moon' is the second full moon in a calendar month.

- There is a two-letter word that perhaps has more meaning than any other two-letter word… and that is 'UP'. If you are not confused after reading this, you must really be messed 'UP'.

  It's easy to understand UP, meaning towards the sky or at the top of the list but when we wake in the morning, why do we wake UP?

  At a meeting, why does a topic come UP?

  Why do we speak UP and why are the officers UP for election, and why is it UP to the secretary to write UP a report?

  We call UP our friends, we use paint to brighten UP a room, we polish UP the silver, we warm UP the leftovers and clean UP the kitchen. We lock UP the house and some guys fix UP the old car.

  People stir UP trouble, line UP for tickets, work UP an appetite and think UP excuses. To be dressed is one thing but to be dressed UP is special.

  A drain must be opened UP because it is stopped UP. We open UP a store in the morning but we close it UP at night. When it threatens to rain, we say it is clouding UP. When the sun comes out, we say it is clearing UP. When it rains, it wets UP the earth. When it doesn't rain for a while, things dry UP. We seem to be pretty mixed UP about UP.

  To be knowledgeable about the proper uses of UP, look UP the word in the dictionary. In a desk-size dictionary, UP takes UP almost a quarter of the page and definitions add UP to about thirty.

  If you are UP to it, you might try building UP a list of the many ways UP is used. It will take UP a lot of your time, but, if you don't give UP, you may wind UP with a hundred or more.

- Of the 17,677 words Shakespeare used in his plays, sonnets and narrative poems, he was the first to use over 1,700 of them.

- Who said English was easy?
  The bandage was wound around the wound.
  The farm was used to produce produce.
  The dump was so full that it had to refuse more refuse.
  We must polish the Polish furniture.
  He could lead if he would get the lead out.
  The soldier decided to desert his dessert in the desert.
  Since there is no time like the present, he thought it was time to present the present.
  A bass was painted on the head of the bass drum.
  When shot at, the dove dove into the bushes.
  I did not object to the object.
  The insurance was invalid for the invalid.
  There was a row among the oarsmen about how to row.
  They were too close to the door to close it.
  The buck does strange things when the does are present.
  A seamstress and a sewer fell down into a sewer line.
  To help with planting, the farmer taught his sow to sow.
  The wind was too strong for us to wind the sail.
  After a number of injections, my jaw got number.
  Upon seeing the tear in the painting, I shed a tear.
  I had to subject the subject to a series of tests.
  How can I intimate this to my most intimate friend?

- In Finnish, pääjääjää, meaning 'the main stayer', has fourteen dots in a row.

- And for an apt anagram finale:

  DORMITORY rearranged is DIRTY ROOM.

  PRESBYTERIAN rearranged is BEST IN PRAYER.

  ASTRONOMER rearranged is MOON STARER.

  DESPERATION rearranged is A ROPE ENDS IT.

  THE EYES rearranged is THEY SEE.

  GEORGE BUSH rearranged is HE BUGS GORE.

  THE MORSE CODE rearranged is HERE COME DOTS.

  SLOT MACHINES rearranged is CASH LOST IN 'EM.

  EVANGELIST rearranged is EVIL'S AGENT.

  ANIMOSITY rearranged is IS NO AMITY.

  ELECTION RESULTS rearranged is LIES – LET'S RECOUNT.

  SNOOZE ALARMS rearranged is ALAS! NO MORE ZS.

  A DECIMAL POINT rearranged is I'M A DOT IN PLACE.

  THE EARTHQUAKES rearranged is THAT QUEER SHAKE.

  ELEVEN PLUS TWO rearranged is TWELVE PLUS ONE.

  MOTHER-IN-LAW rearranged is WOMAN HITLER.

26

THE BEATLES

- Over the course of their career, The Beatles spent more than 400 weeks in the music charts.

- John Lennon was born to Julia Lennon after thirty hours of labour.

- Only 6 per cent of the autographs in circulation from members of The Beatles are estimated to be real.

- George Harrison had a 14.5in (36.8cm) neck.

- John Lennon was expelled from school for misbehaviour at age five.

- John and George always went to the dentist together because they were both scared of the experience.

- In the 1960s, Paul had three cats named Jesus, Mary and Joseph.

- John Lennon's mother taught him how to play an old Spanish guitar like a banjo.

- Paul used the working words 'scrambled eggs' before coming up with 'yesterday' while composing this song.

- Ringo cannot swim, except for a brief doggie-paddle.

- John Lennon was raised by his mother's sister, Mimi Smith.

- Brian Epstein made The Beatles have their hair cut short after he signed them in 1962.

- By age 15, John Lennon was a big fan of Elvis.

- In 1965, John's dad Alfred made a record called 'That's My Life'.

- It has been reported that John Lennon got a big thrill out of shoplifting when he was young.

- The Beatles featured two left-handed members: Paul, whom everyone saw holding his Hofner bass left-handed, and Ringo, whose left-handedness is at least partially to blame for his 'original' drumming style.

- John Lennon's mother died after being hit by a car.

- George was afraid of flying in an airplane.

- Six Brazilians were turned away by immigration officials at Heathrow Airport after failing a quiz about The Beatles. The group claimed to be travelling to the UK for Liverpool's Mathew Street Festival, which celebrates the lives of the Fab Four.

- John used to envy his cousin Stanley for his Meccano set.

- An American firm wrote to The Beatles asking if they could market their bath water at a dollar a bottle. They refused the offer.

- 'Dear Prudence' was written about Mia Farrow's sister, Prudence. Grown withdrawn from prolonged meditation, at one point she wouldn't leave her chalet to join the rest of the company at a religious retreat in Rishikesh, India.

- Later in life, John Lennon discovered that he had dyslexia.

- Throughout their career, Ringo received far more fan mail than any of the other Beatles.

- 'Lovely Rita' was inspired by Paul's parking ticket from a female warden on Abbey Road in London.

- In 1962, a Merseyside newspaper held a contest to see who was the biggest band in Liverpool. One of the main reasons that The Beatles won was because they called in posing as different people and voted for themselves.

- In 1996, Ringo Starr appeared in a Japanese advertisement for apple sauce, which coincidentally is what 'Ringo' means in Japanese.

- John Lennon named his band The Beatles after Buddy Holly's 'Crickets'.

- Paul was regularly the first Beatle dressed for performances.

- John Lennon hated the band The Hollies.

- George Harrison didn't like The Hollies either, and had a specific distaste for Graham Nash.

- Without glasses, John Lennon was legally blind.

- At the end of 'A Day in the Life', an ultrasonic whistle, audible only to dogs, was recorded by Paul McCartney for his sheepdog.

- At exactly 2.58 seconds into 'Hey Jude', you can hear John say in the background 'Fucking hell'.

- John Lennon's favourite food was cornflakes.

- Paul and Pete Best were arrested in Hamburg because they stuck a condom to the wall and set it on fire.

- The song 'A Day in the Life' ends with a chord that sustains for around forty seconds.

27

FOOD AND DRINK

- Americans consume about 10lb (4.5kg), or 160 bowls, of cereal per person each year. But America ranks only fourth in per capita cereal consumption. Ireland ranks first, England is second and Australia third.

- The biggest pumpkin in the world weighed 1,337.6lb (606.7kg).

- Bubble gum and candy floss were invented by dentists.

- The longest sausage made in Australia was 6.9 miles (11.1km) long.

- Before Prohibition, the most common form of drinking beer at home was to sup it out of a bucket filled at a local pub or brewery.

- In the 19th century, people believed that gin could cure stomach problems.

- Fifty-eight per cent of American school kids say pizza is their favourite cafeteria food.

- McDonald's calls frequent buyers of their food 'heavy users'.

- All fruits have three layers: exocarp (skin), mesocarp (pulp) and endocarp (pit).

- The chicken is one of the few things that can be eaten before it's born and after it's dead.

- Thirty-two out of thirty-three samples of well-known brands of milk purchased in Los Angeles and Orange counties in California contained trace amounts of perchlorate, which is the explosive component in rocket fuel.

- As a nation, Britain eats nearly 10 billion eggs a year; that's 26 million every day, which placed end to end would reach from the Earth to the Moon.

- Hershey's Kisses are called that because the machine that makes them looks like it's kissing the conveyor belt.

- Chocolate contains phenyl ethylamine, the same chemical that your brain produces when you fall in love.

- If you place a T-bone steak in a bowl of Coke, it will be gone in two days.

- The heaviest hen's egg weighed 16oz (454g) – that's six times heavier than an average large egg from the shops.

- Pour a can of Coca-Cola into the toilet bowl and let the 'real thing' sit for one hour, then flush clean. The citric acid in Coke removes stains from vitreous china.

- There is a bar in London that sells vaporised vodka, which is inhaled instead of sipped.

- Before 1989, the dark-brown Smartie had a plain-chocolate centre and the light-brown Smartie tasted of coffee.

- To cure hangovers, boozers in the Middle Ages would down a plate of bitter almonds and dried eels after drinking.

- The world's oldest piece of chewing gum is 9,000 years old.

- The world's largest omelette was made in Madrid from 5,000 eggs by chef Carlos Fernandez. It weighed 1,320lb (598kg).

- The average American drinks 3.4 cups of coffee a day.

- The peach was the first fruit eaten on the Moon.

- In the USA, 49 per cent of Americans start each morning with a bowl of cereal, 30 per cent eat toast, 28 per cent eat eggs, 28 per cent have coffee, 17 per cent have hot cereal and fewer than 10 per cent have pancakes, sausage, bagels or French toast.

- In Outer Mongolia, drunks slurp down a pickled sheep's eye in tomato juice to stave off hangovers.

- The Ancient Greeks slaughtered a sheep and ate its entrails while they were still warm.

- The eight original colours of Smarties – red, orange, yellow, green, mauve, pink, light-brown and dark-brown – remained the same until the replacement of the light-brown one with a blue Smartie following a successful promotion in 1989. There have since been complaints that the colouring made children hyperactive.

- The Ancient Romans considered flamingo tongues a great delicacy. The birds' existence was threatened by hunters, so the Romans made a law making it illegal to hunt them, but it failed.

- In Ancient Rome, it was considered a sin to eat the flesh of a woodpecker.

- Also in Ancient Rome, oysters were so highly prized that they were sold for their weight in gold.

- The early American Indians of the south-western United States only ate the organs of the animals they hunted for food, and left the muscles for predatory animals. Their meat-eating habits were changed by European influences.

- The Ancient Greeks considered parsley too sacred to eat, while Romans served it as a garnish and to improve the taste of food. They believed it had special powers and would keep them sober.

- Peas will lose their bright-green colour if cooked in a covered pot with acidic ingredients, such as lemon juice, wine, or tomatoes.

- Paper can be made from asparagus.

- In the Middle East, and later in Europe, doctors blamed the aubergine for all sorts of things, from epilepsy to cancer. In the 5th century, Chinese women made a black dye from the aubergine skins to stain and polish their teeth, while some people in medieval Europe considered it an aphrodisiac.

- The Egyptians ate mustard by tossing the seeds into their mouths while chewing meat.

- Pears ripen better off the tree, and they ripen from the inside out.

- The first bottles of Coca-Cola sold for a mere 3 pence per bottle in 1899.

- Pecan crops need a freeze to help loosen the nuts from their shells.

- In ancient times, parsley wreaths were used to ward off drunkenness.

- In the Middle Ages, sugar was a treasured luxury, costing nine times as much as milk.

- The can opener was invented forty-eight years after cans were introduced.

- The first beer brewed in England was made by the Picts in about 250 BC. The beverage was made from heather and may have had hallucinogenic properties.

- In early 1999, General Mills launched an 'Around the World Event' promotion with internationally known marshmallow shapes in its Lucky Charms cereal. These shapes included a purple Liberty Bell, a pink-and-white Leaning Tower of Pisa, a green-and-yellow torch, a gold pyramid, a blue Eiffel Tower, an orange Golden Gate Bridge, a green-and-white Alps, and a red-and-white Big Ben clock.

- The first-known pizza shop, Port Alba in Naples, opened in 1830 and is still going today.

- About 27 per cent of food in developed countries is thrown away each year.

- Onions, apples and potatoes all have the same taste. The differences in flavour are caused by their smell.

- With two forks and a charge, a pickle will emit light.

- Tibetans drink tea made with salt and rancid yak butter.

- Nachos are the food most craved by American mothers-to-be.

- The average French citizen eats 500 snails a year.

- One pound (0.45kg) of tea can make nearly 300 cups to drink.

- In the Middle Ages, chicken soup was believed to be an aphrodisiac.

- Bananas are consistently the number-one subject of complaint of grocery shoppers. Most people complain when bananas are overripe or even freckled. The fact is that spotted bananas are sweeter, with a sugar content of more than 20 per cent, compared with 3 per cent in a green banana.

- Milk is considered to be a food and not a beverage.

- The cashew nut, in its natural state, contains poisonous oil. Roasting removes the oil and makes the nuts safe to eat.

- The strawberry is the only agricultural product that bears its seeds on the outside.

- Cheese is the oldest of all man-made foods.

- There is more alcohol in mouthwash than in wine.

- Four per cent of the food you eat will be eaten in front of a refrigerator with its door open.

- Tomatoes with a strawberry inside have been successfully grown.

- There is a wild edible plant called hernandulcin that is a thousand times sweeter than sugar.

- The boysenberry is a mixture of the blackberry, loganberry and raspberry.

- The carob can be used to replace chocolate in cooking.

- The word 'whisky' comes from the Gaelic *uisge beatha*, meaning 'water of life'.

- The globe artichoke belongs to the daisy family.

- The turnip originated in Greece.

- Grasshoppers are the most popular insect snack in some parts of the world.

- Corn is the only cereal crop with American origins.

- Kohlrabi is a cross between a cabbage and a turnip.

- Tea bags were first launched in the 1920s.

- One in five chickens in the supermarket are infected with Campylobacter, a bacterium that can cause food poisoning.

- Swiss steak, chop suey, Russian dressing and the hamburger all originated in the USA.

- Tequila is made from the root of the Blue Agave cactus.

- Jeff Chiplis, from Cleveland, has a collection of over 10,000 carrot items.

- The Agen plum, which became the basis of the US prune industry, was first planted in California in 1856.

- The longest carrot recorded, in 1996, was 16ft 10.5in (5.2m).

- The Californian grape and wine industries were started by Count Agoston Haraszthy de Moksa, who planted Tokay, Zinfandel and Shiraz varieties from his native Hungary in Buena Vista in 1857.

- The colour of a chilli is no indication of its spiciness, but size usually is – the smaller the pepper, the hotter it is.

- The daughter of confectioner Leo Hirschfield is commemorated in the name of the sweet he invented. Although his daughter's real name was Clara, she went by the nickname 'Tootsie' and, in her honour, her doting father named his chewy chocolate logs 'Tootsie Rolls'.

- The heaviest carrot recorded in the world, in 1998, was a single root mass weighing 18.985lb (8.611kg).

- Potato chips were invented in Saratoga Springs in 1853 by chef George Crum. They were a mocking response to a patron who complained that his French fries were too thick.

- As much as 50 gallons (227.3 litres) of maple sap are used to make a single gallon (4.5 litres) of maple sugar.

- The difference between apple juice and apple cider is that the juice is pasteurised and the cider is not.

- The dye used to stamp the grade on meat is edible and is made from grape skins.

- The English word 'soup' comes from the Middle Ages word 'sop', which means a slice of bread over which roast drippings were poured. The first archaeological evidence of soup being consumed dates back to 6000 BC, with the main ingredient being hippopotamus bones!

- Pearls melt in vinegar.

- The US FDA allows an average of thirty or more insect fragments and one or more rodent hairs per 3.5oz (100g) of peanut butter.

- The Greek foot soldiers who hid in the Trojan Horse were said to have consumed ample quantities of raw carrots to make their bowels inactive.

- The city of Denver in Colorado claims to have invented the cheeseburger.

- Americans eat an average of 18lb (8.2kg) of fresh apples each year. The most popular variety in the United States is the Red Delicious.

- Watermelon, considered one of America's favourite fruits, is really a vegetable (*Citrullus lanatus*). Cousin to the cucumber and kin to the gourd, watermelons can range in size from 7lb to 100lb (3.2–45.4kg).

- In early Celtic literature, the carrot is referred to as the 'Honey Underground'!

- The first ring doughnuts were produced in 1847 by a 15-year-old baker's apprentice, Hanson Gregory, who knocked the soggy centre out of a fried doughnut.

- The Japanese word for carrot is *ninjin*.

- The fungi called truffles can cost £450 to £850 per pound. They are sniffed out by female pigs, which detect a compound that is also in the saliva of male pigs. The same chemical is found in the sweat of human males.

- The hamburger was invented in 1900 by Louis Lassen. He ground beef, broiled it and served it between two pieces of toast.

- The herring is the most widely eaten fish in the world. Nutritionally, its fuel value is equal to that of a beefsteak.

- The best-selling chocolate bar in Russia is Snickers.

- It is alleged that Nero ate the last remaining root of the ancient carrot 'sylphion'.

- The ice-cream soda was invented in 1874 by Robert Green. He was serving a mixture of syrup, sweet cream and carbonated water at a celebration in Philadelphia. He ran out of cream and substituted ice cream.

- The largest item on any menu in the world is probably the roast camel, sometimes served at Bedouin wedding feasts. The camel is stuffed with a sheep's carcass, which is stuffed with chickens, which are stuffed with fish, which are stuffed with eggs.

- People in Sweden eat about 2.2lb (1kg) of ham per person each Christmas.

- The largest living organism ever found is a honey mushroom (*Armillaria ostoyae*). It covers 3.4 miles^2 (8.8km^2) of land in the Blue Mountains of eastern Oregon, and it's still growing.

- Popcorn was invented by the American Indians.

- Potatoes, pineapples and pumpkins originate from Peru.

- The vintage date on a bottle of wine indicates the year the grapes were picked, not the year of bottling.

- Milk delivered to the store today was in the cow two days ago.

- There is a carrot-pie flavour jelly bean.

- The white potato originated in the Andes Mountains and was probably brought to Britain by Sir Francis Drake in about 1586.

- The world's first chocolate sweet was produced in 1828 by Dutch chocolate-maker Conrad J. van Houten. He pressed the fat from roasted cacao beans to produce cocoa butter, to which he added cocoa powder and sugar.

- Carrots have the highest vitamin A content of all vegetables.

- The world's deadliest mushroom is the *Amanita phalloides*, aka the death cap. The five different poisons contained by the mushroom cause diarrhoea and vomiting within six to twelve hours of ingestion. This is followed by damage to the liver, kidneys and central nervous system – and, in the majority of cases, coma and death.

- Van Camp's Pork and Beans were a staple food for Union soldiers in the American Civil War.

- Vanilla is the extract of fermented and dried pods of several species of orchids.

- Over 1,200 varieties of watermelon are grown in ninety-six countries worldwide. There are about 200 varieties of watermelon throughout the USA.

- There are more than 15,000 different kinds of rice.

- When Catherine de Medici married Henry II of France in 1533, she brought forks with her, as well as several master Florentine cooks. Foods never before seen in France were soon being served using utensils instead of fingers or daggers. She is said to have introduced spinach, used in dishes 'à la Florentine', as well as aspics, sweetbreads, artichoke hearts, truffles, liver crépinettes, quenelles of poultry, macaroons, ice cream and zabagliones.

- When honey is swallowed, it enters the blood stream within a period of 20 minutes.

- Carrots are not always orange and can also be found in purple, white, red or yellow colours.

- When potatoes first appeared in Europe in the 17th century, it was thought that they were disgusting, and they were blamed for starting outbreaks of leprosy and syphilis.

- As late as 1720 in America, eating potatoes was believed to shorten a person's life.

- The white part of an egg is called the albumen.

- When Swiss cheese ferments, a bacterial action generates gas. As the gas is liberated, it bubbles through the cheese leaving holes. Cheese-makers call them 'eyes'.

- Carrots were first grown as a medicine, not a food.

- Although the combination of chilli peppers and oregano for seasoning has been traced to the Ancient Aztecs, the present blend is said to be the invention of early Texans. Chilli powder today is typically a blend of dried chillies, garlic powder, red peppers, oregano, and cumin.

- Fresh herbs can be preserved by chopping them up and freezing them in ice-cube trays.

- A 'black cow' is a chocolate soda with chocolate ice cream.

- In South Africa, termites are often roasted and eaten by the handful, like pretzels or popcorn.

- Table salt is the only commodity that hasn't risen dramatically in price in the last 150 years.

- The milk of reindeer has more fat than cow milk.

- Grapes explode when you put them in the microwave.

- The Chinese used to open shrimp by flaying the shells with bamboo poles. Until a few years ago, in factories where dried shrimp were being prepared, 'shrimp dancers' were hired to tramp on the shells with special shoes.

- Native Americans never actually ate turkey; killing such a timid bird was thought to indicate laziness.

- Pigturducken is a pig stuffed with a turkey, which is stuffed with a chicken, then deep fried in oil.

- Americans eat more than 22lb (10kg) of tomatoes every year. More than half this amount is eaten in the form of ketchup and tomato sauce.

- The only food that does not spoil is honey.

- In Suffolk, carrots were formerly given as a remedy for preserving and restoring the wind of horses.

- A turkey should never be carved until it has been out of the oven for at least thirty minutes. This permits the inner cooking to subside and the internal meat juices to stop running. Once the meat sets, it's easier to carve clean, neat slices.

- Ancient Greeks and Romans believed asparagus had medicinal qualities that helped prevent bee stings and relieve toothaches.

- Worcestershire sauce is basically an anchovy ketchup.

- When tea was first introduced in the American colonies, many housewives, in their ignorance, served the tea leaves with sugar or syrup after throwing away the water in which they had been boiled.

- Worldwide consumption of pork exceeds that of any other type of meat.

- From 1lb (0.45kg) of carrots, we can obtain 1oz and 11 grains (29g) of sugar.

- During the Middle Ages, almost all beef, pork, mutton and chicken was chopped finely. Forks were unknown at the time and the knife was a kitchen utensil rather than a piece of tableware.

- There are 2 million different combinations of sandwiches that can be created from a Subway menu.

- The wheat that produces a 1lb (0.45kg) loaf of bread requires 2 tons (2.03 tonnes) of water to grow.

- There are more than 7,000 varieties of apples grown in the world. The apples from one tree can fill twenty boxes every year. Each box weighs an average of 42lb (19kg).

- Soy milk, the liquid left after beans have been crushed in hot water and strained, is a favourite beverage in the East. In Hong Kong, soy milk is as popular as Coca-Cola is in the USA.

- There are professional tea tasters as well as wine tasters.

- There are thousands of varieties of shrimp, but most are so tiny that they are more likely to be eaten by whales than people. Of the several hundred around the world that people do eat, only a dozen or so appear with any regularity in Western fish markets.

- Thin-skinned lemons are the juiciest.

- Though most people think of salt as a seasoning, only 5lb (2.3kg) out of every 100lb (45.4kg) produced each year gets to the dinner table.

- Goat's milk is used to produce Roquefort cheese.

- The Anglo-Saxons included carrots as an ingredient in a medicinal drink to guard against the Devil and insanity.

- Sixty cows can produce a ton of milk a day.

- A mere 2 per cent drop in body water can trigger fuzzy short-term memory, trouble with basic maths and difficulty focusing on the computer screen or on a printed page.

- It takes more than 500 peanuts to make one 12oz (0.3kg) jar of peanut butter.

- In Australia, the number-one topping for pizza is eggs. The favourite topping in Chile is mussels and clams, while in the United States it's pepperoni.

- Spinach is native to Iran and didn't spread to other parts of the world until the beginning of the Christian era.

- When American children were asked what they would like on their hot dogs if their mums weren't watching, 25 per cent said they would prefer chocolate sauce.

- The Chinese developed the custom of using chopsticks to eat because they didn't need anything resembling a knife and fork at the table: they cut up food into bite-sized pieces in the kitchen before serving it. This stemmed from their belief that bringing meat to the table in any form resembling an animal was uncivilised and that it was also inhospitable to ask a guest to cut food while eating.

- Camel's milk doesn't curdle.

- The dark meat on a roast turkey has more calories than the white meat.

- The most widely eaten fruit in America is the banana.

- Beetles taste like apples, wasps taste like pine nuts and worms taste like fried bacon.

- The original recipe for margarine was milk, lard and sheep's stomach lining.

- Most common food plants contain natural poisons. Carrots, for example, contain carotatoxin, myristicin, isoflavones and nitrates.

- Chocolate chip cookies are the baked goods most likely to cause tooth decay. Pies, un-iced cake and doughnuts are less harmful to the teeth.

- Most nuts will remain fresh for a year, if kept in their shells.

- The Uruguayan Army once won a sea battle using Edam cheeses as cannonballs.

- In 1987 a 1,400-year-old lump of still-edible cheese was unearthed in Ireland.

- Buttered bread was invented by the astronomer Copernicus. He was trying to find a cure for the plague at the time.

- In 1983, a Japanese artist made a copy of *The Mona Lisa* completely out of toast.

- Washing a chicken egg will strip it of natural coatings that keep out bacteria; it will rot very quickly thereafter.

- During Thanksgiving and the Super Bowl, food consumption is larger than on any other day in the USA.

- A bee produces only one-twelfth of a teaspoon of honey during its entire lifetime.

- There are over 225 different kinds of bread in Germany.

- Humans are the only species that drink milk from the mothers of other species.

- Preliminary research indicates that eight to ten glasses of water a day could significantly ease back and joint pain for up to 80 per cent of sufferers.

- China produces more apples than the rest of the world put together.

- Even mild dehydration will slow down one's metabolism by as much as 3 per cent.

- It is illegal to import pork products into Yemen, with a maximum punishment of death.

- A single sausage measuring 5,917ft (1,803.5m) in length was cooked in Barcelona, Spain, on 22 September 1986.

- Over 180 million Cadbury's Creme Eggs are sold between January and Easter each year.

- Caesar salad has nothing to do with any of the Caesars. It was first concocted in a bar in Tijuana, Mexico, in the 1920s.

28

Crime and Criminals

- You can be imprisoned for not voting in Fiji, Chile and Egypt — at least in theory.

- 0.7 per cent of Americans are currently in prison.

- Frank Wathernam was the last prisoner to leave Alcatraz Prison, on 21 March 1963.

- Quebec City, Canada, has about as much street crime as Disney World.

- Police in Finland issued a £116,000 fine to a man who was caught exceeding a 25mph (40km/h) speed limit.

- An Argentinian burglar who got stuck in a chimney was ordered to rebuild it himself.

- Russian police stopped women drivers to hand out flowers instead of speeding tickets to mark International Women's Day.

- The average length for a criminal sentence in Colombia is 137 years.

- Police officers in India have invited the public to post jokes about them in a bid to improve the image of the force.

- Two-thirds of the world's kidnappings occur in Colombia.

- Al Capone's older brother Vince was a policeman in Nebraska.

- A drug-sniffer dog working at a UK prison has received death threats because it's so good at its job.

- More than 400 policemen in a Mexican city have been ordered to go on a diet.

- A German man faced up to ten years in a Turkish prison because his 9-year-old son picked up pebbles from a beach. He was charged with smuggling archaeologically valuable national treasures.

- A Czech prisoner locked up on theft charges was freed and allowed to go back home to his wife after getting a permanent erection.

- A robber was jailed for twelve years in Illinois – despite singing to the court in an effort to get a reduced sentence.

- America puts more of its citizens in prison than any other nation.

- An Argentinian man was cleared of urinating on the steps of a museum because they were already dirty.

- The average number of cars stolen per day in Mexico City is 124.

- A magician's rabbit was 'liberated' mid-act by a suspected animal-rights activist in Brighton.

- The prisoners of a small Brazilian jail are paying the bills in exchange for better conditions.

- The United States has 5 per cent of the world's population, but 25 per cent of the world's prison population.

- An Indian police chief is asking bank managers to feed stray dogs to encourage them to guard their premises.

- Two-thirds of the world's executions occur in China.

- British customs officers have arrested an air passenger carrying more than her own weight in edible snails.

- Post-office staff in Malaysia once found 21,000 undelivered letters stored in an apartment that used to be rented out by one of their colleagues.

- A Texas prisoner who threw his faeces over a prison officer was given an additional fifty years in prison for harassment.

- Germany has drawn up blueprints for Europe's first jail specifically to house OAPs – old-aged prisoners.

- Classical music and aromatherapy are being used in a Mexican jail to try to calm down some of the most dangerous prisoners.

- The Belgian news agency Belga reported that a man suspected of robbing a jewellery store in Liège said he couldn't have done it because he was busy breaking into a school at the same time. Police then arrested him for breaking into the school.

- A couple caught on camera robbing a store could not be identified until the police reviewed the security tape. The woman had filled out an entry form for a free trip prior to robbing the store.

- A man was arrested and charged with the robbery of vending machines. The man posted his bail entirely in quarters.

- A Romanian man jailed four years earlier for burgling a wealthy neighbour's flat was caught by the same policeman robbing the same property hours after he was released from jail.

- In a stroke of irony, the maximum-security prison in St Albans, Vermont, was responsible in 1996 for sending out public-relations brochures enticing tourists to visit Vermont.

- Wayne Black, a suspected thief, had his name tattooed across his forehead. When confronted by police, Black insisted he wasn't Wayne Black. To prove it, he stood in front of a mirror and insisted he was Kcalb Enyaw.

- Overweight policemen in the Philippines were ordered to take an anti-obesity drug to help them slim down.

- A Bolivian man spent two months in jail charged with smuggling cocaine before tests revealed he had in fact been carrying talcum powder.

- In Texas, an anti-crime law requires criminals to give their victims twenty-four hours' notice, either orally or in writing, and to explain the nature of the crime to be committed.

- A gentleman mugger in Austria was jailed despite his elderly victim's pleas for him to be let off because he was so polite.

- The prison system is the largest supplier of mental-health services in America, with 250,000 Americans with mental illness living there.

- In Bangladesh, kids as young as 15 can be jailed for cheating in their finals.

- Former enemies America and Russia now have a great deal in common – they both lead the world in locking people up.

- You're sixty-six times more likely to be prosecuted in the USA than in France.

- The Chico, California, City Council enacted a ban on nuclear weapons, setting a £300 fine for anyone detonating one within city limits.

- In September 2004, a Minnesota state trooper issued a speeding ticket to a motorcyclist who was clocked at 205mph (330km/h).

- A Chinese truck driver was arrested for kidnapping two toll station operators to save the equivalent of 70 pence.

- In Ancient Egypt, killing a cat was a crime punishable by death.

- In Hong Kong, a betrayed wife is legally allowed to kill her adulterous husband, but may only do so with her bare hands.

- Men in Costa Rica can now be sent to prison for trying to chat up women.

- Russians reportedly pay out more than £19 billion a year in bribes, with the average person paying almost a tenth of their wages in bribes.

- In Ancient Greece, an adulterous male was sometimes punished by the removal of his pubic hair and the insertion of a large radish into his rectum.

- In Alaska, it is legal to shoot bears. However, waking a sleeping bear for the purpose of taking a photograph is prohibited.

- A drunken German who bought three hand grenades at a flea market in Bosnia was arrested after throwing one out of the window to see whether it worked.

- Duelling is legal in Paraguay as long as both parties are registered blood donors.

- Police in Canada impounded an ambulance after arresting the driver for trying to pick up a prostitute.

- It is a criminal offence to drive around in a dirty car in Russia.

- A prisoner in Decatur, Georgia, fell through the roof of a courthouse and into a judge's chambers while trying to escape.

- A woman was chewing what was left of her chocolate bar when she entered a Metro station in Washington, DC. She was arrested and handcuffed; eating is prohibited in Metro stations.

- A sketch of a burglar drawn by an 11-year-old schoolboy was so good that it helped Austrian police to catch the thief less than an hour later.

- Four jails in Brazil are using geese to help prevent prisoners from escaping.

- To help reduce budget deficits, several states have begun reducing the amount of food served to prison inmates. In Texas, the number of daily calories served to prisoners was cut by 300, saving the state £3,000,000 per year.

- Hondas and Toyotas are the most frequently stolen passenger cars because they have parts that can be readily exchanged between model years without a problem.

29

DOCTORS' NOTES

- Patient has chest pain if she lies on her left side for over a year.

- The patient was examined, X-rated and sent home.

- On the second day the knee was better, and on the third day it disappeared.

- The patient is tearful and crying constantly. She also appears to be depressed.

- The patient has been depressed since she began seeing me in 1993.

- Discharge status: alive but without my permission.

- Healthy appearing decrepit 69-year-old male, mentally alert but forgetful.

- The patient refused autopsy.

- The patient has no previous history of suicides.

- The baby was delivered, the cord clamped and cut, and handed to the paediatrician, who breathed and cried immediately.

- The patient has left white blood cells at another hospital.

- She is numb from her toes down.

- The patient had waffles for breakfast and anorexia for lunch.

- The skin was moist and dry.

- Occasional, constant, infrequent headaches.

- The patient lives at home with his mother, father and pet turtle, who is presently enrolled in day care three times a week.

- The patient's past medical history has been remarkably insignificant with only a 40-pound weight gain in the past three days.

- The pelvic examination will be done later on the floor.

- Patient was released to outpatient department without dressing.

- The patient expired on the floor uneventfully.

- The patient was alert and unresponsive.

- Examination reveals a well-developed male lying in bed with his family in no distress.

- Rectal examination revealed a normal-size thyroid.

- She stated that she had been constipated for most of her life until she got a divorce.

- I saw your patient today, who is still under our car for physical therapy.

- Both breasts are equal and reactive to light and accommodation.

- Examination of genitalia reveals that he is circus sized.

- The lab test indicated abnormal lover function.

- The patient was to have a bowel resection. However, he took a job as a stockbroker instead.

- Skin: somewhat pale but present.

- The patient was seen in consultation by Dr Blank, who felt we should sit on the abdomen and I agree.

- Large brown stool ambulating in the hall.

- Coming from Detroit, this man has no children.

- Patient has two teenage children, but no other abnormalities.

- By the time he was admitted, his rapid heart had stopped, and he was feeling better.

- I have suggested that he loosen his pants before standing, and then, when he stands with the help of his wife, they should fall to the floor.

- The patient will need disposition, and therefore we will get Dr Blank to dispose of him.

- She slipped on the ice and apparently her legs went in separate directions in early December.

- The patient experienced sudden onset of severe shortness of breath with a picture of acute pulmonary oedema at home while having sex, which gradually deteriorated in the emergency room.

- The patient was in his usual state of good health until his airplane ran out of gas and crashed.

- Since she can't get pregnant with her husband, I thought you would like to work her up.

- The bugs that grew out of her urine were cultured in Casualty and are not available. I WILL FIND THEM!!!

- Many years ago, the patient had frostbite of the right shoe.

- The patient left the hospital feeling much better except for her original complaints.

- When she fainted, her eyes rolled around the room.

30

MISCELLANEOUS

- John C. Holmes, a 1970s porn star, had a penis that measured 13.5in (34.3cm) long.

- Men are more likely than women to carry sexually transmitted diseases.

- In 1978, Ralph Lauren created the 'prairie look' with denim skirts worn over white petticoats.

- Ten books on a shelf can be arranged in 3,628,800 different ways.

- Bright yellow and bright blue are the safest and most visible colours to paint cars.

- Nearly 100 per cent of the dirt in the average home originated from outside – 80 per cent of that comes in on people, stuck to their clothes and their feet.

- The odds against a person being struck by a celestial stone—
  a meteorite—are 10 trillion to 1.

- The world's most valuable Barbie doll is the 40th Anniversary
  De Beers customised doll that was worth £455,000 and wore
  22-carat diamonds. At around £10,000, the second most
  valuable Barbie is an original prototype. Next, if in mint or
  never-removed-from-box condition, is a brunette 1959
  ponytail Barbie that may fetch up to £5,250.

- The odds against flipping a coin head's up ten times in a row
  are 1,023 to 1.

- On average, more animals are killed by motorists than by
  hunters with guns.

- Monday is the favoured day for people to commit suicide.

- The odds against hitting the jackpot on a slot machine are
  889 to 1.

- Deep-sea diving from oilrigs is among the world's most
  hazardous occupations, averaging a death rate of 1 out of
  every 100 workers each year.

- The manuals used for launching the first Space Shuttle
  would, if all the copies were piled on one another, reach
  almost twice the height of Chicago's Sears Tower.

- Virgin Atlantic discovered that it takes in an average of 10 pence per passenger per flight in loose change found in the plane's seats. If that figure holds for the approximate 320 million people who fly from one country to another worldwide each year the total is about £32 million. Lost coins on domestic flights don't amount to much, however. Chicago O'Hare cleaning crews said they found only about 3 pence per flight. It is suggested that more travellers to other countries 'accidentally' leave foreign coins behind to avoid dealing with them once they get home.

- Car accidents rise 10 per cent during the first week of daylight saving time.

- Half of all murders are committed with handguns.

- There are forty-eight teaspoons in a cup: three teaspoons make a tablespoon and sixteen tablespoons make a cup.

- The odds of someone winning a lottery twice in four months is about 1 in 17 trillion. But Evelyn Marie Adams won the New Jersey lottery twice in this period during 1985–86.

- About 66 per cent of all traffic death rates occur at night. It is believed that more fatalities occur at night because of more people driving under the influence, even though there are fewer cars on the road than during the day.

- There are more than 200 different types of Barbie doll.

- Every time you lick a stamp, you're consuming one-tenth of a calorie.

- Sixty-nine per cent of accidents occur within 25 miles (40km) of home.

- Money isn't made out of paper; it's made out of cotton.

- Most car horns honk in the key of 'F'.

- Some toothpaste and make-up contains crushed volcanic stone.

- University studies show that the principal reason to lie is to avoid punishment.

- The colour combination with the strongest visual impact is black on yellow.

- The popular Barbie doll was without a belly button until the year 2000.

- Tablecloths were originally used as towels with which dinner guests could wipe their hands and faces after eating.

- The name of the camel on the Camel cigarettes pack is Old Joe.

- It takes fifteen months of instruction at the Pentagon's School of Music to turn out a bandleader, but merely thirteen months to train a jet pilot.

- Whether or not you are relaxed or braced during a car accident makes little difference to the severity of your injuries.

- The distinctive smell that you experience upon opening a box of crayons comes from stearic acid, which is the formal name for processed beef fat.

- The art of map-making is older than the art of writing.

- Crayola crayons come in 120 colours: twenty-three reds, twenty greens, nineteen blues, sixteen purples, fourteen oranges, eleven browns, eight yellows, two greys, two coppers, two blacks, one gold, one silver and one white. In early 2001, US president George W. Bush voted for his favourite colour – blue bell. Teen pop star Britney Spears chose robin's egg blue.

- The world's most valuable coin was the Sultan of Muscat 1804 Silver Dollar, which sold for $4.14 million dollars at a New York City auction because of its condition and its rarity. The coin is thought to be one of eight silver dollars presented as proofs to the Sultan of Muscat in 1835.

- It takes the same amount of time to age a cigar as wine.

- The 'sad' emoticon :-(gets the same trademark protection as a corporate logo or other similar intellectual property. The mark is owned by Despair – an 'anti-motivational' company that sells humorous posters about futility, failure and repression to 'pessimists, losers and underachievers'.

- An anemophobic is someone afraid of high winds.

- The longest recorded swim was by Martin Stel who swam 2,360 miles down the Mississippi River in 2002. He spent 68 days in the water.

- The longest jail sentence passed was in the United States – 10,000 years for a triple murder.

- Levi Strauss made the first pair of blue jeans in 1850. They were intended as work trousers for American miners looking for gold.

- In Ancient Rome, only important people wore purple clothes. This is because the purple dye came from a particular kind of shellfish and was very expensive.

- The Christmas tree tradition was started in 16th-century Germany by Martin Luther, a German theologian.

- If you could count the number of times a cricket chirps in one minute, divide by 2, add 9 and divide by 2 again, you would have the correct temperature in degrees Celsius.

- If you had fifteen cubes numbered 1 to 15 and you tried to line them up in every possible sequence, and if you made a change every minute, it would take you 2,487,996 years to do it.

- If you stroke a cat 70 million times, you will have developed enough static electricity to light a 60-watt light bulb for one minute.

- If you travelled at the speed of light, it would only take you 0.0000294 seconds to climb Mount Everest.

- Being unmarried can shorten a man's life by ten years.

- Adults have, on average, 2 gallons (9 litres) of air in the space between their skin and their clothes.

- A forgetful grandfather won £200,000 in Australia after he accidentally bought three tickets for the same lottery draw.

- A Googol is the mathematical term for a 1 followed by 100 zeros.

- World War II veterans are now dying at the rate of about 1,100 each day.

- In 2002, the most popular boat name in the USA was *Liberty*.

- The Amazon rainforest produces half the world's oxygen supply.

- If you were to go on holiday for eleven days, you'd have less than 1 million seconds to enjoy it.

- Beaver Lake, in Yellowstone Park, USA, was artificially created by beaver damming.

- Off the coast of Florida, there is an underwater hotel. Guests have to dive to the entrance.

- Over 4 million cars in Brazil are now running on gasohol instead of petrol. Gasohol is a fuel made from sugar cane.

- In the USA, firearms and tobacco are the only consumer products available on the market not subject to any federal health and safety standards.

- The longest throw of a fresh egg – without breaking it – is 323ft 2.3in (98.51m). The record was achieved in Texas in 1978.

- The world record for pancake flipping is 349 flips in two minutes and the largest pancake ever tossed measured 49ft (15m) in diameter.

- An average ballpoint pen can write a line 2 miles (3.2km) long.

- The significance of the number 21 in a 21-gun salute is derived from adding the digits of 1776.

- The Empire State Building has 6,400 windows.

- It is considered an insult to tip at a restaurant in Iceland.

- Names for Atlantic hurricanes can be only French, English or Spanish.

- Twelve per cent of lightning strikes occur at golf courses.

- A light bulb at a fire station in Livermore, California, has been burning since 1901.

- Queen Isabella of Spain was the first woman to be featured on a US postage stamp.

- Times Square was originally called Long Acre Square.

- The 'F' word is used 246 times in the movie *Goodfellas*.

- Fifty-seven per cent of women would rather go on a shopping spree than have sex.

- Sixty-three per cent of pet owners sleep with their pets.

- The average American receives their first romantic kiss at age 13.

- There are twice as many billionaires in the USA today as there were ten years ago.

- More than half a million trees are used every Sunday to produce America's Sunday newspapers.

- Forty-eight per cent of men think balding has a negative effect on business and social relationships.

- In 1948, 2.3 per cent of American households had televisions. Today, 99 per cent do.

- The name Jeep came from the abbreviation used in the army for the 'General Purpose' vehicle, 'GP'.

- One million Americans wear false teeth. Approximately half of these are radioactive. There is a tiny amount of uranium in these teeth to make them whiter in incandescent light.

- In 1998, 58 per cent of American adults were married and living with their spouses, an all-time low.

- The top three products for coupon redemption are cold cereal, soap and deodorant.

- Once every month, *National Geographic* publishes enough magazines to create a pile 52 miles (83.7km) tall if stacked.

- A special matchmaking agency has been set up in China to cater to people who want sexless marriages.

- Forty-six per cent of violence on TV occurs in cartoons.

- Only about 5 per cent of people dream in colour.

- Eighty-five per cent of parents use child safety seats incorrectly.

- The ratio of people to TVs in the world is 6 to 1.

- The average American male laughs sixty-nine times a day, whereas the average woman laughs fifty-five times a day.

- Males make 85 per cent of all obscene calls.

- The life expectancy for Russian men has actually gone down over the past forty years. A Russian male born today can expect to live to be 58, on average.

- Five per cent of Americans never get married.

- If a girl owns one Barbie, she most likely owns seven.

- Fifty per cent of American adults attended an arts activity in 1997.

- People aged 24–35 worry less than adults of other age groups.

- Five per cent of Americans say they 'never' make their beds.

- The average person moves their residence eleven times in their life, about once every six years.

- Thirty-five per cent of people watching TV yell at it.

- A surprising 1 in 7 Americans can't locate the USA on a map.

- Only 30 per cent of US adults actually have dandruff while 50 per cent are 'self-conscious about it'.

- Thirty-two per cent of women and 8 per cent of men say they are better at doing laundry than their spouse.

- In 1985, the most popular waist size for men's trousers was 32. By 2003, it was 36.

- A Brussels Airlines flight to Vienna was aborted because the pilot was attacked in the cockpit. The attacker was a passenger's cat that had got out of its travel bag.

- Thirteen per cent of the letters in a given book are 'e'.

- The average age at which kids begin to use a microwave is 7 years old.

- The average American has used 730 crayons by the age of 10.

- Sixty-three per cent of American adults will rent at least one video this month.

- The average sleeper rolls over twelve times in bed per night.

- The Pentagon uses an average of 666 rolls of toilet paper each day.

- More babies are conceived in December than any other month.

- About 8 per cent of the students at the Dunkin' Doughnuts training centre fail the six-week course.

- The average speed of a golf ball in flight during the PGA tour is 160mph (257.5km/h).

- Eight-five per cent of phone calls are conducted in the English language.

- Ninety-nine per cent of India's truck drivers can't read road signs.

- There are 47,355 female millionaires aged between 18 and 44 in Britain.

- You can now buy a coffin that can be used as a wine rack, table, and/or bookcase before you are buried in it.

- Three per cent of all photos taken in the USA are taken at Disneyland or Disney World.

- Nearly 6 per cent of all marriage proposals are made over the telephone.

- A chef's hat is shaped the way it is to allow air to circulate around the scalp, keeping the head cool in a hot kitchen.

- Sixty per cent of American babies are named after relatives.

- Over 15 billion prizes have been given away in cracker jack cereal boxes.

- Chicago mayor Richard J. Daley commemorated St Patrick's Day in 1965 by pouring 100lb (45.4kg) of emerald-green dye into the Chicago River.

- In response to the criticism that his reviews always praised Broadway openings, Walter Winchell replied, 'Who am I to stone the first cast?'

- While in Alcatraz, Al Capone was inmate #85.

- If Barbie were life-size, her measurements would be 39-23-33. She would stand 7ft 2in (2.18m) tall and have a neck twice the length of a normal human.

- The war of 1812 is the only war in American history of which Congress debated the merits.

- There are more Samoans in Los Angeles than on American Samoa.

- Soccer legend Pelé's real name is Edson Arantes do Nascimento.

- There are 2.5 million new gonorrhoea cases a year among Americans.

- If you could magnify an apple to the size of the Earth, the atoms in the original apple would each be about the size of an apple.

- Hong Kong has the world's largest double-decker tram fleet.

- Hip-hop star Ice Cube's real name is O'Shea Jackson.

- There are 207 spottable mistakes in *Star Wars*, the most in any movie. Second highest is *Harry Potter and the Chamber of Secrets*, with 203 mistakes, and third is *Pirates of the Caribbean: The Curse of the Black Pearl*, with 201.

- On average, a hedgehog's heart beats 300 times a minute.

- More people are killed each year from bees than from snakes.

- Slugs have four noses.

- Owls are the only birds that can see the colour blue.

- The Mongol emperor Genghis Khan's original name was Temujin, and he started out life as a goatherd.

- Louis IV had a stomach the size of two regular stomachs.

- A scholar who studies the Marquis de Sade is called a Sadian, not a Sadist.

- Ralph Lauren's original name was Ralph Lifshitz.

- A person from the country of Nauru is called a Nauruan; this is the only palindromic nationality.

- Slugs use their slime trails to find one another. One cubic metre (35.3ft³) of garden soil can harbour up to 200 slugs.

31

LAST WORDS

- 'I don't know.'

  Peter Abelard, philosopher

- 'Is it not meningitis?'

  Writer Louisa M. Alcott

- 'I am sweeping through the gates, washed by the blood of the Lamb.'

  Tsar Alexander II

- 'There are no more other worlds to conquer!'

  Alexander the Great

- 'Give the boys a holiday.'

  Philosopher and scientist Anaxagoras, referring to the school he ran

- 'I see my God. He calls me to Him.'

  St Anthony of Padua

- 'Pardonnez-moi, monsieur.'

  Queen of France Marie Antoinette, after accidentally stepping on the foot of her executioner as she approached the guillotine

- 'For the name of Jesus and the protection of the Church, I am ready to embrace death.'

  Martyr St Thomas a Becket

- 'Wait 'til I have finished my problem!'

  Archimedes of Syracuse, mathematician

- 'The ladies have to go first... Get in the lifeboat, to please me... Goodbye, dearie. I'll see you later.'

  John Jacob Astor IV, the richest man in the world, saying farewell to his lover as he gave up his seat on an escaping lifeboat from the sinking Titanic *for a female passenger*

- 'Am I dying or is this my birthday?'

  Lady Nancy Witcher Langhorne Astor, the first female Member of Parliament, in response to being surrounded by her family on her deathbed

- 'Don't worry, be happy.'

  Indian guru Meher Baba, whose last words in 1925 were followed by forty-four years of silence before his death in 1969

- 'How were the circus receipts in Madison Square Gardens?'

  Phineas Taylor Barnum, US showman

- 'Ah, that tastes nice. Thank you.'

  Johannes Brahms

- 'Are you happy? I'm happy.'

  American actress Ethel Barrymore (Blyth)

- 'Oh, I am not going to die, am I? He will not separate us, we have been so happy.'

  Charlotte Brontë, speaking to her husband of nine months,
  Reverend Arthur Nicholls

- 'Beautiful.'

  Poet Elizabeth Barrett Browning, in reply to her
  husband who had asked how she felt

- 'Now comes the mystery.'

  Evangelist Henry Ward Beecher

- 'Friends applaud, the comedy is over.'

  Ludwig van Beethoven

- 'Bless you, Sister. May all your sons be bishops.'

  Brendan Behan, Irish playwright and member of the IRA

- 'What's this?'

  Leonard Bernstein

- 'Who is it?'

  Outlaw Billy the Kid as he was tracked and cornered
  by Sheriff Pat Garrett

- 'Mine eyes desire thee only. Farewell.'

  Catherine of Aragon, first wife of Henry VIII

- 'I am about to – or I am going to – die: either expression is correct.'

  Dominique Bouhours, French grammarian

- 'Don't let the awkward squad fire over my grave.'

  Robert Burns, referring to the military recruits who were not yet sufficiently drilled to take their place among the regulars

- 'How gratifying!'

  Poet Robert Browning

- 'Do you know where I can get any shit?'

  US comic Lenny Bruce, who later died of an overdose

- 'Now I am master of myself.'

  Marcus Porcius Cato (the Younger), committing suicide after Julius Caesar's victory over Pompey at Thapsus

- 'Never forget it; decay is inherent in all things.'

  The Buddha

- 'And so I leave this world, where the heart must either break or turn to lead.'

  French writer Nicholas-Sebastien Chamfort, in his suicide note

- 'All I want to say is I'm innocent. I'm here on a framed-up case. Give my love to my family and everything.'

  Louis Buchalter, the highest-ranking member of organised crime ever to be executed

- 'Good night.'

  Lord Byron

- 'Stay for the sign.'

  Charles I, warning his executioner to wait for his cue to behead him

- 'Don't let poor Nelly starve.'

  Charles II, in reference to his mistress Nell Gwynne

- 'I hope never again to commit a mortal sin, not even a venial one, if I can help it.'

  Charles VII of France

- 'Why not? After all, it belongs to him.'

  Charlie Chaplin, in response to the priest who, attending his deathbed, said 'May the Lord have mercy on your soul.'

- 'It's been a long time since I've had champagne.'

  Anton Chekhov

- 'Tell the mayor I'm sorry to be causing the city so much trouble.'

  US murderer Frederick W. Cowan, speaking into a telephone before shooting himself

- 'The sleep of the tomb will press on my eyclid.'

  French poet and political journalist Andre Chenier, guillotined in 1794

- 'Take a step forward, lads. It will be easier that way.'

  Irish patriot Erskine Childers, executed by firing squad

- 'I'm bored with it all.'

  Winston Churchill, before slipping into a coma

- 'Damn it... Don't you dare ask God to help me.'

  Movie star Joan Crawford, speaking to her housekeeper, who had begun
  to pray aloud

- 'So here it is!'

  Cleopatra, the 'it' being the small asp that she allowed to bite her

- 'Let's forget about it and play high five. I wish Johnny
  would come.'

  Wild West icon Buffalo Bill Cody

- 'Doctor, do you think it could have been the sausage?'

  French poet, playwright and diplomat Paul Claudel

- 'You sons of bitches. Give my love to Mother.'

  American bank robber and murderer Francis 'Two-Gun'
  Crowley, before being electrocuted

- 'I am not sorry.'

  US president William McKinley's assassin Leon Czolgosz

- 'I'm bored. I'm bored.'

  Gabriele D'Annunzo, Italian poet, novelist, playwright,
  playboy, war hero and fascist adventurer

- 'Show my head to the people. It is worth seeing.'

  Georges Jacques Danton, the acknowledged leader
  of the French Revolution

- 'KHAQQ calling Itasca. We must be on you, but cannot see you. Gas is running low.'

  Aviator Amelia Earhart, whose plane wreck was never found

- 'Carry my bones before you on your march, for the rebels will not be able to endure the sight of me, alive or dead.'

  Edward I

- 'I am not the least afraid to die.'

  Charles Darwin

- 'Too late for fruit, too soon for flowers.'

  English writer Walter De la Mare

- 'I'd hate to die twice. It's so boring.'

  Richard Feynman, physicist

- 'Swain, can't you stop this [pain]? Swain!'

  Twentieth president of the United States James A. Garfield, calling to his doctors who couldn't locate the bullet after he was shot

- 'All my possessions for a moment of time.'

  Elizabeth I

- 'Remember, the death penalty is murder.'

  Wrongfully convicted murderer Robert Drew, executed by lethal injection

- 'Yes, I have heard of it. I am very glad.'

  Edward VII, upon being told by his son that one of the king's horses, Witch of the Air, had won the 4.15 race at Kempton Park

- 'This is the happiest moment of my life.'

  German anarchist Adolf Fischer, before he was hanged for his crimes

- 'Watch out, please.'

  Viennese author, critic and theatre director Egon Friedell, whose opposition to the Nazis led to him jumping to his death from an office window, to avoid capture from the Gestapo

- 'Who the hell tipped you off? I'm Floyd all right. You've got me this time.'

  US bank robber Charles 'Pretty Boy' Floyd

- 'I love you.'

  Convicted murderer Sean Flanaghan, speaking to his executioner

- 'People want to know if I still love Martha. But of course I do. I want to shout it out. I love Martha. What do the public know about love?'

  'Lonely Hearts Killer' Raymond Fernandez handed this note to a guard as he walked to the electric chair. His lover and accomplice, Martha Beck, had died only a few minutes before

- 'I've had a hell of a lot of fun and I've enjoyed every minute of it.'

  Errol Flynn

- 'A dying man can do nothing easy.'

  Benjamin Franklin

- 'No, not quite naked. I shall have my uniform on.'

  Frederick William I, King of Prussia

- 'Why fear death? Death is only a beautiful adventure.'
  Pre-eminent American theatrical director Charles Frohman. The phrase
  was replicated in J.M. Barrie's Peter Pan

- 'I'd like to thank my family for loving me and taking care of
  me. And the rest of the world can kiss my ass.'
  Convicted nun murderer Johnny Frank Garrett, upon being executed

- 'It is nothing. It is nothing.'
  Austrian heir to the throne Archduke Franz Ferdinand,
  on his mortal gunshot wound

- 'Southerly gales, squalls, lee rail under water, wet bunks,
  hard tack, bully beef, wish you were here – instead of me!'
  Global traveller and adventure writer Richard Halliburton's
  final signal before his vessel disappeared in a storm

- 'Dying is easy. Comedy is difficult.'
  Oscar-winning British actor Edmund Gwenn

- 'You promised me that you would help me when I could no
  longer carry on. Tell Anna about our little talk.'
  Sigmund Freud, reminding his friend Dr Schur of his agreement
  to carry out a mercy killing. Schur gave Freud a little opium,
  and he died two days later

- 'That's good. Go on. Read some more.'
  Twenty-ninth US president Warren G. Harding, commenting on some
  favourable editorials his wife was reading to him when he died
  suddenly of a heart attack

● 'Let not my end disarm you, and on no account weep or keen for me, let the enemy be warned of my death.'

Genghis Khan

● 'Wally, what is this? It is death, my boy. They have deceived me!'

George IV

● 'I came here to die, not to make a speech.'

US outlaw Crawford 'Cherokee Bill' Goldsby, prior to being hanged

● 'My friend, the artery ceases to beat.'

Swiss physician, scientist and poet Albrecht von Haller

● 'I have loved justice and hated iniquity: therefore I die in exile.'

Pope Gregory VII

● 'All is lost. Monks, monks, monks!'

King Henry VIII

● 'Now let the world go as it will; I care for nothing more.'

King Henry II

● 'God will pardon me, that's his line of work.'

Heinrich Heine

● 'Open the second shutter so that more light may come in.'

Johann Wolfgang von Goethe

- 'I know you have come to kill me. Shoot, coward. You are only going to kill a man.'

  Ernesto 'Che' Guevara

- 'I only regret that I have but one life to lose for my country.'

  US revolutionary Nathan Hale

- 'Let us now relieve the Romans of their fears by the death of a feeble old man.'

  Hannibal

- 'Let's see if this will do it.'

  Actor Jon-Erik Hexum as he shot himself with a blank-loaded pistol on the set of TV spy show Cover Up. *The concussion forced a chunk of his skull into his brain; he died six days later, an accidental suicide*

- 'Hold the cross high so I may see it through the flames!'

  Joan of Arc as she burned at the stake

- 'I see black light.'

  Victor Hugo

- 'Leave the shower curtain on the inside of the tub.'

  Hotelier Conrad N. Hilton's response, upon being asked for any words of wisdom

- 'I am about to take my last voyage, a great leap in the dark.'

  Thomas Hobbes

- 'I'm tired of fighting! I guess this thing is going to get me.'

  Harry Houdini

- 'Does nobody understand?'

  James Joyce

- 'Kill me, or else you are a murderer!'

  Franz Kafka, speaking to his physician, whom he begged
  to end his pain

- 'On the contrary.'

  Henrik Ibsen, upon hearing his nurse inform a visitor
  that he was feeling better

- 'That is indeed very good. I shall have to repeat that on the Golden Floor!'

  Poet A.E. Housman, speaking to his doctor, who told
  him a joke just before he died

- 'The prettier. Now fight for it.'

  English playwright Henry Arthur Jones, upon being asked who
  he would prefer to have at his side during the evening between
  his nurse and his niece

- 'And now, in keeping with Channel 40's policy of always bringing you the latest in blood and guts, in living colour, you're about to see another first – an attempted suicide.'

  American newscaster Chris Chubbuck, before killing herself
  during a live broadcast in Florida

- 'It came with a lass and it will go with a lass.'

  James V of Scotland, referring to the Crown of Scotland
  as his only child, Mary, was only six days old

- 'Don't worry, it's not loaded.'

  Rock group Chicago's Terry Kath, playing Russian roulette

- 'I wish I'd drunk more champagne.'

  Economist John Maynard Keynes

- 'Mind your own business.'

  Artist Wyndham Lewis, speaking to his nurse, who had asked about the state of his bowels on his deathbed

- 'Such is life.'

  Australian outlaw Ned Kelly, executed by hanging

- 'That's obvious.'

  John F. Kennedy, in reply to the comment of the Texas governor's wife, 'Mr President, you can't say that Dallas doesn't love you.'

- 'My dear, before you kiss me goodbye, fix your hair. It's a mess.'

  George Kelly, American playwright and uncle of Grace Kelly

- 'I'll be in hell before you start breakfast, boys! Let her rip!'

  US train robber Thomas 'Black Jack' Ketchum, whose head came flying off as he reached the end of his rope when hanged

- 'No one can be more willing to send me out of life than I am desirous to go.'

  Bishop Hugh Laud, executed because of his support of Charles I and his opposition to Parliament

- 'Why do you weep? Did you think I was immortal?'

  Louis XIV of France

- 'Why not? Why not? Why not? Why not? Yeah.'

  LSD guru Timothy Leary

- 'Turn me. I am roasted on one side.'

  St Lawrence as he lay tied face down on a gridiron suspended over a bed of coals, and slowly burned to death

- 'They won't think anything about it.'

  Abraham Lincoln, reassuring his wife that it would be all right to hold hands just before John Wilkes Booth sneaked into his theatre box and shot him from behind

- 'They tried to get me – I got them first!'

  Poet Vachel Lindsay, before suicide by drinking Lysol

- 'I wonder why he shot me.'

  Democrat politician Huey P. Long, Jr, upon being hit by the son-in-law of a former political opponent

- 'I deserve this fate. It is a debt I owe for a wild and reckless life. So long, everybody!'

  Convicted murderer William P. Longley

- 'Is this dying? Is this all? Is this what I feared when I prayed against a hard death? Oh, I can bear this! I can bear this!'

  Cotton Mather, New England minister and Puritan preacher

- 'Shoot straight, you bastards! Don't make a mess of it!'

  Australian Anglo-Boer War soldier and poet Lt Henry H. Morant, speaking to the firing squad that executed him

- 'Frenchmen, I die guiltless of the countless crimes imputed to me. Pray God my blood fall not on France!'

  Louis XVI

- 'No, but comfortable enough to die.'

  Maria Theresa, Empress of Austria, speaking to her son Joseph, who attempted to comfort her saying, 'Your Majesty cannot be comfortable like that.'

- 'It has all been most interesting.'

  Lady Mary Wortley Montagu, English writer and world traveller

- 'I am a queen, but I have not the power to move my arms.'

  Queen Louise of Prussia

- 'Let's cool it, brothers...'

  Malcolm X, speaking to his three assassins, who shot him sixteen times

- 'Dying is a very dull and dreary affair. And my advice to you is to have nothing whatever to do with it.'

  W. Somerset Maugham

- 'Go on, get out! Last words are for fools who haven't said enough!'

  Karl Marx, in response to his housekeeper who asked if he had any last words

- 'My soul I resign to God, my body to the earth, my worldly goods to my next of kin.'

  Michelangelo

- 'You will find the word "Calais" written on my heart.'

  Queen Mary I

- 'Hold your tongue! Your wretched chatter disgusts me.'

  French minister Malesherbes, speaking to his priest uttering last rites

- 'My Lord, why do you not go on? I am not afraid to die.'

  Queen Mary II, speaking to Archbishop Tillotson, who had paused while reading a prayer for the dying

- 'Why should I talk to you? I've just been talking to your boss.'

  US writer and gambler Wilson Mizner as he briefly awoke to find a priest standing over him

- 'Last of all, we must die.'

  St Phillip Neri, at the end of a long day seeing visitors

- 'This hath not offended the king.'

  Sir Thomas More

- 'I don't want to survive myself.'

  Guy de Maupassant

- 'Tomorrow, I shall no longer be here.'

  Nostradamus

- 'Human life is limited; but I would like to live forever.'

  Right-wing Japanese writer Mishima Yukio who killed himself after failing to convince the Japanese military to overthrow the civilian government

- 'We are all going.'

  Assassinated US president William B. McKinley, responding to his wife as she cried, 'I want to go too, I want to go too!'

- 'Shoot me in the chest!'

  Benito Mussolini, speaking to his executioners

- 'I do not have to forgive my enemies. I have had them all shot.'

  Spanish Prime Minister Ramon Maria Narvaez

- 'I don't know what I may seem to the world. But to myself I seem to have been only like a boy playing on the sea-shore and diverting myself in now and then finding a smoother pebble or prettier shell than ordinary, whilst the great ocean of truth lay all undiscovered before me.'

  Sir Isaac Newton

- 'You'll have to drive. I'm hit.'

  Mobster George Nelson, aka Lester Gillis or 'Babyface', hit by seventeen bullets while on the run

- 'What an artist the world is losing in me!'

  Nero

- 'I am just going outside and may be some time.'

  Lawrence Oates, member of the ill-fated Scott Antarctic expedition, walking out of the tent and vanishing into a blizzard so that his companions wouldn't be hindered by his lameness

- 'Born in a hotel room – and God damn it – died in a hotel room.'

  Eugene O'Neill

- 'You wouldn't hang your own sheriff, would you?'

  Crooked sheriff Henry Plummer, lynched for corruption by the townspeople of Bannock, USA

- 'Hurry it up, you Hoosier bastard. I could hang a dozen men while you're fooling around!'

  US serial killer and rapist Carl Panzram, after spitting in the face of his executioner

- 'Here am I, dying of a hundred good symptoms.'

  Alexander Pope

- 'Die, my dear doctor! That's the last thing I shall do!'

  Lord Henry John Temple Palmerston, British prime minister and Liberal politician

- 'If I had two lives to give, I'd give one gladly to save Mrs Suratt. I know that she is innocent and would never die in this way if I hadn't been found in her house. She knew nothing about the conspiracy at all.'

  Lincoln assassination conspirator Lewis Paine, speaking about cohort Mary Surratt, executed at the same instant

- 'This isn't *Hamlet*, you know, it's not meant to go into the bloody ear.'

  Laurence Olivier, speaking to his nurse, who spilt water over him while trying to moisten his lips

- 'I'm tired. I'm going back to bed.'

    George Reeves, American actor who played Superman in the classic 1950s television series. Angry that visitors had awakened him, he announced that he was going back to bed. Instead he went to his bedroom and shot himself in the head with a 30-calibre Luger

- 'Goodbye… Why am I haemorrhaging?'

    Boris Pasternak

- 'Dear World. I am leaving you because I am bored. I feel I have lived long enough. I am leaving you with your worries in this sweet cesspool. Good luck.'

    Oscar-winning British actor George Sanders before taking an overdose of sleeping pills

- 'I will be glad to discuss this proposition with my attorney, and that after I talk with one, we could either discuss it with him or discuss it with my attorney if the attorney thinks it is a wise thing to do, but at the present time I have nothing more to say to you.'

    JFK assassin Lee Harvey Oswald, speaking to Inspector Thomas Kelly of the US Secret Service before being assassinated himself by Jack Ruby

- ''Tis well.'

    George Washington

- 'I am curious to see what happens in the next world to one who dies unshriven.'

    Italian painter Pietro Perugino, giving his reasons for refusing to see a priest as he lay dying

- 'Bring down the curtain, the farce is played out.'

  French satirist Francois Rabelais

- 'Youth, I forgive thee! Take off his chains, give him 100 shillings and let him go.'

  King Richard I, referring to Bertrand de Gourdon, who had shot him with an arrow at Chalus, precipitating his death

- 'Bury me where the birds will sing over my grave.'

  Alexander Wilson, the father of American ornithology

- 'Please don't let me fall.'

  Alleged Lincoln assassination conspirator Mary Surratt before she was hanged as the first woman ever executed by the US Government

- 'Why yes, a bullet-proof vest!'

  US criminal James W. Rodgers, giving his final request before the firing squad

- 'You can keep the things of bronze and stone and give me one man to remember me just once a year.'

  Writer Damon Runyon

- 'Woe is me, I think I am becoming a god.'

  Roman Emperor Titus Flavius Sabinus Vespasian

- 'So little done, so much to do.'

  Gold and diamond mining millionaire Cecil John Rhodes

- 'Never yet has death been frightened away by screaming.'

  Turkish ruler Tamburlaine

- 'I feel this time they have succeeded. I do not want them to undress me. I want you to undress me.'

    Leon Trotsky, exiled from Stalin's Russia, speaking to his wife while preparing for surgery due to wounds from one of Stalin's spies

- 'Everybody has got to die, but I have always believed an exception would be made in my case. Now what?'

    Pulitzer Prize-winning writer William Saroyan, speaking on the telephone to the Associated Press

- 'I feel certain that I'm going mad again. I feel we can't go through another of those terrible times. And I shan't recover this time. I begin to hear voices.'

    Virginia Woolf's suicide note

- 'The car seems OK...'

    Formula One driver Ayrton Senna, seconds before his steering column broke and his car hit a wall, killing him

- 'Good people, be not hurried. I can wait a little.'

    William 'Skitch' Snow, British criminal hanged at the second attempt in 1789, as the rope broke the first time

- 'Hell no! No one ever did anything for me. Why in the hell should I do anything for anyone else?'

    Mass murderer Charles Starkweather, when asked to donate his eyes to an eye bank

- 'Crito, I owe a cock to Asclepius. Will you remember to pay the debt?'

    Socrates

- 'Even in the valley of the shadow of death, two and two do not make six.'

  > Leo Tolstoy as he rejected his friend's pleas to reconcile with the
  > Orthodox Church

- 'They couldn't hit an elephant at this dist—'

  > General John Sedgwick, mocking the Confederate soldiers in the
  > Army of the Potomac during the American Civil War

- 'Don't let it end like this. Tell them I said something.'

  > Mexican bandit, revolutionary and folk hero Francisco
  > 'Pancho' Villa, speaking to newspaper reporters as he was
  > assassinated by supporters of his enemy

- 'Had I but served God as diligently as I have served the King, He would have not given me over in my grey hairs.'

  > Cardinal Thomas Wolsey, English prelate and statesman

- 'Tell mother, tell mother, I died for my country… Useless… useless…'

  > Abraham Lincoln's murderer, John Wilkes Booth

- 'Curtain! Fast music! Lights! Ready for the last finale! Great! The show looks good. The show looks good.'

  > Broadway producer Florenz Ziegfeld, hallucinating that
  > he was directing one last show